How to Build an Internet Service Company

From A to Z...

How to Build

an

Internet Service Company

From A to Z...

Charles H. Burke

Social Systems Press
A Division of Systems 2000+, Inc.

HOW TO BUILD AN INTERNET SERVICE COMPANY
Copyright © 1996, 1997 by Charles H. Burke

SECOND EDITION, April 1997
Printed in the United States of America.

Library of Congress Catalog Card Number 96-069435

Publishers Cataloging in Publication
(Prepared by Quality Books Inc.)

Burke, Charles H., 1970-
    How to Build an Internet Service Company : From A to Z / Charles
H. Burke.
    p. cm.
    Includes bibliographical references and index.
    ISBN 0-935563-03-2

    1. Internet (Computer network) 2. New business enterprises--
Management.   I. Title.

TK5105.875.I57B87 1996   004.6'7
                            QBI96-20472

Acknowledgments
All photos and pictures have been reprinted with permission from their respective copyright holders.

A NOTE ON GRAPHICS:
Many of the pictures in this book have been collected directly from the World Wide Web (with permission). The grainy texture seen on many of them have to do with the way Web graphics are optimized for viewing as opposed to a print medium.

Grateful thanks go to the following:

Tom Sumner for suggesting the idea and being a good friend.
Kurt Risser, the most talented programmer in Kentucky.
The whole Lucia crowd.
Kevin Cotton and Michael Boyd, while often at a distance but
    still close at hand.
Jack Rickard for always speaking the truth.
Brad Hobbs, a real professor and renaissance thinker.
Michael Polly, a friend and mentor.
The amazing team at MISnet.
David Hamilton Johnson, for excellent technical support.
Kanti Busch, my beautiful sweetheart, for putting up with me.

…and my loving family.

TABLE OF CONTENTS

INTRODUCTION

What a long strange trip...

What I'm going to share with you is the hardest won experience and knowledge that I have to offer. When I first started down the road to becoming an Internet Service Provider (ISP) I would have gladly paid twenty times the cost of this book for the information that it contains. That would have been impossible though, as I began this journey long before the 'Information Superhighway' (the last time I will use this cliché, I promise) was a marketable asset.

I began working with personal computers in the late seventies and early eighties on a Commodore CBM. The first computer I owned was a Commodore Vic-20. I progressed through all the early days of the personal computer owning at one time or another a Commodore 64, a TI 994a, a Tandy and even a Timex Sinclair. I jumped on the IBM platform in the mid eighties where I have happily lived ever since. The most fascinating peripheral of personal computers was always the modem. When I first made a 300 baud connection, horrifyingly slow in retrospect but bleeding edge at the time, I was hooked. I dialed into a local BBS (computer based Bulletin Board System) that was being run on a kit computer that someone had built up in their basement. The BBS offered a number of instructional files for computer hobbyists and a message base where a handful of local computer aficionados communicated with each other. The thought of conversing with strangers who I had never met in person was almost too much for this poor soul to fathom. Computer based communications also broke down all the barriers and allowed people to talk to each other with no preconceived notions or prejudices built in. Just as today, age, race and appearance don't play a role in your online communications. You are judged by the content of your message alone. Being young at the time this was extremely advantageous. It was love at first 'byte.' I stayed active in the local BBS circles for the next decade until I had the opportunity to take over a local thriving BBS system that was being shut down due to the owner being unable to subsidize its existence any longer. In 1989 'The Dance of Shiva' became my labor of love for the next three years.

Help! I've gotten online... and I can't hang up!!!

During those years BBS's were mostly free services. The idea of charging for one was a bit ludicrous. Although it was being done successfully on a few systems in North America they were by far the exception. Of course Compuserve and a few other large national services date back to those early days of computer communications as well. There were not that many people interested in computer communications in my local market (Louisville, Kentucky) and the technology was still far from pretty. Only in the years after 1989 did locally operated online systems become popular to the wider audience of computer users.

The growth of the personal computer closely matches the growth of online systems. As individuals bought these expensive boxes they longed for a way to connect them to ever widening bodies of information. So, computer enthusiasts needed an inexpensive way to communicate with each other. The technical hurdles seemed to be endless as both users and companies pushed the envelope of technology. It was only natural that computer users valued each others advice like gold, there simply weren't that many of us. By the time 1992 rolled around the 'online industry' was already in full tilt. Seeing the opportunities that existed, myself and an early partner invested a bit more money into the BBS to see what we might be able to build with it. Working it part time and on a very limited budget we were able to grow the system at a slow but steady pace until we reached eighteen dial up lines. At the peak of our achievement, modest as it may have been compared to larger national systems, the Internet became the new 'frontier' to be explored in computer communications. By 1993 we were providing Internet Email and limited Usenet message bases on the local BBS. However, this would not be enough to stem the interest in full Internet services that was obviously just on the horizon. My partner left the fray and I continued on with The Dance of Shiva making preparations to become a full Internet Service Provider (ISP).

I experienced a tremendous learning curve while I was building my ISP business even though I had years of computer experience. We had entered what I like to call 'the world of UNIX.' Unix is an operating system that is ancient, but quite alive, in computer circles. Unix was developed to be an open ended system that would allow many people to use the resources of just one computer simultaneously. The forerunner of today's Internet (ARPANET) was a computer network that was used on the forerunner of today's Unix operating systems. Therefore, one would assume that if you wanted to be an ISP you would have to know UNIX? Thankfully this is only partially true today. Learning an entirely new operating system and hundreds of new commands and their thousands of possible relationships to each other is not necessary any more. For whatever it may be worth, experienced Unix system administrators command upwards from $35k yearly in salary. I could not hire one nor did I desire particularly to become a Unix expert to achieve my goals. My own particular route for overcoming this obstacle was to use a proprietary server, a computer designed to do most of the Internet services without me having to actually know Unix in any great detail. Since that time many new turnkey operations have arisen that take the pain out of using UNIX and later in this book we delve into one such system. A turnkey system, regardless of what solution you go after, will make your move into the business fast and painless. Utilizing a turnkey system you are guaranteed to be working with a company that has already worked all the kinks out of the hardware/software combination. Building up a system from scratch only places you in the position of hitting many (if not all) of the pitfalls that those who came before have already traversed.

I will describe alternate methods in this book on how to achieve the goals you will need to meet to become an ISP. One of these methods involves a Unix specific operating system and another will discuss using a proprietary server. However, don't mistake what you hold in your hands for a technical manual. THIS IS NOT A TECHNICAL MANUAL...those are included with whatever particular hardware and software products you decide upon. Setting up the hardware and software is the easy part. You will pay someone for the equipment it will take for you to provide Internet services and they will be able to instruct you on how their particular solution functions. We will include a list of resources and how to contact a myriad of vendors who supply this market throughout the chapters where appropriate. To focus too specifically on one particular answer would be a disservice to you at this point. The world of hardware and software changes in dog years. One year in human terms will see many years of advances in these areas. What will not change so rapidly is how you will piece all of this equipment together and formulate a winning strategy to enter this market. With that said, the recommendations I do make between these pages are reliable, tried and tested and have worked successfully for me. Your mileage may vary.

What is the Internet and what Internet services are being sold? What types of equipment will you need? How do you get connected to the net and what are the pros and cons of differing methods? How can you best market these services? I also hope to give you a crash course in all of the jargon that accompanies the Internet, worthy of a book unto itself.

If you do not currently have *true* Internet access you will need to get an account ASAP. I'm not talking about Compuserve or Prodigy or

America Online either. I mean a *real* Internet account. You want to be connected using the PPP protocol. If you don't know of any local Internet providers then call a couple of the locally owned computer stores and they should be able to help you. If you don't have a local provider yet (a terrific problem to have, for you) get a long distance account with a provider in a nearby state. Dialing out of state is often less expensive than intra-state toll charges. This account will serve two purposes. First, you will get much needed experience from the user's point of view. You will also use this account to access a number of Internet web pages that I will refer to in this book. I'm not sure that it is possible to become an Internet Service Provider without becoming a bit of a user first. In order to make this book as valuable as possible without filling it with information that will be outdated the day of the printing I rely heavily upon resources that are maintained on the Internet itself. Examples include FAQ (frequently asked question) lists and other informative web pages. These are ever changing as the technology itself expands. These resources have been around for many years on the Internet. Tying it all together is the hard part. It *is* difficult getting the big picture of how an ISP goes about getting started. There are many pitfalls and snags that you can avoid and this is what I hope to help you accomplish.

With these questions in mind we will begin the real meat of the book. What you are about to read is very personal to me. I've lived all of the mistakes in order to get the right answers. In sharing these with you I feel as though I'm giving away the family recipes. Something so hard won is never easy to give away at any price. I hope this helps you on your road to financial success in this new market.

Happy surfing...

Chuck Burke

CHAPTER I

WHAT IS THE INTERNET?

The Ghost of Internet Past

The original 'Internet' was a defense department project to build a data communications grid over a distributed network. This was initiated in the late sixties and called the Advanced Research Project Agency Network (ARPANET). It was designed to connect distant computers together through a patchwork of connections. The intent was to have the information that flowed through these computers accessible to any other computers in the network even if one of the destination computers failed. Computers have a nasty habit of failing when subjected to nuclear explosions and the Department of Defense was keenly aware of this flaw in their design. The National Science Foundation (NSF) and a number of accompanying universities involved in their programs began to rely upon this early internet (not to be confused with today's Internet, capital 'I') to relay files and email between themselves. This spread until many universities outside of the original DOD and NSF group began to use the Internet as well.

The Ghost of Internet Present

What the Internet is *not*
Thus, out of this early defense spending we have today the world's largest network of computers tied together and a wonderful business opportunity to boot. Let me start by telling you what (and who) the Internet is *not* and then we can proceed to talk about what the Internet really is. There are many misconceptions in this area. The Internet is not one of the major long distance carriers. The Internet is not Compuserve, Prodigy, America Online (AOL), Delphi, Netcom or any of the other large national online services. Netscape Communications, makers of the popular Netscape Navigator world wide web browser, is not the Internet. Microsoft is not the Internet, even though they would love for you to believe so. Your phone company is not the Internet. What I am basically saying is that no one company is *the* Internet. All of the aforementioned companies are however part of the Internet. If you successfully get your ISP business started you too will be part of the Internet and fully capable of competing with the best of them. Let's now talk about what the Internet *is*.

The Physical Internet
The Internet is the world's largest collection of computers ever tied together. Computers owned by universities, businesses, non-profit organizations, government bodies, casual users and that nerdy kid that lives down the street. The Internet is also the connections between these computers. Leased lines, ISDN circuits, ethernet connections, satellite signals, cell packet networks, cable coax systems and dial up connections over plain old telephone service (POTS) form the connections between these computers. These connections are provided by local regional Bell operating companies (RBOC) and all of the major long distance carriers and even a new breed of connection provider, the CAP, which we'll discuss later. The hardware and the accompanying connections to other computers form the physical body of the Internet.

The grid or patchwork that makes up all of these connections is why we have the World Wide Web today. The Web is a distributed body of documents, graphics, audio and even video that reside at many of the ISPs and universities in the world. Most ISPs will provide Web services in house, meaning that they have a computer or computers that serve up web documents. If the patchwork of connections were not so spread out we might be surfing the 'world wide tunnel' or the 'world wide line' today. This distributed nature of connections, as opposed to a linear connection between the first and last of the computers on the net, allows for faster travel time for data and a much more robust or 'stay alive' instinct. This topic and how you can use this knowledge to your advantage is discussed in greater detail in the chapter on connections later in the book. For now, a small diagram will help to make this clear.

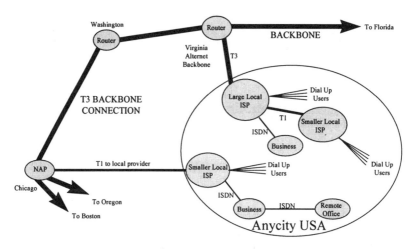

This diagram shows the relationship between a backbone and local ISP companies. Don't worry about understanding the types of connections at this point as they will be explained later in the book. Note how one city can be connected to different parts of the Internet 'backbone'. If the Washington router were to 'go down' then data may still be able to make it to and from its destination using alternate paths. (not to be confused with 'Alternet' a backbone provider)

If you are connected to 'small local ISP' and you wish to access a World Wide Web page on a computer connected to the MCI backbone in Oregon, your request would travel to Chicago and then directly to Oregon. If someone wished to access a Web page on the 'large local ISP' and they were connected to the 'small local ISP' their request would travel to Chicago then to Washington then to Virginia and finally to the computers at the 'large local ISP' site.

Although the computer hosting the Web pages may be just down the street you are confined to taking this roundabout path due to the way the connections are laid out. Even though this seems highly inefficient it does not necessarily mean that it must be slow. Data can travel quite rapidly through high performance connections even over thousands of miles. Although I used Web pages as an example of data sent over the Internet this same principle applies to all Internet services. Telnet, Gopher, FTP and all of the other possible uses of Internet connections consist at the basic level as just packets of data. Packets are packets, and so they all move through the Internet according to rules of traffic and the connections between computers.

The Post Office Internet - IP Addresses and Domain Names
IP Addresses - How do these data packets know where to go? They do not. However, they do have an 'IP address' or Internet Protocol address that accompanies each and every one of them. This address is read by routers as the packet comes in. The router contains tables of IP addresses that it knows and 'default routes' for IP addresses that it does not know. Think of routers as the local post offices of the Internet. When packets come in a router will either know exactly where that packet should go or it will use the default route for packets that have addresses it does not know. It gets a bit stickier than this though. IP addresses are ugly and fairly unusable for most people. They are in the form of numbers separated by periods, such as 204.189.85.1 There are classes of IP addreses as well. A class defines how many IP addresses are in a particular group. As an ISP you will want to begin your business with at least one Class-C address. A Class-C address gives you 256 IP addresses to work with. Sounds like a lot? It isn't. You can use up 256 addresses in your first six months of business. This is because every resource on your network (on the entire Internet for that matter) requires an IP address. Every dial up user, every workstation and every unique domain (see below) on your network requires an IP address. Now, there are ways to 'save' IP addresses too.

Dynamic / Static IP Addressing

If your server supports it, and it will, your dial up customers can be provided with what are called 'dynamic IP addresses' as opposed to 'static IP addresses'. Static IP addresses are addresses that do not change, they always point to the same resource or connection on the Internet. Web servers are a good example of a resource that needs a static IP address. Dynamic IP addresses are simply IP addresses that you've set aside in a pool for dial up users to be assigned upon logging in to your system. In this way you only use as many IP addresses as the maximum number of simultaneous connections you can support. An ISP who supports 40 dial up lines can use a maximum of 40 IP addresses when utilizing this method. Another ISP with 40 lines and 400 dial up customers would run out of IP addresses in their first Class-C group if he attempted to assign one to each user. Some users will request their own static IP address, so that regardless of what line they log into they will always be assigned the same address. Why is this? Because some Internet services are easier to use when your IP address never changes. For instance, some of the audio or conferencing software on the Internet requires that you connect to another user's IP address. If this address changes depending on what line they connect to when dialing your system it is more difficult for friends and relatives to contact them 'voice' as they will not know what address to 'call'. If users request this service be sure to charge an extra $5 or more monthly for the service as it does require additional setup on your part and uses your resources (IP addresses).

Sub-Netting

Sub-Nets are slices of a larger IP class addressing. For instance, a Class-C group, discussed earlier, is a sub-net of a Class-B group. Class-B groups are made up of many Class-C groups. A Class-C address can also be sub-netted further by using what is called a 'Net-Mask'. A net mask allows you to define how large a sub-net is. By applying a net-mask to a single IP address you can enlarge the number of addresses that this particular IP address refers to. Leased line customers of yours will generally require a sub-net, or perhaps even an entire Class-C group from you so that they in turn can service a number of Internet connections such as workstation, web servers, dial up users, etc.

Domain Names

If 204.189.85.1 was an IP address that pointed to your Web server which held hundreds of great Cajun recipes and you wanted others to be able to find this resource easily you wouldn't want them to have to remember the IP address. This is where 'domain names' come into play. Domain names are the word representations of IP addresses. If you can dream up a domain name that has not been taken already you can register this with the Internic, the body that oversees domain name registrations. Currently domain names cost $100 which hold them for you

> **TIP:** To check whether or not a domain name has been registered simply follow this procedure. TELNET to 'internic.net'. Once there you will be presented with a command prompt. Type in the following command: **WHOIS DOMAIN.COM** If this domain has not been taken it will not appear in the database search you are performing. If it has, a bit of information concerning the owner will appear. (See your ISP if you do not know how to 'telnet') Alternatively you can use the Internic's web based form at www.internic.net.

for two years and then $50 each year thereafter. This is the current 'true' cost, what a local ISP may charge you is another matter entirely. Instructions on how to register a domain name will be given by your connection provider so there is no point in getting deeply involved in that. It's a fairly straight forward process that involves you filling out a form and Emailing it to the concerned parties. Registering a domain name basically points that name to a specific IP address. That IP address will be exactly where the information is contained or it will point to your own in house router which will know where the information is contained. The correlation of IP addresses to domain names is called DNS, Domain Name Service. A computer that handles this function is called a domain name server. As an ISP you will be registering LOTS of domain names, both for Web and leased line customers of your own.

Let's talk about the structure of domain names now. Domain names are words (as opposed to numbers) separated by periods. If you wished to have a Cajun web page with its own address you might wish to have the domain name of 'cajunrecipes.' However, you must have an extension to the word to dictate what type of resource this is. These are also known as Top Level Domains or TLDs for short. Common extensions you will find on the Internet are:

- com   Commercial site (generically used as well)
- mil   Military
- edu   Educational institutions
- gov   Government body
- org   Organization, popular with non-profit groups
- net   Network (ie. a provider of Internet services)
…and many more

Domain name extensions may also reflect a country of origin:

- us   United States
- ky.us   Kentucky, United States
- jp   Japan
…and so on

Most likely you will just give your site the 'com' extension and thus you would register 'cajunrecipes.com' with the Internic. On your local domain name server you would place cajunrecipes.com and tell it what IP address that name specified. This address would be a dedicated IP address that would point to your Web server. Your web server in turn would be configured to know that address and when requests came to it for that particular address it would serve up the appropriate web pages. Perhaps a dynamite gumbo recipe would pop up on the users screen. Now, if this is truly a World Wide Web site you would probably tell your domain name server that 'www.cajunrecipes.com' was the domain name of the web site. Why? Because this has become common practice to separate Web pages from other types of Internet services. It would be fairly intuitive to an experienced Internet user that this address referred to a Web page that contained Cajun recipes. You have created what is called a sub-domain name by adding the 'www' prefix to the beginning of your domain name. Cajunrecipes.com is still the domain name, but www.cajunrecipes.com is a sub-domain of the parent name. The Internet at large only knows that cajunrecipes.com points to your own in house network. Your in house network can make as many sub-domains from this parent name as you like. Ie. www.cajunrecipes.com, ftp.(your_domain), private.(your_domain) etc. This is discussed in detail later in the chapter on marketable services. An excellent resource for learning more about DNS is a book called <u>DNS and BIND</u> from O'Reilly and Associates. Their web address is www.ora.com or you can order this from any good local bookseller.

Now that you have a basic understanding of the physical body of the Internet and how data flows over it, let's discuss the meat of your market, the applications that this network are being used for today.

The Useful Internet

What do people actually use the Internet for? Although an understanding of how the Internet is tied together is necessary for any budding ISP, the marketable services that the net provides is where the money lies. The actual marketing analysis of each of these services follows later but for now let's get a basic understanding of what the Internet is used for. First, however, we need to discuss how one actually connects to the Internet.

Connecting to the Net
Winsock, also known as a TCP/IP (protocol) 'stack', says it all. Windows is the operating system you will first cater to. It has the largest market share of any platform available and will comprise the largest percentage of your user body. Windows is expandable by use of dynamic link libraries, or .DLL files. These files contain code that expands the connectivity and capabilities of the Windows operating system. The term 'winsock' almost universally refers to a transmission control protocol / Internet protocol (TCP/IP) dynamic link library, or .DLL file that assists in connecting your PC to an ISP. Remember that TCP/IP is the protocol or language of the Internet.

A SNAPSHOT OF THE ISP ACCESS INDUSTRY

The figures from Boardwatch Magazine's ISP directory were announced at the August, 1996 ISPcon (Internet Service Provider's Convention) by Jack Rickard, editor in chief. The following figures were derived from their ISP poll and apply to access providers only, as opposed to organizations that just provide web markup or some other peripheral Internet service. These figures do not include information from Sprint, MCI or AT&T:

ISPs in North America (Includes Canada):	3,030+
States with the most ISP organizations:	

California	406
Florida	169
Texas	161
New York	143
Illinois	110

ISP Company Demographics:

Median age of company	14 months
Average number of employees	12
Median number of employees	5
Average number of area codes	3 serviced
% of ISPs in only one area code	56%
(42 serve more than 15 area codes)	

Dial Up account information:

Average # of users	1,303
Median # of users	400
Average access price	$21.37
Median access price	$19.95

Revenue:

Average monthly gross	$27,845
Median monthly gross	$7,980
Cumulative monthly gross	$81 million
Cumulative yearly gross	$980 million

T1 service:

# of ISPs offering T1 service	725
Average monthly price of service	$1,366
Median monthly price of service	$1,200
Average price from a major backbone:	$2,367

Note: These are port fees only and do not include the wire's cost

Dial up connections to the TCP/IP Internet network are accomplished using one of two protocols, SLIP or PPP. SLIP is the serial line interface protocol. It's older than PPP and is less reliable as well. SLIP has no inherent compression built into it whereas PPP does. Using what is called Van Jacobsen's header compression with SLIP, where allowed, makes for a faster connection to the Internet. This is often called C/SLIP for compressed SLIP connections. If at all possible, use the PPP, point to point protocol, when connecting to the Internet. It's faster by a tiny margin but is also more robust than SLIP. Trumpet Winsock is by far the most popular shareware winsock program in the world. It supports both types of connections. As an ISP you will not have to worry about providing SLIP connections any longer as PPP has become the de facto standard. New variations on PPP are coming out that allow for encrypted communications to an Internet server as well as other enhanced features. Windows 95 and Windows NT both support PPP internally, that is, they have an inherent winsock included with them. For Win 3.x you will need a third party stack.

There are a number of commercially available winsock 'stacks' that will accomplish the task of logging you into an Internet server with a PPP connection. The most prevalent one is called the Trumpet Winsock. Trumpet and it's author, Peter Tattam, were awarded the Dvorak Award for outstanding TCP/IP connectivity software at the 1995 OneISPcon. This was well deserved as Mr. Tattam's Trumpet winsock revolutionized (and popularized) Internet connectivity almost overnight. Trumpet's home page can be reached at www.trumpet.com.au Although if you can reach this home page it's assumed you're using some sort of dialer and winsock already. You'll want to have Trumpet handy for your customers who do not have an internal dialer and TCP/IP stack. If your customers are using Windows95 or Windows NT this part of the puzzle is much easier as these two operating systems can be configured for an Internet connection internally. They can dial into your Internet service and establish a TCP/IP connection with no additional software. After that of course they will have to have some other software to make use of the functions of the Internet.

To get the latest information on how Windows95 can be connected to the net try these web addresses:

- www.windows95.com/connect/tcp.html
- www.microsoft.com

For information on connecting Windows NT to the Internet via SLIP/PPP try one of these web addresses:

- www.microsoft.com
- www.windows.net/ispfaq/

One final note about dialing software and TCP/IP stacks. A number of companies have released Internet suites for use by ISPs. Many of them offer very shoddy applications that do not stack up well against the recommended software list at the end of this section. However, there are some of them who offer quite flexible packages. Shop around when deciding what software you will distribute and support.

Email

Email is the most popular activity on the Internet. Email allows you to send and receive messages, in almost real time, to and from other users who have access to Internet Email. Email will usually contain the ability to 'attach' files to the recipient as well. This depends of course on the particular software and service that you are connected to. In this way you could send a message and a copy of your latest manuscript to a publisher or your professor and have them review it. You could send this message at 8am and they might pick it up at 9am when they check their email. By noon you have a letter waiting for you in your email with commentary from them. Now, if your professor in this scenario is in Hawaii and you are in Alabama you can imagine the cost savings as well as the convenience. Make no mistake about it, Email is the fax of the future.

Your e-mail has been returned due to insufficient voltage.

Who has access to Internet email? It's estimated currently that about 35 million users have access to this resource. All the users of the large national online services have Internet email capabilities too and they account for 8 to 9 million users alone.

The World Wide Web

The web is the largest body of documents ever assembled in one accessible format for public consumption. It consists of text, links to other documents, graphics, audio, video and virtual reality simulations. To be exact, virtual reality and audio portions of the web are not truly hyper text markup language (HTML), the language of the world wide web. These two portions are accomplished by what are called helper applications or 'plug-ins.' The web has become almost endlessly extendible via these plug-ins.

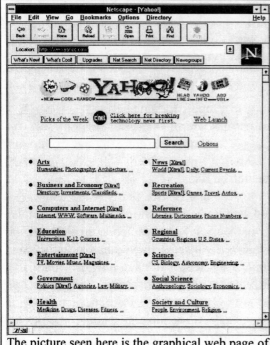

The picture seen here is the graphical web page of the popular Yahoo search engine located at www.yahoo.com. Yahoo allows you to type in key words and then returns lists of web pages that fit your search criteria. It is the equivalent of an Internet yellow pages.

Since these add-ons are doing their work almost seamlessly within Web browsers the difference between the browser and the add-on begin to fade. Soon there will be hundreds of these plug-ins that will allow you to see everything from real time stock quotes across the top of a web window to video conferencing with your friend down the street. The Web is the 'coolest of the cool' Internet applications. The Web was the application that really made the Internet what it is today. Barely three years ago there WAS NO graphical world wide web. The browser was called Lynx and surfed what was an entirely text based digital ocean. You would move your arrow keys to select key words on the screen, hit enter, and jump to that topic. This does not sound too intriguing does it? It wasn't. This is why it took the graphics razzle dazzle portion of the web to get a real audience interested. What can you find on the Web? Anything…if you don't believe me go to Yahoo (www.yahoo.com) or choose the NET SEARCH button at the top of the Netscape browser to access the Infoseek search engine. Search engines are like the 'yellow pages' of the Internet. Type in anything you may be interested in and you will be presented with not a few but literally piles of Web addresses. Some of the search engines on the Internet contain millions of document addresses. Here is a listing of popular web search engines and their associated web addresses:

- Infoseek   guide.infoseek.com/NS
- Yahoo   www.yahoo.com
- Lycos   www.lycos.com
- Superpages   superpages.gte.net
- Alta Vista   www.altavista.digital.com
- Excite   www.excite.com
- C|Nets Search   www.search.com   (Excellent! A database of search engines)

With so much information available at your fingertips it's no wonder that people are falling over themselves to get access to the web. It reminds me of the old joke, why do they put fences around cemeteries? Because people are just dying to get in. There are many people in rural areas just dying for Internet access.

USENET
Usenet is the public sounding board of the Internet. The Usenet consists of 19,000+ newsgroups and growing. Newsgroups are an odd term for these conferences however, outside of some pay-for-play news services available through Usenet the majority of the conferences are made up of individuals participating in them. These

conferences are based on topic names that identify (to some degree) what they are based upon. Some popular identifiers and their categories are listed below:

alt.whatever		Alternative, anything goes.
		Ie. alt.sadistic.dentists.drill.drill.drill
soc	Social	Ie. soc.problems
sci	Scientific	Ie. sci.medicine
talk	Talk, miscellaneous	Ie. talk.politics
rec	Recreation	Ie. rec.woodworking
comp	Computers	Ie. comp.modems

Usenet differs from Email in the fact that any message you send to a conference (a/k/a newsgroup) is posted for all to see. Likewise, any message that anyone else sends to the conference is open for you to see. In this way a public 'conversation' based on stored messages is created. You come in at noon and check out your favorite conference and you reply to a few of the new messages. You post a new message yourself and follow up to one message through private email by replying to the sender's email address and then sign off. Usenet is international and you'll find people from almost every nation participating in one conference or another. The Usenet is a way to network with distant individuals who share your personal or professional interests and its usefulness should not be underestimated.

Just as Email can hold file attachments an entire sub-class of Usenet newsgroups have been created to carry nothing but files in the form of message attachments. This is mainly to allow those who do not have other means available to them to exchange files with the larger body of Internet users. An interesting phenomenon developed out of this however in that the Usenet is by far the largest repository of pornographic images publicly available today. These are the infamous 'alt.binary.pictures…' category of newsgroups. Using the latest Usenet readers one simply has to click on a message that contains a picture and the reader will download the message text and save it as a file with the proper name and extension in place. The Usenet client software then calls the file and if you have the proper viewer associated with the file's extension the viewer will launch and display the graphic. (There is a fine line between being informative and being criminally encouraging. I probably just stepped over it.) Due to the fact that the Usenet is a distributed 'echo' network, just as IRC is (see below), systems that carry these newsgroups carry all the pictures that are deposited in them as well. The only differences being how much history is 'archived' or saved from server to server. Some Usenet servers carry weeks of older messages while some only carry a couple of days worth. A user simply has to make up a fictitious handle and Email address, feed it to their news reader, and they have almost complete anonymity on the Usenet conferences…and thus very little chance of prosecution if the images are found to be obscene. You will have a sub-set of users who will literally demand that you carry these newsgroups. If you don't carry them you face a hidden loss maker in the number of users who will leave your service for another ISP that does carry them. If you do carry them you put yourself in the legal fray with the hundreds or thousands of other ISPs that do carry them. No prosecution has resulted due to carrying these (that I know of) but with the latest telecommunications bill just passed through Congress you can expect the political and legal landscape to be changing rapidly from this point on.

One more note on Usenet servers and we'll save the rest for the how-to aspects of the book…to carry the Usenet newsgroups you need a doozy of a machine and a good high capacity connection. We'll go into the details later.

For now, become acquainted with the following Usenet newsgroups, they will help you on your way to becoming an ISP.

- alt.culture.internet
- alt.internet.services
- alt.bbs.internet

FTP
File Transfer Protocol. This is the protocol that is used to send and receive files across the Internet. Games, utilities, word processing documents, software drivers and more can all be stored in an FTP

site. Using an FTP program you can access tremendous stores of these files. You can also create an 'FTP Site,' a place where others may pickup files. This has a number of advantages in certain situations which we'll discuss in the marketing chapter. Netscape Navigator, the popular Swiss army knife of browser, has built in FTP abilities. To access a public FTP site using Netscape use the following syntax in the LOCATION or URL box: **ftp://address.com** Some popular FTP sites are: Microsoft at ftp.microsoft.com, the SimTel archives at ftp.coast.net, and the Garbo archives in Finland at garbo.uwasa.fi.

TELNET
Although not used as much as in the past Telnet is still an important part of the Internet. When you 'telnet' you log into a remote computer system through the Internet and use its own interface to interact with it. Telnetting to internic.net was suggested earlier as a way for you to find if domain names have been registered. You'll want a good Telnet program that supports Zmodem and ANSI emulation as well. This way you'll be able to log into BBSs through the net and see their menus in the format they were designed to be seen (ANSI). You'll also be able to download files from them using the popular Zmodem protocol. Another great place you may wish to telnet to is boardwatch.com. This is the BBS for Boardwatch Magazine, a fantastic resource for entrepreneurial ISPs.

IRC
Internet Relay Chat is an increasingly popular service. IRC, once discovered, traps a certain percentage of users who are never able to leave! IRC is where people 'chat' or type to each other in real time. There are many publicly available IRC servers which you can log into. There are three popular IRC networks, and any server you log into will 'echo' or carry many if not all of the conferences or chat 'rooms' that the other servers on their IRC network carry. It's not uncommon to log into an IRC server and find 3,000+ conferences with anywhere from 1 to 50+ people in each one. Conference rooms are organized according to title and can be created on the fly by users as well. If you'd like to start a discussion on CAJUN

RECIPES you could do just that. All you have to do then is hope that there are others out there that would like to join in on your discussion. IRC has also been extended beyond its original intentions and programs have developed that give IRC new functionality without necessarily using the IRC server to perform these feats. For instance, you can send and receive files to others in IRC while you are chatting with them, and some programs allow the display of user's pictures. Publishing a list of publicly available IRC servers would be useless as it would be out of date the moment I finished typing it. To find a current list of available IRC servers do a NET SEARCH using one of the Internet search engines listed earlier in this chapter. Search on 'IRC SERVERS' and you should have more than you can contend with.

It's important to note though that IRC servers, like any public good, are 'over grazed.' There are times when it will be impossible to access a public server due to the crowd. The same rule applies to the public Usenet servers. Establishing an in-house IRC server for your network can be very trying to coordinate but it can be done. There are a number of IRC networks in existence. The largest is EFNet with others such as DALNet (www.dal.net) and UnderNet following behind.

Video Conferencing

CUSEEME is a video conferencing program now commercially available through White Pine Software. Using a supported video card and camera and/or audio board you can send and receive audio and video to others on the Internet. You will not want to try this with anything less than a 28.8 modem however. It is a very intriguing service indeed. Although it's a bit of a diamond in the rough at this point expect to see major advances in this technology as White Pine and others continue to push the edge of the envelope in this area.

Just another night on the Internet. This user, going by the handle Bulldog, was found on one of the publicly available CuSeeMe reflectors.

Audio

Audio is becoming a hot commodity on the net. A new technology called RealAudio from Progressive Networks has made a big splash by allowing RealAudio servers to broadcast audio clips to web users. You install the RealAudio player as a helper or plug-in application to your favorite web browser and whenever you click on a RealAudio link a broadcast comes over your PC audio speakers.

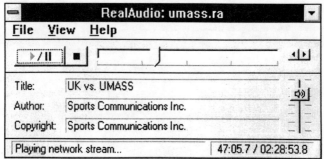

Seen above: The entire audio of UK vs UMASS, being played through the RealAudio plug-in (www.uksports.com)

What does this mean for the end user? Well, for starters, how about listening to the NPR news broadcast whenever *you* feel like it, as opposed to at the top of the hour. Specialty news services are opening up as well that provide these types of 'net-broadcasts' with computer news being at the top of the stack. Another terrific application for this is listening to a song from a recording artist's latest album in a try-before-you-buy type of scenario.

Where Do I Get the Goodies?

A list of the 'cream of the crop' resides below. These are applications that if you have not already done so, you should acquire quickly and put to good use. They will be excellent choices for your future user base and you should become an expert on each of them. I can't stress enough how important this can be to your future well being as an ISP. By providing the best of breed in client software you will be earning the first notch on your gun to competing effectively with your other local providers. You would be surprised how many ISPs just grab the latest shareware version of the most vanilla software and in turn let their users download it or send it to them on disk. By using the most professional client software you will be sending a message to both your users and the competition.

I will add a quick jargon note here to clarify some of the syntax from the last few service examples. End users use 'client software,' often abbreviated as just 'clients.' If you're unfamiliar with the term we'll explain it here. Servers do the hand outs on the Internet. A web server dishes up HTML (web) documents to users who request those documents. These users are clients to the web server. The software they use is client software which takes the output from the server and turns it into something useful for the end user. A web browser client software package takes HTML documents and turns them into something quite attractive (or quite ugly, depending on the designer) for users to view. An IRC client takes the output from an IRC server and turns it into typed conversation that rolls up the users screen. And so on and so forth... Now you understand the client/server relationship. Clients are not 'dumb,' they do have to do some work once they receive data, but they must have input from the servers to do their job.

Application Company Name / Author	'Best of Breed' Software Web Address
Winsock Trumpet Intl.	Trumpet Winsock Www.trumpet.com.au
Email Client Connectsoft	Email Connection www.connectsoft.com
Web Client Netscape	Navigator home.netscape.com
Usenet Client Forte	Agent / Free Agent www.forteinc.com
Telnet Client InterSoft Intl.	NetTerm Starbase.neosoft.com/~zkrr01
FTP Client Alex Kunadze	CuteFTP www.cuteftp.com
IRC Client Khaled Mardam-Bey	mIRC www.mirc.co.uk
Video Conferencing White Pine	CuSeeMe www.wpine.com
Audio Player Progressive Networks	Real Audio www.realaudio.com

In my humble opinion (IMHO, an oft abbreviated term on the net), these are the best that the net has to offer. This list in no way encompasses all of the various Internet clients that are available however, just the most popular ones. Visit the sites and read the most current licensing policy arrangements. You'll want to acquire any freeware/shareware versions available so that you can in turn distribute them to your end users. Many of these are available in both 16bit and 32bit versions as well. The 16bit versions work with Windows 3.x. The 32bit versions work with Windows 95 and Windows NT only. True 32bit software takes advantage of multitasking and new speed capabilities built into these operating systems and inherently should work faster than their 16bit counterparts. Offering both in separate categories, depending on the platform being used, shows your customers that you understand the technology.

Integrated Packages

Distributing all of these packages in a cohesive manner is more easily said than done. Having your users install them individually is out of the question. It would be far too daunting a task for most novices. You should offer them in this à la carte manner for those that are 'in the know,' but the majority of your customers will want an easy installation that walks them through the entire process. The easiest route to take is to use an integrated package offered by Netscape Communications or Microsoft. The Microsoft bundle includes their Internet Explorer web browser and a basic email and news client bundled with a dialer to make the connection to your system. It's available free of cost and can even be downloaded from their web site at www.microsoft.com/isp. Once you license it you can customize it to your liking. I have little love for Internet Explorer but the price is hard to argue with. The Netscape bundle comes with the Netscape Navigator browser which has integrated Email, FTP and Usenet functionality. A dialer is included in the bundle to make the connection. Write to moresales@netscape.com for information. Depending on how many you believe you can sell in a year, you purchase a license that obligates you to a price point per package. This route can be a bit expensive but it will get your clients the best web browser on the market. The cost of course can be amortized over the life of the clients subscription or you may want to charge for the package. The email client and Usenet software that is integrated into Netscape leave a lot to be desired but there's always a tradeoff somewhere. For customizing your own package you might want to take a look at 'InetMgr,' a product from Commercial Computer Solutions (www.ccsweb.com). This package allows you to integrate client software into a nice installation and menu system for your customers. Also see the nice bundle entitled Internet Valet from Intercon (www.intercon.com). Another alternative is to navigate through the various licensing arrangements with the authors of the products you would like to distribute and then have a programmer put them all into one neat package for distribution. This is exactly what Mindspring, the nations largest dial-up Internet provider, has done. There are no easy answers to this one. However, the better and more abundant the tools you empower your users with the more grateful they will be. I can recount endless complaints from customers accusing us of being an incomplete service provider because we did not offer telnet on our network (when in fact any PPP session is capable of using Telnet). A slight variation of an old saying comes to mind here, 'It's the software stupid!'

Just a quick note on 'shareware'. The 'try before you buy' concept of shareware is on the honor system. All of the applications mentioned above are available on the net as a shareware or demonstration release. Many programmers work long hours to build outstanding applications. If you find their programs useful you should register them to support the people who worked so hard to bring them to you. Please encourage your users to do likewise and support the shareware concept.

The Ghost of Internet Future

What is it Worth?
As of this writing the Internet is already a TEN BILLION dollar industry as estimated by a number of sources. There's no point in arguing this, if you have read this far you have some sort of feeling for the type of opportunity the net is presenting to entrepreneurs and investors alike. Regardless of how many billions of dollars this market is currently worth I assure you it will be worth twice as much by the end of the millennium. It appears that there will be plenty of business to go around for quite some time.

The future of the Internet is one thing if nothing else, BIG. Consider a resource like the telephone and a medium such as newspapers and television. Now take the best that all of them have to offer and imagine where it may go…. The Internet will be as popular as the telephone in 20 years; most houses and the vast majority of the population of the planet will have access to it in one form or another. You simply can't take a low cost 'best of all possible worlds' and not expect it to grow like Bill Gate's checking account. The opportunities are almost limitless; it's as if we all suddenly became potential newspaper publishers and TV broadcasters all rolled into one, but at an extremely low cost (comparatively). Currently there is little regulation concerning the Internet. It will take a number of years for the latest telecommunications bill to be shaped and molded by the courts. Current issues that concern ISPs are copyright infringement and obscenity claims that have and will be made in the future. However, more regulations, licensing and taxes are on the way, you can bank on it. A good book that covers online legal issues is listed in the last chapter and it will behoove the new ISP to read it.

What about the future of dial up access? Many ISPs fear that dial up access will become a commodity product that everyone will offer. This may be true, everyone may very well attempt to offer it. Who will offer it successfully though? Compuserve has seen just a portion of the subscribers it expected to gain with its WOW Internet service. MSN, the Microsoft Network, was to be the mouse that roared but has made just a squeak. Those who provide outstanding customer support will be able to compete. Those who do not offer terrific support will fail. The price on unlimited dial up access is falling almost monthly in every major metropolitan area. If you can offer excellent customer service and otherwise differentiate your company you will be able to carve out a potentially very large chunk of this business, even in the most competitive city. Even if the phone companies and everyone else jumps on this band wagon I think you can take a lot of customers and give them something very special for their money, TLC, tender loving care. They will stay with you through thick and thin and they may even pay more for the service if you do this well enough. Outside of the large cities rural areas offer a gold mine for ISPs. The rural areas are almost always last to be serviced by anyone, including the largest national providers! A small town of 15,000 can still provide enough customers to make an ISP fly if there are not already five other competitors for the business. Don't be discouraged by competition though, if you plan your business right and take care of the user base you will persevere. As change occurs and competition increases, the smaller, single territory provider will be presented with many opportunities to join with larger regional networks if they so desire. One way or the other, the bright ISPs future looks good.

ISPs who can offer comprehensive programming services at good fees will make a killing in the coming years. Simple HTML and dial up access *can* be offered by anyone, although whether it is done with the proper service is another story. Programming however will continue to remain a niche area for quite a while. The learning curve is much steeper in this area and it is not for the faint of heart. If you know good programmers in your area, especially hungry ones, jump on them now! This business is not locale specific either, a good programming shop can offer custom services from anywhere. They can also develop programs that can be sold nation-wide or even worldwide. Five years from now I believe that this will be *the* top revenue producing area, not dial up and not simple web services. Do not get me wrong though, there will still be a market for these services and any qualified group will be able to make money from them, but the competition will be much stiffer. Prepare for the future now by becoming a programming and content resource, these are services that can not be duplicated verbatim.

If debugging is the process of removing bugs, then programming must be the process of putting them in.

CHAPTER II

BUSINESS OPPORTUNITIES ON THE NET

When I first started an ISP I had no concept that there were so many varied services that users would request. Due to this inexperience and the sophistication of our users our product mix and pricing structures were constantly undergoing updates and total overhauls. During our first three months of operation it was impossible to find a 'total price list' which we could present to a potential client. Any price lists we had on hand were thrown out the door within three weeks as we revised our fee structures. This amounted to a tremendous loss of time. It also showed our customers that we were not clear on what our pricing was and made us 'appear our age.' The following conversation is similar to ones I hear on a weekly basis as we continue to price our competition's service;

Customer: Do you offer FTP sites for companies?
ISP: Uhhh, sure.
Customer: What are your rates?
ISP: Hmmm, what sounds fair to you?

If I had a better understanding of all of the potential services available, even to the most green ISP, I could have priced them according to our market situation. The type of conversation shown above should be avoided at all costs. In this chapter you will receive a crash course in Internet services. Although pricing is discussed here, don't be tempted to put a price on these just yet or begin to contemplate what you can charge for these varied options. The next chapter deals with your competitive market picture and after you've followed the directions there you will be much better positioned to begin pricing your future services.

I've broken down potential revenue streams for an ISP into four categories as seen here:

Internet Revenue Streams

Access

Access is whereby you as an ISP provide Internet connectivity for your clients. Your customers either want access to the Internet individually or wish to tie a larger network of computers to the Internet full time. This access does not have to entail any other single option other than a connection to your Internet network, but in many cases it will. All of the considerations will be discussed. If you do not have a thorough understanding of the equipment and services that are discussed next, do not become discouraged. The end of this section discusses more details on leased lines (for dedicated services) and the chapter on equipment will discuss CSU/DSUs and routers.

Dial Up Access - Analog Modems

This is your 'swarm.' Dial up customers are out there in droves, just waiting for Internet access. Many of them may already be on one of the larger national services and looking for a more affordable local alternative. If you have existing competition there is sure to be a number of users who are dissatisfied with their existing provider. You do have an account on their system, don't you? I knew you did. Find out what their users are saying. What are their weak points? The larger national services tend to be much slower than local ISPs due to the filtering they do to pass Internet information to their proprietary client software and the sheer bulk of their user base traffic. This will be changing and we can expect them to provide faster access to their

While dial up access is by far the most popular method of getting online, it's worth mentioning that a new breed of access is popping up in major cities. The 'public terminal' offers rented time on the Internet. Nowhere is this shown in greater detail than in the emerging cyber cafes. Here you can get coffee, tea, and web access, all at a price. Visit the granddaddy of all cyber cafes, Cybersmith, at www.cybersmith.com. If you're interested in building a cyber café, the Cyberdiner system makes this as easy as brewing a new pot of coffee. Take a peek at: www.cyberplace.com/cyberdiner.html

customers in the near future. After they get up to speed you can still beat the pants off of them in service so don't lose any sleep over this. Your dial up customers will be using modems from speeds of 14,400bps up to the latest standard of 33,600bps (BPS is a measurement of data speed, bits per second). Anything slower than 14,400bps is really impractical for graphical access and I highly recommend you don't sell to these customers but rather suggest a modem upgrade first. Dial up customers will make up the majority of all of your headaches as they will fill your tech support phone line(s) with endless calls. For now, let's get a grip on what they want and what you will have to provide to them. Dial up users want speed! Don't start your new ISP with anything less than 28.8 modems. Preferably you will be able to get the new 33.6 or 56k modems instead. Modems will be discussed in detail in the hardware chapter.

Commonly bundled with dial up access: Dial up customers will also want a 'POP' email account which is almost always bundled with access. This is a standard email box that takes incoming mail for users and stores it on your local server until they are able to pick it up at their next call. Many ISPs are now offering multiple mail accounts to their clients as a value-added service. Dial up users will want *you* to provide them with Usenet access as well. Many of them will wish to have their own home page on the world wide web and whether or not you can charge for this depends really on your market conditions. Potential customers will call you and will want to know the procedures for getting connected, a/k/a 'Where do I get the software.' You will have to be prepared to answer that question for them.

Dial Up Access - 56k Modems
New advances in modem technology have again chased the critics away with tails tucked firmly between their legs. Almost every advance in modem speed has been greeted with skepticism and the unfailing statements that this is 'the limit.' No longer will advances be possible over POTS, we will have to turn to a different technology to get faster speeds. Nothing gives me more satisfaction when these types are proven wrong. Rockwell International, the

largest maker of modem chip sets in the world, is now locked in a race with U.S. Robotics, the largest modem maker in the world, for dominance of a new speed standard in modems. X2 technology, capable of delivering 56kbps access to the end user, is right around the corner. Just as it was with the 33.6 standard, all the big players want their methodology to be dominant. After all, what works for Microsoft... Undoubtedly the early adopters of this new technology will be those who get the worst of the cross fire. When early standards were attempting to hash out the 33.6 standard we ended up with such hybrids as v.FastClass and v.32Terbo. These protocols are never mentioned anymore but users who thought they were getting a long lasting product from purchasing a modem equipped with one of these protocols were sadly disappointed.

There is no doubt that 56k modems are on the way down the pipe, but what can the ISP do to hedge the bets? First, keep in mind that not all ISPs can offer X2 technology. This is because the higher speeds rely on the fact that many ISPs have digital connections for servicing their user base. Digital connections such as channelized T1's and ISDN PRI type circuits (discussed in detail later) can carry many 'voice' or analog modem calls digitally from the RBOC service office to the ISPs site. These types of transport mediums carry your user's data to you digitally with signals made up of 1s and 0s, as opposed to analog transport mediums where the modem's data is transported mainly via electrical pulses representing sound. Plain old telephone services (POTS) carries your data calls to you via analog signals. Making a digital connection to your RBOC is both a function of the equipment you use (it must support digital connections) and the type of wires you order for servicing dial up calls.

Next, if you're not using 56k capable modems from the beginning, be certain that the modems you purchase are software upgradeable. Modems equipped with EPROM chips are able to be reprogrammed by running a simple software program which 'uploads' the new protocol into the chipset. Modems without EPROMs must either be upgraded via a chip replacement or worse, are unable to be upgraded. For instance, the US Robotics consumer line, the Sportster modems, must be upgraded by replacing chips. Their justly named v.Everything Courier class (commercial class) of modems are software upgradeable. When the new 56k standards are finalized you can be sure I'm going to take my home modems and get them 'souped up' in this way. The same goes for our rack modems, we'll simply apply a software patch and presto, a nice *old* rack of 56k capable modems.

56K modems also foretell of the increasing bandwidth needs that an ISP must support. This however is nothing new as the quest for speed is an unstoppable desire. Advanced multimedia applications such as video conferencing and streaming audio need a lot of bandwidth to do their job.

Just to take a quick look at the numbers: Jupiter Communications (www.jup.com), famous for technology research, has estimated that 56k modems will command 50% of the net access market by 1998. They further estimate that 56k will be the norm for 65% of the market by the year 2000. Don't spend a fortune too early in this game by getting 56k modems before they are offered everywhere. It will take some time for the consumer market to catch up with the new standard. Just be sure to get easily upgradable modems and you'll be in good shape (and probably save a bundle.)

Seen on the Net: Technical Support is a race between your staff to build bigger and better idiot-proof systems, and the Universe trying to produce bigger and better idiots. So far, the Universe is winning.

Access Pricing Plans

Pricing plans are a love hate relationship with providers. You want to offer more than one plan so as to extract the most revenue from the largest number of customers possible. If you offer too many however you will find that your pricing plans become unclear to potential users and are an accounting nightmare. I suggest you offer two plans, one low end and one unlimited, or nearly so. These unlimited plans generally run in the

USER TO LINE RATIOS:
There is a mathematical formula that describes how many phone lines an online service provider should have to service x number of customers. I heard about it for years, and I even saw it once though it made no sense to me. The industry average is between 8 to 13 users per phone line. One thing is certain, the more phone lines you have, the more users you can support per phone line. A ten line provider cannot support ½ as many users as a twenty line provider. The same applies to a twenty line provider compared to a forty line provider. When first starting your service I recommend a ratio of no more than ten customers per line until you get a good feel for how many 'busies' your users will be getting.

area of $15 to $30 monthly for users, dependent upon your market and the quality of your service. Unlimited usage has become almost universally the most desired access. However, the problems arise when you have users who stay online beyond human endurance. They leave their mail programs hooked up when they go to eat dinner. They stay connected to IRC when they are asleep. When designing your 'super' plan or unlimited access plan keep these problems in mind. It will be necessary to police your system to some extent and you must be prepared to deal with problem users. Having policies in place makes this job much easier for you. Many providers offer 'super' plans of 200 or 300 hours per month after which they charge a per hour fee. Some simply say, "You can have unlimited access but we police this usage. Please do not abuse the system so that all of our customers may enjoy this service." Make certain that the users know that this is for PERSONAL USE only, not for 24/7 connections that need Internet access. The environment of your service and the number of busy signals or 'busies' that users encounter depend upon how you create and enforce these policies and your user to line ratio.

For a second tier price plan, or a low usage plan, I recommend something in the area of $10 monthly for 15 to 30 hours of usage. Once again, what you can charge is largely dependent on your cost structure, what your competition charges and how well they run their own systems. For extra hours something in the area 50 cents to $1.50 can be found in use today. You must have a user accounting system to enforce this hourly billing however. Trying to achieve this billing feat manually is not possible once you're past 40 or 50 users. Keep this in mind when designing your own price packages.

Setup Fees
Another fee I highly recommend you charge your new customers is a setup charge. Charging for a setup accomplishes a number of tasks; you receive a small amount of up-front income to support this new user as well as add all of their information into your accounting system. You also create a small psychological barrier to exit (and entry) for the customer. This is because the first month is the 'hardest' for them in terms of cost, each additional month is easier due to no additional fees other than their service charge. Most ISPs will charge a setup fee and if this is the case in your own locale then users who wish to 'shop around' and try other services encounter this setup fee as a barrier to entry at every stop they make, thus discouraging them from switching systems too often. Current setup fees range from $5 to $30. The systems with no or low setup fees, all other things being equal, will experience more 'churn' as users come in and exit to try other systems. These ISPs also encounter many flaky users who come in for a month and then refuse to pay their bills thereafter. You've heard the saying 'you get what you pay for.' I'll add to this and say that 'you get what you charge for.' I recommend a standard setup fee of $10 to $20 for most new ISPs.

High or Low Cost
Keep this in mind when developing your own pricing plans; it's easier to lower your costs than to raise them. Don't get stuck in a rut by starting out too low-ball to attract users. Run a 'special' or a two month 'discount' in the beginning. Waive your setup fees for the

first two months as an incentive. Just make certain it's clear to the users that this is a special short-term offer. Also, don't do anything so odd that your accounting system will be unable to handle it or you'll end up doing a lot of manual work to figure out your billing.

Credit Cards -vs- Checks: Charging dial up customers can be one of the easiest or one of the hardest tasks you will face. The preferred method to charging these users is to use their credit card. You will have to have a merchant account to do this (see the chapter on equipment). If they wish to pay by check I have a number of suggestions as to good policies for you. Customers who pay by check are notorious for getting their payment to you late. In addition, they will want you to bill them so that they receive a reminder in the mail each month. This is both time consuming and expensive on the ISPs part. You should design a policy whereby customers you must bill pay an extra $1 to $2 each month. Call this your 'billing' sur-charge. Customers will therefore be tempted to pay with their credit card making your billing procedures mostly automated and thus much easier to handle. Additionally, when a customer contacts you and wishes to pay in this manner you should request that you receive their first check before the account is setup for them. This will save you a lot of back tracking and follow up later as customers tend to 'forget' to send in that first check and yet use your service for the first few weeks to their heart's content.

Voice Support

Access is your primary service for dial up users but it may feel as though technical support is your sole business. Once you reach a couple of hundred users your phones will ring off the hook. It will be important that you have a very open policy for user support. Voice mail, email, phone support, and even possibly fax back services are all necessary for a successful support shop. Keep in mind that many of your callers will be working day jobs so it is important to offer at least a couple of hours of evening support. A good place to start for new ISPs is to offer phone support from the hours of 10am to 7pm. In this way you are available to the bulk of potential callers.

As you begin to develop your help-desk procedures be sure to track the questions you hear the most. If you can discern a pattern then you need to take steps to make this information more readily available. Perhaps you could alleviate 10% of your calls by simply noting a bit of information to the user at the time of singup? Use your help-desk as a pulse on your clientele and their problems and be proactive for your future clients. Help-desks, much like Web server space and Usenet services, can be outsourced. This is a very attractive option for the new ISP. Outsourced services are offered with one of the turn-key solutions mentioned later in the book.

Rollover and Line Costs
There are many nuances when ordering your phone lines that you should keep in mind. If you are setting up your ISP business within your home you may be eligible to use personal lines. These are generally much cheaper than business lines. In some areas this is considered illegal so check with the local regional bell operating company (RBOC), a/k/a the telephone company. If you are locating in a business site you will have to install business lines regardless of their use. For business line customers you may be able to save money by taking advantage of a number of pricing options many Bell companies offer. 'Outbound tariffed' or 'metered' service allows you to deduct a few dollars per line per month for basically charging you for any outbound calls you make on these phone lines. You will not be making many calls on these lines (if any) so check into this. Also, you will not need dial tone and some RBOCs still charge for this service, depending on how backwards they are ($3.00 per line in Kentucky). See if this is an option you can deduct as well. Finally, you will need to add rollover service of some sort to your phone lines so that when the first one is busy the next caller will get your number two modem. For rollover service and phone lines that are being ordered in bulk check with your local RBOC business office on the availability of 'Essex' or 'Centrex' service. These services give you dial tone phone lines but may involve the installation of some equipment in your premises. Depending on local tariffs and the distance of your office from the telco POP you may be able to save a considerable amount of money over the long term.

The Copper Shortage 'Gotcha'
One issue that comes up often with new ISPs is how the phone wires are delivered to their business site. When ordering POTS lines into your site for your dial up customers there often arises a shortage of 'copper' or wiring to deliver these lines. Plain copper pairs, the two pairs of wires that run phone service into a location, are universally offered as the default way of running voice traffic into a location. For one, two or even ten phone lines this is usually acceptable. What happens though is that as an ISP grows the available 'copper' to a location runs out. The phone company only has so many copper pairs available in any particular area and once they are gone new cables have to be installed. If the wiring is underground, as it is in most new areas, this might require digging up roads, driveways and yards. Your neighbors will not appreciate this to say the least and it could delay the installation of new voice circuits by weeks! The RBOCs do not always mention it but there is a solution to this. There is a class of equipment known generically as 'Channel Banks' that take two pair of copper wires and break the signal out of them into 24 separate voice channels. As you can see, this is a fantastic way of conserving the existing copper wiring. The installation requires that a channel bank be installed at the telco CO (central office) that supplies your site with phone service. Another channel bank is installed at your location and this box breaks the signal out into individual voice circuits. The channel banks require additional electricity to do their magic so an uninterruptible power supply (UPS) is usually included with them in the event that you lose power to your facility. This class of service is also called 'channelized T1.' This is due to the fact that a T1 data circuit is used to transport the voice traffic over the 24 data channels that a T1 makes available. Some Remote Access Servers, highly integrated hardware solutions, incorporate channel banks into their existing circuitry. You'll see this later in the Ascend solution for an ISPs POP.

When dealing with your RBOC representative you may want to mention your expectations of expansion and subsequent need for more voice circuits in the future. Bring up the topic of a channel bank and see what they have to say. I've heard that tariffs for this type of service vary from city to city but in Louisville we were able to get them at absolutely no additional cost. This made our expansions relatively painless and fast while other ISPs played 'beat the clock' when installing additional circuits. They just didn't know what to ask for. If they do insist that you pay for them be certain to investigate the options. Your RBOC may be allowed to charge for channel banks but may also be required to supply you with as many copper circuits as you request. If so, you have a loophole here with which to leverage your request for channel banks. They do not really look forward to digging up streets and laying more wires if they do not have to.

While we're on the topic of the local telcos, I'll give you another bit of advice that can make your life easier down the road. Establish a major rapport with your service technicians. Give them free net access, home-pages and software. Send tech support to their house to install the whole package. Invite them to all of your parties and when they visit your site take them out to lunch! The amount of tips and technical support you will receive in return will surprise you. In addition to having all of the answers, these people encounter hundreds of individuals and businesses every single month. You get the gist. Just don't lose their business card!

Dedicated Access - Modems
There will come a time when you will receive requests for dedicated or 'nailed up' 28.8 (33.6 or even 56k) modem lines. These are useful for groups who desire a continuous connection to the net but do not have a need for a lot of bandwidth (yet!). BBSs are prime candidates for this type of access. They purchase it from you and in turn supply two to three phone lines of their system with Internet access. In Kentucky you can currently get 28.8 full time connections for $100 to $150 monthly. Setup charges are generally in the area of $50 to $150 as well. For customers who need this type of access you will often be asked to supply a domain name and a certain number of sub-netted IP addresses. This can be another source of revenue (see the section on DNS in this chapter). When pricing this service's monthly cost and the setup charge keep in mind what a modem will cost, how valuable that port is to you, and what the phone line installation and the monthly charges will run you. I recommend a monthly pricing of 3 to 5 times the monthly cost of the phone circuit.

This is the big variable in this equation. If your costs are higher it's difficult to extract this from your customers and the RBOC gets a lot of your potential share of revenue.

Dial Up Access - ISDN

ISDN stands for Integrated Services Digital Network. ISDN is a high speed switched data circuit that carries both voice and/or data. Although ancient in origins, the RBOCs have just recently begun to formulate a standardized strategy for rolling it out to customers. This is partially market driven as users beg for more bandwidth in their data connections and partially as a response to the coming data networks that the cable companies intend to roll out.

ISDN is High Speed

ISDN has two 'B' or bearer channels and one 'D' or data channel. This is why ISDN service is often referred to as '2B+D'. The two bearer channels can move up to 64kbps per second (compared to a 28.8kbps on a standard modem) each and the D-channel can move 16kbps of data. Kbps is Kilo Bits per second, a measurement of data speed. This type of ISDN line is referred to as 'basic rate interface', or BRI for short. You will also hear of PRI, 'primary rate interface,' which refers to a larger ISDN circuit that consists of 23 64k 'B' channels and one 64k 'D' channel. As with any data circuit, you need to be armed with all of the semantics when requesting the service. It was originally intended that the two B-channels would carry two voice lines and the D-channel would carry digital signaling (also known as 'out of band') information. The D-channel's bandwidth is still used in this way so as an ISP you should be concerned with the possibilities of the bearer channels. Making a data connection with one of the B channels will give you a very snappy 64kbps data throughput. However, utilizing what is called inverse multiplexing you can bond the two bearer channels together for an effective throughput of 128kbps. This is an Internet user's dream connection. At roughly 5 times the speed of a standard modem web pages tend to snap on screen and downloads seem to just fall onto your hard-drive.

ISDN - A Switched Circuit?
A 'switched' circuit refers to a data or voice line that can basically make and receive calls. You can originate a call from a switched circuit to another end point of the same type of connection. As an end user you will be most familiar with POTS, plain old telephone service, which is a switched network of phone lines. You can originate a call from one end to any other voice line in the world (well, sometimes). The same is true (mostly) for ISDN circuits. The two bearer (B) channels have what are called SPIDS, or telephone numbers in layman's terms. Using the known SPIDS of another ISDN circuit you can make a call to that line. Switched circuits are the opposite of hard-wired or 'nailed up' circuits that only run from one location to another. T1 and 56k circuits are two examples of 'nailed-up' lines.

ISDN - Voice or data?
Yes, given your particular ISDN terminal equipment and the type of ISDN service you order you can use one or both channels for voice or data. For instance, on channel 1 you could make a 64kbps connection to a local provider and on channel 2 you could call someone down the street who does not have to have ISDN to talk with you. You could make two simultaneous phone calls to different people, or you could have a full 128k connection to an Internet provider who offered inverse multiplexing that was compatible with your ISDN adapter.

ISDN - Analog and Digital
Much of the ISDN equipment on the market offers one or two analog ports built in. As we've mentioned before, these ports offer the user the convenience of standard analog equipment tied to their ISDN equipment. Ie. standard phones, fax machines and modems can all use one or both of the ISDN circuits to make a connection to other analog devices. Originally it was envisioned that ISDN-enabled devices (phones, faxes, etc.) would make use of the ISDN circuit directly. Who wants to upgrade when their existing handset works fine? Due to the lack of enthusiasm for upgrading current equipment the conversion circuitry for digital-to-analog translation has been incorporated into most ISDN boxes.

ISDN - Availability and Pricing

ISDN is not yet universally available. You will have to check with your local RBOC on availability and pricing. There are many nuances to ISDN availability as well. Some RBOCs do not offer flat rate ISDN service, which makes it very unattractive for 24/7 connections. Some charge you more depending on your distance to their POP (point of presence). If you're within a ¼ mile radius of their POP they charge you their standard rate each month, if you're further from the POP they may charge you in increments based on ¼ mile distances. There are almost always different prices for personal use versus business lines as well. And finally, if the local RBOC does offer flat rate service you may be able to get ISDN circuits for your ISP business that are 'tariffed outbound' or metered. Once again, this means that you only pay extra when you make outbound calls from your lines. This is a money saver for ISPs as you can order all of your phone lines and ISDN lines this way and save a few dollars each per month. Your customers will be calling you, not the other way around right? Likewise, from a customer's point of view, flat rate is almost always more desirable than metered service. A new twist on this scenario is where the telcos offer PRI with unlimited outbound service and only meter the end-user's BRI. As an ISP you could acquire a PRI circuit and have your equipment setup for 'dial-back.' In this way, the customer initiates the call but only uses a few seconds of metered time. The ISP is thus able to utilize this handy loop-hole to continue to offer dedicated ISDN service. Just a little something to consider.

ISDN - Differing Connectivity Methods

ISDN adapters can interface with your network in one of two ways. You can have an ISDN 'terminal adapter' which plugs into an RS-232 type serial port or you can have an ISDN router which plugs directly into your ethernet. The Motorola Bitsurfer pro is an RS-232 type ISDN adapter and the Ascend Pipeline 50 is an ethernet type ISDN adapter. The terminal adapter variety have the drawback that they can only communicate at an effective throughput of 115kbps, the top speed of a 16550 buffered UART or COM port. A new breed of low cost internal ISDN adapters that can break this barrier are offered by some vendors. These adapters are on a PC card which will need to be inserted into a free slot inside of the computer they are attached to. One current problem with ISDN is that the adapters do not necessarily work with each other perfectly if they're not made by the same company. Most all of them will talk to each other at 64kbps utilizing one B channel. However, if you want to get compression between the two adapters you had better first check with the manufacturers and see if their compression schemes are compatible. Compression effectively increases your throughput when sending and receiving uncompressed data such as plain text. Likewise, if you hope to get both B channels connected for 128kbps throughput you will need to do the same. This is one of the main stumbling blocks for ISPs when rolling out ISDN service to businesses. The best rule of thumb is to standardize on one type of adapter for business use and one type for personal use and then learn what other adapters they are compatible with. For all practical purposes, an ISP will desire to use the more sophisticated ethernet enabled equipment, either via individual units or in more sophisticated packages that rack many ISDN adapters together. This is both for manageability purposes and efficiency reasons. Ascend Communications (www.ascend.com) offers a full range of ISDN equipment.

When ordering ISDN equipment be sure that they have NT1 or a 'terminator' built into them. Older ISDN equipment did not have these built in and you see many 'fire sale' type prices on this older equipment today. Don't be fooled into buying one of these older adapters, the NT1 will cost you close to $100 alone.

Throughput: What you feel like doing with your foot and your computer screen after seeing the message, "General Failure Reading Drive C:".

ISDN - Dial Up Pricing
Prices for dial up ISDN Internet service depend on your ISDN equipment costs and ISDN line charges, both of which must be factored into your Internet service fees. ISDN service can be obtained in Tennessee for as low as $25 monthly for residential use while in Louisville, Kentucky, the price is $65 monthly for residential service. You most assuredly will pay more for business lines and it is worth noting that Tennessee is definitely the low end

exception. To effectively provide ISDN dial up service you must be in an area that has ISDN prominently advertised and inexpensively available from the local RBOC. California and Tennessee are two states that are quickly converting to ISDN en masse. You must also consider that the equipment will definitely cost you more than standard analog modems. To make full use of the two ISDN B channels you will need ISDN equipment that can take two different calls for 64kbps connections and connect both of them to your Internet server. Many terminal adapters will not allow this so you'll most likely have to standardize on the higher priced ethernet type adapters. Check with your specific hardware vendors to find out what they recommend. It's a terrible waste to have two B channels on an ISDN line but only one of them available to dial up callers.

ISDN - Dedicated Access
Dedicated ISDN access is a very attractive alternative to companies that need a full time connection to the net where 28.8 speeds are too slow and fractional T1 costs too much. Be certain that you include a setup fee to cover your line installation costs. You'll also want to have pricing for both dedicated 64kbps and 128kbps. When companies don't want to make the leap to a full 128kbps you can really make a good revenue stream from selling two ISDN 64k channels. You will get to charge two setup fees and draw in two different customers. Don't make your 64kbps pricing exactly half of the 128kbps option, something in the area of 70% is closer to what you will want to charge. This gives companies incentive to go the entire distance and take the full ISDN circuit. If they do not, you make more by selling off the two separate B channels than you would by selling the entire line. This is only right as you will have to service not one but two customers so the extra revenue is more than justified.

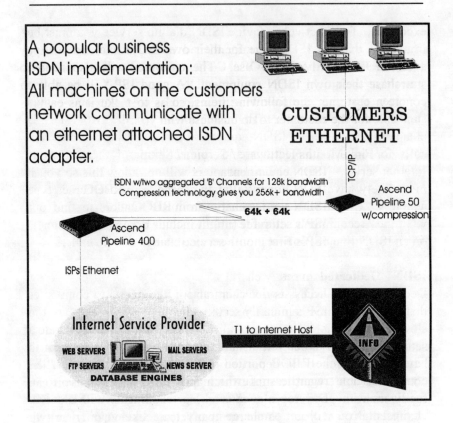

A popular business ISDN implementation: All machines on the customers network communicate with an ethernet attached ISDN adapter.

CUSTOMERS ETHERNET

TCP/IP

ISDN w/two aggregated 'B' Channels for 128k bandwidth
Compression technology gives you 256k+ bandwidth

64k + 64k

Ascend
Pipeline 50
w/compression

Ascend
Pipeline 400

ISPs Ethernet

Internet Service Provider

WEB SERVERS   MAIL SERVERS
FTP SERVERS   NEWS SERVER
DATABASE ENGINES

T1 to Internet Host

INFO

ISDN - Dedicated Access Pricing

Take into account a good startup fee when figuring a pricing schedule for dedicated ISDN service. You will need to purchase an ISDN adapter and have an ISDN line installed at your site to service this customer. Although you do not need to cover the entire cost of the ISDN adapter and the installation, the setup fee should take a major chunk of this burden away from you. Your monthly charges should be enough to cover the ISDN line on your side and provide a reasonable pay back time for the equipment. After the pay back period you own the equipment knowing that the customer has funded this. All monthly charges after this period include a good portion of revenue that falls directly to your bottom line. Additional services that the customer may request include domain names and multiple IP addresses. These can be additional sources of revenue for the ISP.

Unless you opt to roll the circuit's cost into your own fee, the customer will be responsible for their own ISDN line and will pay the RBOC directly for its use. The customer will also need to purchase their own ISDN equipment. A good ISP will be able to quote a customer the following items, so as to make it as easy as possible for the customer to do business with you:

> First Months Hardware / Service / Setup
> > ISDN equipment
> > ISDN line installation charge from RBOC
> > ISDN service charge from RBOC
> > ISP's setup fee (might include domain name, etc.)
> > ISP's first month service charge
>
> Recurring monthly charges
> > ISDN service charge from RBOC
> > ISP's monthly service charge

Make it clear to the customer that you are doing this as a service to them and that the RBOC portion of the bill is something that they cannot escape regardless of which ISP they may choose to do business with. Develop a good working relationship with a service representative at your phone company (just like your friend, the technician). They will assist you in getting fast price quotes on ISDN installation and monthly charges for your customers. This extra service will be much appreciated as you help the customer realize the full extent of the charges they will be paying.

YET MORE JARGON	
CAP	A 'competitive access provider,' an alternative to the RBOC for local in-state voice or data traffic.
Carrier	Anyone who handles leased lines and data/voice traffic, usually a long distance company.
Crook	One who steals, with or without the consent of the law.
POP	Point of Presence, an equipment location or access point for voice and data carriers.
RBOC	Regional Bell Operating Company, the phone company
Local Loop	The run of a data wire from a business site to a POP

56k, T1 and Fractional T1 Dedicated Access

56kbps wires are called DS0s (Data Service 0) in the RBOC infrastructure. They are without a doubt one of the worst deals on the market today for everyone but the RBOC. A 56kbps wire requires that you as an ISP provide two very expensive pieces of equipment to talk with this line. A CSU/DSU will be needed to interface the 56k wire to a free port on a router, another pricey component. (Routers and CSU/DSUs will be explained in the equipment chapter) A cheap CSU/DSU that handles only 56k lines will cost you a few hundred dollars and a router can run $800.00 on the low low end. Even integrated solutions will run near a thousand dollars. Additionally, most 56k wires are nailed-up lines, originating at one point and terminating in another. Switched 56k, as opposed to a nailed up wire, does exist but is also on the way out. The installation costs on these lines can vary widely from one city to another. Costs for 56k wires (as well as T1s and other slices of a T1) consist of two 'local loops.' The local loop is the portion of the wire that runs from the wire carrier's POP to an end point for the circuit. Since there are two destinations, one for each end of the wire, there are two local loops that will be priced for this type of line. The distance from the POP as well as the distance between the POPs is often counted in the monthly costs for this service. The closer the two destinations are to their respective POPs and the closer the POPs are to each other, the less expensive the wire will be. With the advent of ISDN 64k and 128k service, dedicated 56k wires are dinosaurs. They generally cost more than ISDN to install and to maintain on a monthly basis. The equipment necessary costs more than ISDN equipment as well. If you or customers you service are in an area that does not offer good ISDN service this may still be a marketable niche for you for the short term.

T1 wires are referred to as DS1s (Data Service 1) or 'megalinks' in the RBOC infrastructure. More generically, 56k as well as T1 wires are referred to as 'leased lines,' as they are rented from the circuit's provider. A T1 is the preferred way of connecting an ISP to the Internet as they offer a tremendous amount of bandwidth. A full T1 is made up of 24 channels of 56kbps effective throughput. You'll also see them noted as 64kbps total bandwidth per channel with the lost amount used for signalling and synchronization. It is this 'channelized' nature of T1 wires that allows ISPs to offer 'fractional T1' service (sometimes called just 'frac,' pronounced 'frack') to customers. Common configurations for frac service include 4 channels x 64kbps for a total of 256kbps and 8 channels for a total of 512kbps.

Now we can delve back into the eccentricities of the RBOC pricing structure to discuss how frac service works in the real world. In practice you can not always buy a fractional T1 line. Some areas do not have this type of service tariffed, offered in their monopoly pricing schedules. Therefore you may need to run a full T1 wire to a customer's site because you wish to sell them fractional T1 bandwidth. Why is this? The physical wire and interconnections for a T1 is the same as for a fractional T1. Fractional T1s utilize only a certain number of channels, generally limited at the provider's site. So, if an RBOC cannot control the amount of data that passes through the wire they tend to charge you for the maximum potential usage of it. The wire cost is one issue, but what are you concerned with? The Internet service charge to the customer. By utilizing a CSU/DSU you can choose how many channels of 64kbps to open up to the customers site. At the customer's site their CSU/DSU will have to be configured accordingly or the data stream will not be able to be interpreted. Thus, you control the spigot of data flow on your end! Although the customer will have to bear the brunt of whatever a T1 wire costs, you can offer them a spectrum of many different bandwidths of data flow to suit their needs and their budget.

Large businesses and even small to medium size businesses that have a need for a lot of bandwidth will order T1 and Frac-T1 service from an ISP. Video conferencing centers are on the rise and you will find that many of them will need more bandwidth than ISDN can offer. Having a solid pricing schedule in hand, as well as the budgeted money for the equipment, is necessary for an ISP to successfully tap into this access market.

56k, T1 Dedicated Pricing

The setup fees for this type of service are generally quite high, in the area of $500+. This is due to the cost of the connectivity hardware for T1 and Frac T1 services including a CSU/DSU plus a router. The customer will also have to pay for the installation of the leased line, not only to their own site but for your portion of the local loop. The ISP's portion of the local loop price is generally included in the startup fee. The customer usually pays the entire cost of the line directly to a carrier or the RBOC. This is opposed to a common variation in the way that ISDN dedicated service is sold. In ISDN dedicated service the ISP can incorporate the price of the ISDN installation and monthly charges into their fees. This is because the costs for ISDN wires are not nearly as expensive as T1 wires. It makes it easier on the customer to understand their monthly billing and allows them to conveniently write just one check per month. With T1 service the line costs are so high that the ISP does not want to be responsible for this if there were to be a default on the charges by the customer. Your customers for these high bandwidth services are going to almost always request a domain name and many IP addresses to support a network on their end of the pipe. In some cases you will need to provide an entire Class-C address (256 IP addresses) to them.

Be prepared to offer a high level of service to these customers, perhaps even visiting them on-site numerous times to close a deal like this. This customer will be paying you a large amount of money on a monthly basis and they will want to be assured of your abilities to provide them reliable and timely service. Network monitoring is a must for these customers. You must be constantly vigilant to keep the bandwidth optimized for their service. A quote to a customer for this type of service will often include the equipment as well, regardless of whether or not you will be directly selling it to them. If they do not have the technical expertise in-house to install this type of connection you may be requested to do a lot of on-site work and this should be included in your setup fee. They may not know what type of equipment they will need given their network environment and you will have to get into the network integration business, or at least be knowledgeable enough to point them in the right direction. They will want to know the entire answer and you will have to give it to them. An outline for a typical quote to such a customer should include the following:

> First months hardware / installation / service
>> T1 / Frac T1 Installation (paid to carrier)
>> T1 / Frac T1 monthly service (paid to carrier)
>> CSU/DSU equipment for their end
>> Router for their end
>> Transceiver for router's AUI port
>> ISP's setup fee (standard setup fee plus domain, etc.)
>> ISP's on-site installation charge
>> ISP's first month service charge
>
> Monthly recurring charges
>> T1 / Frac T1 monthly service (paid to carrier)
>> ISP's Internet service charge

Typical T1 Internet service (access fees, not wire costs) charges range from a low of $900 to well over $2000 monthly. The low end is charged by ISPs and the high end is usually charged by the large carriers. Fractional T1 runs the gamut from a full T1 down. Price the service intelligently. Make the first leap larger and progressive steps up in bandwidth less expensive. This encourages customers to 'go for broke,' hopefully not literally, and get a larger feed.

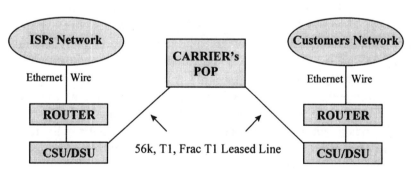

The Virtual Private Network (VPN)

Before we close our discussion of dedicated circuits it is important to note a new service that is being pitched to businesses nationwide. The Virtual Private Network (VPN) is a series of offices tied together via the public network as opposed to directly via leased lines. The offices in this scenario still need dedicated circuits but the cost to run lines down the street to the local ISP and the Internet service charge are generally less than it costs to run them hundreds of miles to tie all the disparate locations together. Outside of a possible windfall of savings the biggest side benefit is all of the Internet services that can now be made use of. There are literally tens of thousands of companies out there with dedicated circuits tying them to remote offices. Because of this legacy of 'islands' in the world you should have no problems targeting potential sales leads.

Security is of the utmost importance when moving corporate data over the Internet so another key phrase you will hear in the same breath as VPN is the concept of the tunneling protocol (TP). TP is the process of wrapping up data in an encrypted envelope within the standard Internet Protocol (IP). In this way, third parties can not hope to make sense of the communications as they travel over the public network. A TP can be implemented in software such as that found in Windows NT 4.0. NT now includes a new variation of PPP with encryption and this is in essence a tunneling protocol. Hardware makers such as Ascend Communications (www.ascend.com) also make a variety of hardware routers and interfaces that encrypt communications before they hit the Internet. By offering VPN's you are extending your services into the realm of the WAN (wide area network) administrator. The LAN (local area network) administrator is thus left to do their job effectively and not worry about how the data is going to get from one campus to the next. In many cases offering a VPN is as simple as swapping out standard components for hardware that is encryption enabled. Managing this is a value added service to the customer and thus commands a value-added charge on top of your normal service fees. If you're comfortable in the role of network integrator and manager this may well be worth looking into.

Caps, Carriers & Crooks
You will be a customer yourself for leased lines if you become an ISP. Leased lines for providing access to ISPs is discussed in the

chapter on getting a connection. If you grow sufficiently you will have customers who will require leased lines from you, or more precisely, Internet service which will travel over leased lines. Once upon a time there was only one game in town for leased lines, your local telephone company. Laws and deregulation have brought about an explosion of alternatives for you. The large long distance carriers burst into the scene early on to take advantage of this market. It was a natural extension of their normal business and all of them will be happy to sell a leased line from you to your customers. In addition to the carriers there is a new breed of provider popping up in many large cities. CAPS, competitive access providers, are moving in to slug it out with your local RBOC. They are providing dial tone, ISDN and leased line services to everyone within reach of their own private fiber and copper networks. Many of these providers are laying wire even as I type, all hoping to get a part of the leased line and dial tone business which has been the sole sanctuary of the baby Bells (the RBOCs) for all of these years.

It is important to stay abreast of the competition in the data and voice markets. Competition lowers prices so Internet service as a whole is more attractive to high bandwidth users as leased lines have become less expensive. It's also advantageous if you wish to assume the responsibility of the leased line contracts for your customers. In this way you can quote a customer the service *and* the leased line and charge a bit extra for the setup and the monthly line costs. Additionally, if you have a full working knowledge of all of the leased line providers in your area you might be able to price the total package lower by finding the most competitive source for the circuit. This will both please and impress your clients and you will win more business this way.

Keep the following long distance providers in mind when pricing your leased lines: MCI, Sprint, AT&T and Worldcom (formerly LDDS and Wiltel). Call the local RBOC, you never know, they may surprise us one day. And finally, to locate the CAPs in your area call some of the major phone systems and network equipment providers. They are an excellent source for information of this sort.

But What About Wireless?
In the never ending battle to remove the 'middleman' (the RBOC) from the ISP equation, some providers have come up with innovative ways to provide access via the airwaves. If you can do away with your own needs for dial up lines you have saved a monthly fortune on your own connectivity costs. If you can do away with your customers need for a dial up line you have made them truly mobile and saved them money and the hassles of sharing their existing voice circuit(s). Although not widely deployed yet, services such as Metricom's Ricochet network are doing just this. Metricom is a Los Gatos, California, company founded in 1985. The original business operation was devoted to wireless data transfer for corporate customers. In 1995 they launched Metricom, their wireless Internet access service. Data is shipped via an unlicensed portion of the 900mhz spectrum from a small transmitter that is hooked to portables or desktop computers through the standard serial port. A network of repeaters captures the data and pumps it back to a network operations center in Texas where it is piped to the Internet at large. Performance is similar to a 28.8 modem although it can vary widely depending on your location. Compared to the standard way of computing on the run, over cellular phones, the performance is comparable or better. The cost however is just a fraction of what a user faces with cellular communications. Metricom now offers access in portions of California, Oregon, Washington state and Washington, DC. For more information visit www.metricom.com.

Although in theory this is a fantastic way to offer access to your customers, the enormous capital outlays for such an endeavor would be far out of reach of most ISP startups. We can hope however that in time the commercialization of the free 900mhz spectrum will bring down the cost of wireless gear and make this an attractive alternative for the end user. Far more feasible today are the larger wireless transmitters that can replace the costly dedicated wires for high bandwidth customers. The monthly recurring costs for frame and T1 connections are the killer for the ISP and customers and these devices can get around this.

The Wi-Lan Hopper - Best of Breed in Wireless

Wi-LAN, a Canadian company based in Calgary, offers a 1.5 mbps solution for wireless communications in the form of their Hopper product line. The benefits of wireless should be readily apparent, no T1 installation costs, no T1 monthly recurring charges, no CSU equipment needed, etc. Makes an ISP kind of water at the mouth thinking about all of these cost savings. The Hopper has the following added benefits: long distance and multiple remote reception points to share the bandwidth. In mild terrain with few physical barriers the Hopper has been tested at up to 6 miles distance with no data loss whereas the densest cities might reduce this to 1.3 miles. Considering that the majority of buildings in a large city will be found in a one to two mile radius this doesn't present a problem. Now, what if you have three customers that need heavy Internet access? With three reception points you can share the 1.5 mbps total bandwidth and each customer could get a theoretical maximum of 500kbps, very comparable to a good fractional T1 offering. When other clients are not utilizing the service a single customer could burst to full T1 speeds as well. Total startup costs about $7000, and when compared to the potential ongoing savings, this is a small price to pay. You can contact Wi-LAN at (800)258-6876 or via the web at www.wi-lan.com.

We see that there are many opportunities for the innovative ISP to become the premiere network access provider in their respective locales. Access is often the most visible service that an ISP offers but there are many other opportunities to generate revenue.

Web Pages

The World Wide Web is the dominant medium for mass communication on the Internet. It is no longer the baby brother on the block. Graphical Web pages came after Email, Usenet, FTP and many other Internet services had long been in existence, yet it's quickly become the major mover and shaker of the net. The web has magazines, news, hobbyist areas, graphical file depots, music archives, company information, personal resumes and more all available at the click of a button. If it's hot you can guarantee it's on the Web.

Browsers and Standards

The Web is composed of what is called HTML documents. HTML is the Hyper Text Markup Language. Not nearly as difficult to master as a true programming language, HTML can be learned by anyone who applies themselves. Within a week you can be churning out web pages with graphics, et al. This does not mean that HTML necessarily means that everyone becomes a graphic designer and layout artist over night. These talents are in much demand as there is a big difference between churning out web pages and designing attractive and functional sites for viewers. The programs that allow end users to view these pages, glorious graphics and all, are called web browsers, or just browsers for short. At the top of the heap of Web browser companies is Netscape Communications with their overnight success, the Navigator. Netscape was an offshoot of individuals that left the original graphical browser endeavor, Mosaic. Mosaic is still alive and kicking but has lost much of its luster as Netscape now leads the market with features and standards.

Standards are a large part of the web. Netscape, with its overpowering market share (65% as of this writing) is a powerful de facto standard maker. If Netscape incorporates a new 'tag' or HTML markup feature into their browser you can bet that other companies will be quick to follow. Many web sites now sport the 'Netscape Enhanced' button that indicates that it uses the latest and greatest features designed specifically for Netscape. Netscape enhanced sites may not come through as they were intended to be seen if viewed from another browser. Following this act is a tough job for the other browser makers. Microsoft has released its' own answer to Netscape in the form of the Internet Explorer. Distributed at no cost with Windows 95 and through their web site, the Explorer is a formidable opponent. This is especially true when one considers Microsoft's programming and marketing muscle. If they are unable to turn the tide of standards creation to their favor however they will always be playing second fiddle to Netscape. Those who create the standards are almost always the leaders. But then again, IBM dropped the ball too, didn't they?

Web Servers

Where Netscape does not have an extreme advantage, but would like to have, is in the web server market. The web servers are the machines and the software that dish up web pages to users who request them. As an ISP you will soon have to make a decision regarding your own web server platform. Since web servers need not interpret the code sent to users, only dish it out, they do not need to constantly change their modus operandi. The browser market can change rapidly within a matter of weeks, the server market is geared more towards an evolutionary scale of months. (See the chapter on hardware and software for more mention of web servers)

HTML Editors

There are a number of editors on the market that can make the job of creating HTML pages much less formidable. A number of these are listed below. In addition to these companies Netscape has come out with their own editor intertwined with their Navigator browser product. Netscape Navigator **Gold** includes not only the standard browser but what first reviews say is a very nice GUI (graphical user interface) layout and designer for web pages. Keep an eye on this one. If Netscape applies itself to the editor market the way they have done with the browser market this will be a solid product.

- HoTMetaL   www.sq.com
- Hotdog Pro   www.sausage.com
- Netscape Navigator Gold   home.netscape.com
- Microsoft's FrontPage   www.microsoft.com/isp

```
WANTED
FUTURE INTERNET WEB MASTER!

Candidates for this job will have a background
in desktop layout and design or communications
with an emphasis on graphical layout.  Past
work must be shown with a proven track record.
Experience in PC based computers and
computer based graphical design is a must, you
tell us what programs you're familiar with!
Lucid communications skills and clean type
editing is also necessary.  Successful candidate
will be responsible for building and maintaining
the web site for SUPER INTERNET
SERVICES, Inc., in addition to building
customer's web pages. Part Time: $10 hourly.

* NO HTML EXPERIENCE NECESSARY *
LEARN WHILE ON THE JOB!

Call Today: (502) 111-1234
```

Who Will Do The HTML?

I have a piece of good advice for you here. Do not try to be an expert in all areas. You will want to be familiar with HTML but you need not be a pro. As an ISP operator you will have more work than you can handle without having to do the design and layout of web pages as well. If you're starting small hire someone part time. If you're not burdened by budget you can hire a full time position immediately. Outsourcing your web work to your provider or a design firm is another attractive and low cost option for the new startup. An excellent online resource for HTML and web design information can be found at www.webreference.com.

If you do hire an HTML writer one of the responsibilities for this person will be maintaining your own home page. This site should be a showcase of your capabilities and describe all of your service offerings. They will also be responsible for handling your customer's sites. This person should be able to communicate effectively and professionally when handling these accounts. Additionally, they should be self-motivated and a willing participant in the constant learning that is necessary as HTML progresses and changes in the months ahead. Here's a tip for you...DO NOT HIRE A COMPUTER WHIZ for this position. You definitely want someone with computer experience but being a hardware/software guru is not the most important trait of a web master. Hire an individual with desktop layout and design experience or a communications major. There are literally hundreds of students who would give their little finger to have a job in this high tech field. You can be flexible and work around their schedule. In addition, they may be able to get school credit for such work. Designing HTML is not rocket science and anyone can master the basics within a few days. Finessing a page and gracefully laying out an attractive site motif will take longer of course and will require a working knowledge of some computer based graphic applications. Acquire one of the editors listed above and the book listed below or one that you find comparable. Hire your best candidate and pay them for the first few weeks to just learn the ropes. While you're busy building your business they can stay busy building an outstanding web site for your organization until you are ready to go prime-time. You'll be happy you followed this advice! Use the previous ad as an outline, create your own and post it in the following sites: colleges and universities (especially the computer labs), any technical schools with communications or layout programs, comic book stores (artists you know), and in the local paper.

Teach Yourself Web Publishing with HTML in 14 Days
Laura Lemay
Book and CD-ROM
Sams Publishing

User Home Pages
Many ISPs have begun to offer no or low cost web space as a value added feature to user's dial up accounts. Given this space users can create their own web areas concerning whatever suits them and falls within the bounds of the ISPs policies. If you are in the extremely advantageous position of having no or low competition you may be able to apply a small surcharge to user's home pages on top of the standard dial up account costs. Say $5 or $8 per month. These web space areas are almost universally measured in one of two ways by ISPs. You will need to decide how many megabytes of hard drive space on your web server you will give users. If you have the capabilities of doing so you can also track and charge users if they exceed a certain amount of transfers within a given time frame. For instance, you might offer two free megabytes of web space and 100 megs of transfers from this space per month with extra transfers

being billed at 25 cents per meg. The majority of users will not do a home page (yet) so it hurts little to offer them at no cost. Of those that do use the space offered most will not use even half a meg of drive space. So again, it hurts little to offer a lot knowing that there will be few that will take advantage of it all. The same principle works with your standard food buffet, the average consumed is what you base your costs on. Your users that do create home pages, which will be more and more as time goes on, will greatly appreciate the service. I have seen a number of providers who allow users to create home pages but do not allow them to use any graphics in them. This is a terribly short-sighted policy on their part. Their users will not appreciate the fact that the ISP is denying most of the benefits of the web to them. I don't recommend this policy to any potential ISP as it will come back to hurt you later. It costs you very little to let your users do their own graphical home pages. If you wish to police anything you might police the amount of transferred megabytes, and thus the used bandwidth, that the users home pages are utilizing each month and put a cap on this. Also, you may want to make a policy that user home pages are not to be for any commercial purposes whatsoever. Users who wish to design commercial pages themselves could be placed into a special category that costs more than standard home pages. The reason for this is because commercial pages will often draw more interest and use more bandwidth and resources.

An interesting twist on user home pages is what I like call 'the home page machine.' Many ISPs are mimicking a service that has long been offered by some of the larger national providers. A script is placed on your server that allows a user to pick and choose elements to create a home page on the fly. In this way a user need not know any HTML to have their own site. The sites produced are fairly generic but this can still fulfill the needs of many of your clients. Check some of the CGI repositories on the net for publicly available scripts to accomplish this task.

Finally, you will have to create an FTP account for any user that will be getting their own web space. This will allow them to add and update their own web areas with no further intervention from you.

Security is of the utmost importance here as you do not want any stray users trampling on files that do not belong to them.

Although charging users for a personal page is not as competitive in today's market, there are a number of enhancements you can charge for:

- Email forms
- Domain Names and sub-domain names (see below)
- Custom graphics work and initial layout, if they desire it
- Any additional type of enhancement normally reserved for business accounts

Commercial Home Pages

Many companies do not have the expertise or the desire to learn how to layout HTML web pages. This is where the savvy ISP comes into play. As an ISP you can offer even more services than a dedicated ad agency that has recently taken the web banner and run with it. These type of companies may be able to do some hot graphics but they will rarely be able to provide all of the server side enhancements that you can, at least not competitively. Companies are looking for INTEGRATED solutions. Any amount of puzzle piecing that they have to do takes them away from their main business. Keep in mind that the web is just another marketing tool for them. The revenue streams for company web sites come from a number of areas:

Page Design and Layout

Develop a price plan that costs x dollars for x number of pages, links and graphics. Two price plans are a good idea, one low end and one high end. This will give you two starting places to build upon as well as a lot of 'cookie cutter' type sites that will be molded to your pricing plan. Be sure to include stipulations for graphics scanning as many of them will have photos they wish to incorporate into their site. The design and layout charges are your 'setup fee', the initial one time fee for getting a site designed and online.

Domain Name Service (DNS)

Many companies will want to have their own domain name to set them apart from the run of the mill web site. Widgets, Inc. may wish to have www.widgetsinc.com as their domain name. This is sometimes better than having service where their address is an extension of your web server address. If your web server were www.siservices.net this company would most likely be assigned 'www.siservices.net/widgets' as a web address by you. The 'widgets' extension would simply be a sub-directory under your own home directory. The Internic charges $100 the first two years and $50 yearly beginning in year three, as an ISP you can charge anything over and above this that your local market will bear. A domain name will use up one of your IP addresses as well and will require some extra setup on your part so you should charge something extra for this service. Some companies charge $150 setup and $75 yearly thereafter while some charge $100 up front and an additional $5 to $10 monthly. How you price yours will depend greatly on what your competitive situation is.

Sub-Domains

Sub-domains are extensions of your own domain address. Let's say your company, Super Internet Services Inc, has a domain name of 'siservices.net.' Your web server would most likely be named www.siservices.net. The 'www.' prefix creates a subdomain of siservices.net. Likewise, you can create as many sub-domains of your main domain name as you like (while your IP addresses hold out). Widgets, Inc. could be assigned a sub-domain name for their web site such as 'widgets.sisservices.net.' This is only slightly preferable to the standard practice with no domain name services (www.siservices.net/widgets). It does make the Widgets web site address shorter but not by a large degree. Since sub-domains cost you nothing but an IP address and a bit of setup (the Internic doesn't get a cut) you can offer these to your customers at a cut rate. $25 to $50 yearly is quite common for this type of sub-domain service. The shorter your Internet companies real domain name is, the more attractive this service will be to customers!

Web Page Hosting

Hosting is the service you perform after you have designed a site and placed it on your server. Hosting is simply keeping content on your servers so that the world can access the site. You will charge a monthly hosting fee to companies to keep their web site on your server. Make no doubt about it, ISPs live for the monthly fees. The setup fees are nice but they are erratic and can not be counted upon to provide a steady income flow. Just hosting the customer's site with no additional services thrown into the bargain will not get you very far. You will need to include other services to justify the monthly fee you will be charging customers. Common examples of such value added services include but are not limited to: dial up access, x minutes monthly of no charge changes to a site, regular updates to the Internet search engines with the site's address and information, etc.

Take a look at the following page for an example of a commercial web page price sheet.

SAMPLE COMMERCIAL WEB PAGE PRICING SHEET

Super Internet Services, Inc.

512 Bardstown Road
Louisville, KY 40205
Voice: (502) 555-1234
Fax: (502) 555-4321

Commercial Internet Web Service Price List:

All commercial web accounts include the following services to make your Internet Presence a success:

Design and creation of Web pages which includes text and graphics of your choosing. All layout and graphics are done to your specifications in Hyper Text Markup Language (HTML), the language of the World Wide Web. Your web site will be placed on servers maintained at our location and any Internet user in the world may view them anytime by calling up your site's web 'address.' This gives your company a presence on the Internet and allows you to communicate with potential customers or stock holders and provide them with all sorts of information. Ideal uses of this technology are advertising products and services, distributing financial information at a very low cost to thousands of possible investors or shareholders, taking reservations remotely from possible visitors or tourists and soliciting long distance sales leads.

An email 'form' The email form allows your company to ask specific questions of potential customers which allows you to create a detailed picture of who is interested in your company. User can add any comments at the bottom of the form but the ability to gain specific information from someone Emailing your company is a valuable pre-sales qualification tool.

Publication of your Web Site address throughout the Internet is of major importance. This is accomplished by submitting your web address and key information to 18 of the top search engines, or yellow pages, on the World Wide Web. In this way anyone who searches on key words such as *cellular, Louisville, Kentucky, printing,* or other relevant phrases to your company are able to pin-point those web sites which have information of value to them.

Unlimited Dial-Up Internet Access is provided to our web site customers. This includes a visit to your home or office where one of our technicians will install all the software necessary to access all of the Internet services. These include: World Wide Web (aka 'surfing' or 'browsing' the net), Usenet discussion groups covering 15,000+ conferences where people converse on subjects of interest to them, and Internet Email which allows you to send and receive email from any online user in the world (this includes users of the national services such as Compuserve, Prodigy and America Online.) In this way a company not only maintains an Internet presence but also becomes privy to the thousands of potential news and research resources that can be found on this new medium. (Note: A 486 or Macintosh computer is required, in the case of PC compatible computers a 14.4 or faster modem is necessary as is the Windows operating system in any of its various flavors)

Home Page: $45.^{00} per month. Setup fee $100.^{00}

All of the services listed above with up to two pages of content and one company logo, photo or graphic is included. 15 minutes of free design changes monthly.

Web Site Account: $99.^{00} per month Setup fee $225.^{00}

All of the services listed above with up to five pages of content and up to 4 logos, photos or graphic images. 30 minutes of free design changes monthly.

Home Page or Web Site Account Upgrade Options:

Additional Email Accounts	$5.00 each per month
Additional Graphics or Logos	$5.^{00} each per month
Additional Web Pages (text only)	$10.^{00} each per month
Domain Name	$150.^{00} setup, $75.00 per year
Sub-Domain Name	$75.^{00} setup, $35.00 per year
Additional Login Accounts	$20.^{00} each per month
Mapping Graphic Links	$5.^{00} each per month

The following upgrades are available on a special quote basis. Super Internet Services, Inc. features a staff of 4 programmers who can build any online database or catalog application to suit your needs: Searchable databases, shopping cart applications and email response systems.

END OF SAMPLE WEB PAGE PRICING SHEET

NOTE: The preceding information is only intended to serve as an example of web page pricing. Use at your own risk. The lawyer made me say that.

This promotional price sheet shows an integrated solution for business customers. Not only does it explain *what* a company will receive but it explains why these services are important. It is both educational and persuasive at the same time. It justifies the monthly charges which is the bread and butter of an ISP. A similar price sheet was used quite successfully in my own endeavors. Feel free to use whatever ideas you may get out of this for your own flyer or brochure.

Web Site Revenue Models

There will be times when you will need to devise a strategy with potential customers on how to make their web site a success. What we are discussing here is not the type of web site that is simply online as an informative area, but one that is placed in the public eye to actively generate business and revenue. The customer is not the only one who can use this new business medium. Since you can make use of all of these web based services at cost you may want to create your own revenue producing site to augment your other ISP endeavors.

The advantages to web based commerce are many: 24 hour access, automated order taking, low cost, etc. How are people making the web actively pay them today?

The Advertising Model

The Web resembles the periodical industry in many respects. It is no wonder then that so many old publications have now found a comfortable place in the online world. New E-Zines, or electronic magazines, are also given birth online and never know the pleasures of being printed on dead tree pulp. These types of information repositories can gather a lot of traffic if they are updated and maintained properly. Another key is that they must be marketed well in order to gain an initial following. Just as in the real world, if you want to draw customers you must let them know that you exist. This is done via standard and online advertising methods, the same concept that this business model falls into.

If you believe that you can create a strong 'draw' or presence on the web then you may be able to make money by actively selling advertising in your online site. Instances of online advertising exist at all popular web sites today. Just click over to your favorite search engine to see what the 'banner ad' has to pitch. Click on it and you've done the site's administration a big favor as your 'click-through' to their advertiser's site will surely be noted and reported upon. The search engines are probably the largest success in this model to date. Due to the massive amount of traffic they draw each day (millions of viewers!) they can command fees that are beyond most organizations reach. Ten, twenty and even thirty thousand dollars per month can be charged to large corporations for 'prime location' spots. What would be a prime location? The home page, the entrance to any web site, is by far the most popular page you will have at your site. The Netscape home page for instance successfully charges thousands of dollars per month due to the number of daily visitors it greets. Other popular pages at the site might follow closely behind the home page and charge a premium for an ad banner location. Less popular pages bring correspondingly less revenue.

How are advertising dollars chased in the web site business? The first thing you need is a site that draws a lot of traffic. You don't have a marketable asset without a lot of visitors. How will you get your visitors? First, you must have compelling content. Plan on updating your content frequently to get repeat visitors. Second, you must advertise your site. It's almost a perverse irony isn't it? Let's look at some other questions to ask yourself or your customer when creating an advertising supported web site:

- What is our topic of expertise or the focus of our site?
- Who is our target audience?
- What is the current online competition like in this area?
- Where will we derive our content from?

- How often will we update our site?
- How will we keep the users coming back?
- What type of advertising will we sell?
- How will we track advertising for our sponsors?
- How will we charge for advertising?

As we discussed earlier, the largish search engines have made a good business from advertising. Other databases on the web are making a go of it as well. One of the more popular database sites is 'TUCOWS,' The Ultimate Collection of Winsock Software. TUCOWS is one of an emerging breed of software review and repository sites. If there is any type of Internet software to be had it has probably been rated and is available via the TUCOW's site (www.tucows.com). Advertising can be purchased on any number of pages they have available and are priced according to the page's popularity.

As opposed to databases, or pure repositories of categorized information, you may have an online magazine in mind. A database site is easier to maintain and expand than an online magazine due to the extensive writing and copyediting needs of a magazine. Once a database's format is standardized and automated, the update and maintenance process is far easier to cope with on a day to day basis. However, there is nothing stopping you from creating an online magazine. Look at C|Net, the Computer Network, for a good example of an online magazine (www.cnet.com) and news source.

How can you charge? You can charge advertisers in a number of different ways. A few of the more popular methods include; by the month, by the impressions and by the click-throughs. Charging by the month is by far the easiest method but many organizations do not feel comfortable buying their ads this way. Monthly visitors to your site may vary depending on the season, the amount of advertising you do for your site and real world occurrences that coincide with your content. If you do not have a good tracking method for impressions and click-throughs this may be your only alternative.

Selling advertising by the number of impressions, or times the ad is displayed, is by far the most accepted method in the industry.

Generally ads are sold in blocks of 1,000 impressions with a cost-per-thousand (CPM) attached to them. Common CPMs that you will see on the net range between $10 and $50 per with $20 CPM being the average. To manage this type of advertising system you must have a sophisticated tracking tool. Adding up impressions by hand from your web server's log files is not really an option. Web management and tracking systems range from the low hundreds to many thousands of dollars. For a good fit you should consult with your web server's company to find which tracking software works best.

A new breed of advertising has recently arrived on the net. The paradigm shift occurred when Proctor and Gamble™ told Yahoo that they were only willing to pay for impressions that actually produced a visit to their site. This was almost unheard of up until this time. Yahoo agreed to the arrangement and things haven't been quite the same since. This is known as the click-through model. Payment is made only for valid clicks on the advertiser's banner which brings them a visitor to their site. Costs for click-throughs range from 25cents to 50cents per. What you can charge is solely what the market will bear for your services. As in the last method, a solid tracking and reporting system will be required.

For an up to date listing of advertising locales on the Internet and what they are charging you might want to visit Webtrack at www.webtrack.com. Webtrack allows sites that are selling advertising to list all of their details for the potential buyer and then categorizes them according to content type. If you will be selling advertising you will want to be listed here as well as any of the other numerous sites that track outlets for advertising.

Included below is a sampling of links for log analysis software:

- Analog - A solid performer for both NT and UNIX systems. Best of all, it is absolutely free! www.statslab.cam.ac.uk/~sret1/analog/

- NetIntellect - from Webmanage A very thorough log analyzer specifically for Windows NT and 95 servers. www.webmanage.com

- net.Analysis - An ultra high-end package (with a price to match) from net.Genesis www.netgen.com

The Subscription Model

Charging visitors a subscription to your site is by far the hardest method to generate revenue. The net culture generally demands that most information be provided free of charge. This does not mean that there is no information that is worth charging for. It's just very difficult to do so on the web. This has been proven time and again with subscription only sites giving in to market pressure and changing over to an advertising model. If you do have information that is sufficiently difficult to find by other sources than you may have something in this model. Other obstacles to this type of a system is the large amount of technical know-how and maintenance that it requires. By comparison, the advertising model is far easier to administrate. For an example of a subscription model you may want to visit The Wall Street Journal™ online (www.wsj.com). They just recently opened their electronic door to digital commerce and are selling subscriptions via the web. Other news providers are waiting with baited breath to see how their endeavor fares.

The Retail Model

This model can be just as effective or even more so than the advertising model in producing profits. The retail model involves bringing conventional sales into the new medium of the web. Don't be tempted to simply open up a store front to hawk goods however. Web users can be much more sophisticated than standard shoppers and are best courted when you provide a high level of value added to your site. How can you make a knock-out retail web site? Provide lots of additional information about the product, tips for it's usage and perhaps even a lesson on the product's origin. The more information you can provide and the more useful your site is to the potential buyer, the more likely they are to close the deal with you. You are not constrained by printing or postage costs so it really pays to go all out on your site. Many retail sites are even providing peripheral information for their shoppers. For instance, if you had a site that sold spices you might also provide a database of spicy recipes. I've seen a biking accessory site that had a calendar of national bike races and other related events. Many sites simply tell the viewer what's happening in the industry by supplying news snippets. You get the idea, the more value you add the more attractive your site will be to visitors. You will also retain customers and get repeat business in this way. Other necessities for the retail model might include a secured site, meaning that you must have a digital certificate and a secure web server to host encrypted transactions online. Some sort of order processing or what is commonly referred to as 'shopping-cart' software will also make your visitor's transactions painless and provide you with a management system to easily fulfill requests. The retail model can be very lucrative if done properly.

Best of Breed Web Widgets: The Tools for the Task
There are a myriad of options when selecting your web server and there are even more choices to make when it comes time to tack on some extras. The interactive elements of a web site can often times be the biggest draw. What are we talking about here? Online discussions, real time chat systems, calendars, guest books and more. Don't forget that the web is an interactive medium and that users do not always want to have information 'pushed' at them. Web users like to interact with other users and the site's administration. This is the element of the web that really sets it apart from every other type of medium. I can not tell you the frustration I have had when I've found a site where I wish to purchase a product and can not even find an email address to inquire further. It is as though these organizations feel that they can post the information and be done with it, their job is over. It's not even an uncommon error and you will encounter it yourself many times while browsing the net. A common variation on this is where you reach a large corporation's web site and they do not have phone numbers posted for tech support

or pre-sales support. Don't fall into this trap. A company is available at the customer's leisure, not the other way around.

Online discussions are a hot item as well. Many sites have found that they can keep the customers coming back time and again by simply allowing them to discuss issues with each other. Online forums provide an interesting and ever changing element to your site that is impossible to provide with static content alone. Guest books and calendars are common niceties as well. Real-time chat can really make a splash if you host a site that draws a crowd that wants to talk with each other in real time. A specialty clothing site would be a poor choice for a chat forum but a site dedicated to video games might well make the grade. Chat forums also allow you to host visits by celebrities in your field. For instance, a site dedicated to all that is good in cooking might have a famous cook online for a moderated real time chat where users could ask questions. A gaming site might host a conversation with the authors of a hot new title. The possibilities are virtually endless.

I'll give you a totally biased look at some of my favorite tools for site enhancement. These are just my own favorite picks and your mileage may vary:

Cold Fusion from Allaire Software (www.allaire.com)
Cold Fusion is a CGI or API application that works with most common NT web servers today. The best way to describe Cold Fusion is that it is a database language for the web. By incorporating DBML (database mark up language) tags into standard HTML you can build interactive applications. Anyone with a mild programming background can figure this application out and have interactive systems online within a week. It's a frightfully powerful application. Don't be alarmed if you have no programming experience. One of the best reasons to buy Cold Fusion is the Allaire Forums package. This is far and away the best message/conference system for the web I've ever seen. It's easy to administrate while being attractive and intuitive to use. Other add-ons include a calendar and a shopping cart system with more scheduled for release.

Domain Searcher from Insanely Great Software
(www.igsnet.com/igs)
Domain Searcher is one of those utilities that you wonder how you
did without once you begin to use it. For organizations such as ISPs
and web creation companies a common chore that is encountered on
a day-to-day basis is domain research. Since so many domains have
been snapped up it can often be daunting to find an acceptable
alternative for your customer. As opposed to telnetting to the
Internic (as discussed in chapter one) to locate domains that have
been taken, you can just call up Domain Searcher. Once the window
appears you simply type in the first few characters of the domain and
let it do its work. Domain Searcher finds all of the domains that
match your criteria and even brings up their information in a pane on
the right side of the window. This is useful for those times where
you believe that trademark infringement is taking place and you need
to contact the domain holder. You will also find yourself playing the
middle man from time to time in order to buy an existing domain.
For $19.95, Domain Searcher is a real steal. Grab a copy today.

Ichat from Ichat, Inc. (www.ichat.com)
Ichat is by far the most sophisticated chat system I've ever seen. It
wins our Best of Breed badge for a web based chat server. It
integrates into a Windows NT server and users access its magic via
the web. The server is priced according to the number of
simultaneous users you would like to host on your system but the
client software is absolutely free. Free client software is almost a
necessity in getting your service universally accepted by users.
After all, who wants to pay for more software just to visit your site?
Ichat offers the most abundant access options you'll ever find in a
chat system. Users can make use of Ichat by telnetting into your
system, using a standard HTML interface as well as an ActiveX
interface built into Internet Explorer 3.0, a Netscape plug-in and
perhaps even with tin cans and string if they can figure out how to
make it work. The administration options are truly amazing. You
can host top level rooms with sub-level categories. Users can even
create their own private rooms if you so allow it. A very slick Java-
based window can float on your desktop and show you users in all of
the different rooms on a site in real-time. It's really a work of art. If
you'd like to try it out go to their web site and download the plug-in

for Netscape. They have a very rich system online that you can use at no cost and there's usually a crowd so you'll have no problems finding someone to talk with.

Polyforms from O'Reilly and Associates (www.ora.com)
Polyforms is a widget that I just can't get enough of. For the $99 it will take to get this tool you would be doing a crime to do without. Polyforms is the penultimate NT forms tool for web sites. Forms are those pages you see where you enter information into text boxes, check radio buttons and make selections from drop down boxes. Polyforms takes all of this information and turns it into something useful for you. You can have the contents of forms stored in text files, HTML files, comma-delimited databases or sent to one or more recipients via email. You can also have it simultaneously store its input to a file and mail the form to a recipient if you like. It provides for templates on the output side which is very powerful indeed. For instance, using a template you could have the input to a Polyform's page output to an HTML guestbook page. It's hard to describe how many ways you can utilize this little application. It functions as a CGI call and it only works on Windows machines so if you're running Unix it will not be of any use to you.

FrontPage from Microsoft (www.microsoft.com/isp)
FrontPage is the ultimate HTML editing and web server extension package from Microsoft. It is hard to call FrontPage a web widget because it is so quickly encompassing many areas that required specialized CGI applications to handle. It is a cross between an HTML layout program and a CGI application wizard. For full functionality you will need both pieces of this hybrid application, the development tool for the desktop and what are known as the 'extensions' for the web server itself. If you do not have access to a FrontPage server, don't be discouraged, FrontPage is fantastic as a stand-alone editor.

The client side application is where web pages are created in a fully graphical layout. In this way, true WYSIWYG (what you see is what you get) development is done on the desktop. Your entire web site and all associated files can be seen at a glance using a breakout map of all pages and their associated links. Graphics, hyper links and even elements from the MS Office suite are fully drag and drop enabled making for painless integration into your HTML code. Wizards, table and frame tools and a myriad of other options make creating single web pages and full blown sites a real breeze. Some of the hottest features are in what are called 'Webbots,' fully self-contained applications that can be dropped into your web pages. Webbots include such snazzy options as page counters, mail forms, database connectivity and conference systems, with more on the way. The FrontPage client side application can be had on the street for a bit over $100.

The server side extensions for FrontPage are the set of applications and code that is installed on the web server itself. Available for both UNIX and NT based web servers at absolutely no cost, the package is a hard bargain to pass up. The extensions are what allow the FrontPage client side user to really make use of all of the features of this package. Without the extensions package installed on your web server many of the extras, especially the Webbots, are unavailable to the user. If the extensions are installed then you are in development heaven. Many ISPs are now making a good business out of offering FrontPage enabled servers to their clients. Many users are now requesting this feature as they become more familiar with the client side development package and it may be worth considering for your own operation.

Other Server Based Revenue Sources

Outside of access and web pages, an ISP has a number of other services in its revenue toolbox. Outside of the audio server, the following services are relatively easy to provide for even the most green ISP. All of the following can be potential revenue streams for you so be sure to include them in some total price list that you build. You'd be surprised as to how many requests you can get for these.

Email

Email for your dial up users is a necessity. You will have to provide them with an email account when you sign them up to your service. The cost for this must be included with the standard monthly charges as the Internet without email is like Makers Mark™ without ice and a glass. It looks great but you don't want to really partake of it that way. However, dial up customers will often need two or more email accounts. One email connection can theoretically service an almost limitless number of email users, but this is not very attractive to the users who have to manage this feat. If a family is 'net savvy' then perhaps mom, dad, and baby brother will all desire to have their own email account. Charge $5 extra per month for additional email accounts in this case. By pushing the advantages of email for the entire family you can increase the average monthly billing for your dial up accounts. What was a bunch of $20 monthly customers can become $25 monthly customers. Some ISPs are even including additional mail accounts in their premium dial-up packages.

Commercial Email Accounts

Many businesses will desire to get email for their employees without introducing the productivity killers of IRC and the Web into the office. Hooking up a 60 person network for email services can be very lucrative and you should have some standard answers for customers who may desire this type of service. The answers to these types of questions are changing rapidly as software is developed for this booming market. For Novell networks a list of current solutions can be found on the Novell FAQ (frequently asked questions list) on the web at this address: 'www.efs.mq.edu.au/novell/faq/' For information on NT networks refer to the Microsoft home page at www.microsoft.com.

Audio

Audio is one of the latest hot commodities on the net. If you are in a position to be able to afford a dedicated audio broadcast server you can offer real-time songs, speeches, news and more over the Internet. These types of servers are a must for anyone in the music industry and they make a terrific news broadcast system as well. Even the most graphically enhanced text gets old after a while. It's a unique twist to hear audio coming out of your PC's sound card speakers. Even if you cannot afford one you may want to keep the possibility in the back of your mind, if the opportunity for a largish business contract comes your way you will be prepared to tell them, 'Yes, we can most definitely do audio over the Internet.' The current leader is the RealAudio system from Progressive Networks. RealAudio sells dedicated servers on a 'per simultaneous feed' basis. The client software is offered as shareware to anyone who requests it through their web server. Contact Progressive Networks at www.realaudio.com.

FTP (File Transfer Protocol)
FTP is another potential money maker for the ISP. FTP sites are servers that store files that can be retrieved by users. If you have the proper username and password you can log into an FTP server and download any of the material it holds to your own PC. Software distributors often like to maintain shareware depositories of their software so that potential buyers can put the product through its' paces. FTP sites are growing more scarce since the web can deliver files using HTTP (hyper text transport protocol) as easily as it can a web document. Their main use today is for very large file depositories where web pages would be too cumbersome to maintain. If you have a customer for FTP based services you will want to charge by the megabyte of storage required as well as the number of megabytes transferred monthly from their area. Not all FTP servers can track transfer statistics so be sure to check with whatever particular implementation you use before you cap the amount of transfers available at a given cost.

Located Servers
As opposed to FTP sites, located servers are an offering that is on the rise in ISP circles. Companies that wish to run their own secured web server or any server for that matter may wish to 'locate' a server on your premises and connect it to the local ethernet. In this way they can use whatever server software they like and maintain the entire thing remotely. The main concern to ISPs is that any company

that has a need for a dedicated server probably has a need for a lot of bandwidth as well. Price this service accordingly. $500 per month is quite common and is not an unreasonable amount to ask for a secured high bandwidth location where electricity is filtered and backed up with batteries. If you have any ad agencies nearby who wish to become web providers approach them with the idea. It's a lot less expensive for them to locate a server at your site than to get their own T1 dedicated line, CSU/DSU and router.

Miscellaneous Revenue Streams

Seminars & Training

Seminars or training visits can be very lucrative to the ISP. I've seen two basic models, with some variations, in action. Both have their pros and cons. However, before you can host a seminar or a training session you will have to have at a minimum a conference room that can seat ten to twenty people, a computer with a flat panel transparent display, an overhead projector, and Internet access. The flat panel display and overhead projector can be swapped for an integrated unit such as those produced by the Boxlight company, sales: (800) 497-4008. The ideal solution is to have a training room with 10 to 20 Internet connected PC's. The latter is much harder to come by so most ISPs go with the simple seminar type session where it is basically a show-and-tell type of operation.

Contact local colleges and universities to see if they have rooms that are available on weekends. Another good source is to contact any local training facilities and trade them for access and web services in return for the use of one of their rooms (and equipment?) once or twice a month. The training facility will get the extra benefit of being able to hawk their own programs to any attendees who come for the show. Another option is the local computer stores who often have many computers setup and ready to go and yet are not utilized in the evenings or weekends.

You have two choices for how to host these sessions. You can either choose to charge or choose to not charge for these sessions. If you do not charge your attendance will be much higher and you will therefore end up with many more potential subscribers coming for the show. Did I fail to mention that you will be blatantly plugging your own system as the main point of connection for sentient beings in your city? If you do charge for the session be sure to offer some type of access discount for those who attend. Perhaps you can waive their setup fees or even give them the first month of access at no charge.

Programming

To offer programming jobs to potential customers you will need to have a net savvy programmer on hand. If you can not hire a full time programmer try to locate one using the methods described previously for getting a web master.

In the past the CGI, or Common Gateway Interface, was used in conjunction with web servers to produce specialty online sites. CGI is a standard way of interfacing languages such as Microsoft's Visual Basic and Borland's Delphi programming language with HTML and therefore produce some rather intriguing interactive web sites. Today you have even more options for programming languages and interfaces for the web. Java, the new language introduced by Sun Microsystems (see the web site at java.sun.com) is now embedded in the latest versions of Netscape's Navigator and Microsoft's Internet Explorer. Java applications are entirely platform independant and use the client's computer for running the programs as opposed to the web server itself. Microsoft and a number of other large companies have either licensed or endorsed the Java language so expect to see it making big waves in the near future. Another alternative to traditional methods of programming for the net is to use a web server which supports databases or spreadsheets inherently. With these types of products no or low programming is required to get some fairly impressive results quickly. Take a peek at the Purveyor web server from Process Software for this type of functionality. Their web address is www.process.com. Your programming capabilities will be shaped by both the programmer(s) that you have as well as the web servers and database engines that they have to work with. Keep this in mind when shopping for your software.

Programming jobs might include building a searchable database of products for web customers to browse, integrating a legacy system to the Internet and creating web-based inventory query systems for distributed warehouses. Programming projects, even for the smallest ISP who can prove their capabilities, can command hundreds or thousands of dollars per job. Once access to the Internet becomes a true commodity service there will still be programming to be done. There is a tremendous amount of integration to be done today in tying the web to the rest of the world. Get a programmer or outsource some programming jobs and take advantage of this booming market!

Site Visits
Like seminars and training sessions you have two equally viable alternatives for providing site visits and demonstrations. Site visits, included in the cost of the setup, should be one of your value-added services for commercial web pages. However, this is excluding the end user who just wants dial up access to the net. There are *many* individuals out there who do not have the time nor the patience to figure out how to install all of the connection and client software to access your system. These individuals look at site visits in the same way they do delivered pizza. They don't have to leave their home or office to get all of the benefits brought to their door. You can hire someone to do these site visits and then pay them a per job fee if you so desire. Many companies charge $50 for this type of service. There is a draw back to actually extracting money from this type of service however, liability! I have an alternative method you might want to consider. Contact a local computer savvy high school or college student. Perhaps even two of them on different ends of the city. College student employment offices are a great place to begin. Arrange with your students to contract these jobs out. This way, when you receive a request for a site visit you will be undercutting your competition and have no direct liability for problems that may arise. The charge can then be set at $25 and be paid directly to the contractor student who makes a terrific fee for 1 ½ to 2 hours of

work. Be certain to get students who are articulate and can communicate and hold themselves well in such a case. You will also need to be available by pager or phone when the site visits are happening so as to handle any special problems that may arise. Here is a basic outline for providing site visits:

- Get a couple of students lined up and know what their free time schedule is like. Find out what days and hours they would be willing to do site visits and how far they are willing to travel.

- If you do not have professionally packaged software, create a set of disks with all of the applications and any additional instructions needed to get Windows 3.x and Windows 95 up and running on your network. Include any utilities that an installer may need such as PKZIP and a recent copy of a virus detection/cleaning program. WRITE PROTECT THEM! We had a situation where one installer inadvertently carried a virus from one customer's location to another customer's site and destroyed the data on his hard drive. Luckily for us the customer was understanding and had made a backup just before the installer came. (Whew!)

- Create a dual purpose check list and information form that installers will leave at the job site for the customer. Just as any literature you create that represents your company, this form should be professional looking and attractive. Include the following information and check boxes on the form:

  1. Installers Name:
  2. Date:
  3. Users ID:
  4. Users Password:
  5. Users Email Address:

     (Check boxes to be filled in as completed by installer)
  6. Connection software setup (Circle one)
     Trumpet / Windows 95 or NT Internal
  7. Web browser installed
  8. Email software installed

9. IRC software installed
10. FTP software installed
11. Any other software that may be installed
12. Demonstration Completed
13. YOUR ISP INFORMATION, including user policies, voice and email support numbers, mailing address, domain name address, IP numbers, and Usenet news server address, etc. This will save you a lot of customer support headaches in the long run as users will be able to support themselves with this information sheet.

*   Take orders for site visits during your regular office hours. Be sure that the customer has a sufficiently capable machine, no 286's or 2400 baud modems allowed. Get their credit card information, full address and directions to their home or office. Setup a tentative date for the visit. Contact your contractors and verify that they can be there on time. Once all of this has been arranged be sure to get the users information into your servers accounting system so they will be ready to go on the day of the visit.

Site visits can be one of the most fruitful user side endeavors you can engage in. Users who do opt to pay for a site visit come away with a system that is guaranteed to hook up to the Internet reliably. They also have a basic understanding of the tools that were installed on their PC and how to use them. They will have less problems and fewer questions than your regular user base and this translates into longer lasting accounts and less headaches for you!

Equipment
If you so choose you can become an equipment reseller to your customers. In addition to making a little bit extra on the side you will have the advantage of being a vertical integrator, able to quote a customer all of the equipment and answers that they need. A one-stop-shop, so to speak. This can be from the low end if you wish to supply the latest and greatest modems to the high end where you will sell CSU/DSUs, routers, and ISDN adapters. The markup on equipment varies wildly but you will definitely make the most

money on the high end side. To become a reseller you will have to establish accounts with companies that carry the type of equipment you will wish to sell. For starters try Merisel at www.merisel.com. They are one of the largest national distributors for computer hardware. Establishing accounts with smaller companies can also be to your advantage as they sometimes are able to sell equipment at a much lower rate than the larger distributors. Since you will have all of the Internet advertising machinery you need to put up a dynamite web site why not carry a few choice pieces of equipment as well?

As we have seen, the net offers many more services than at first meets the eye. You do not have to offer all of the services mentioned previously to be an Internet service company. Under heavy competitive pressure you might opt to specialize in one particular niche that you would do better than the rest. Even without competitive pressures, you may decide that only one or two particular facets of the Internet industry interest you. Keep your options open. The back of the book features a sampling of Internet service companies and an outline of the services they provide. The variety of services shown there may be beneficial to you as you continue to formulate your own plans.

One thing is for certain, few companies have the benefit of working in a field with no competition breathing down their neck. The next chapter approaches this issue and should help you assess your market situation.

CHAPTER III

ASSESSING YOUR MARKET PRESENCE

You should be fully aware of what type of market you are operating in before beginning down the road to becoming an ISP. The local ISP competition, as well as future competition that will be moving into the region is your main concern. As mentioned before, the big national players cannot offer the type of service, support and quality that you will be capable of as a local operation. The large national online services will be years (if ever) in catching up with the lean local ISP businesses. If they undercut you on price, and you have planned and built your network carefully, then you can be assured that they are skimping somewhere. Their customers will know it and you should educate your own customers as to the competitor's weaknesses. Without insulting anyone you can simply play upon your own strengths in your product literature. Remember, it is very poor form to insult the competition. This type of practice will only discourage your more experienced clients.

Who is the Real Competition?

Local BBSs are moving to the Internet in droves. Keep an eye on any of them that have not yet introduced these services, particularly the larger ones. Check your local newspaper and chamber of commerce to find who the current players are. Call all of the local computer stores, drill them for information on services and competitors. The local shops can be a wealth of tips and gossip about up and coming organizations. Once you believe you have a list of who all of the local competitors are, log into their systems and test drive them yourself. You may have to spend a bit of money but it will be well worth it to get a full understanding of how their operation works. Assessing these competing operations is absolutely necessary to understand what your future positioning will be! You will not be able to out-do all of them on every service and price level but you must understand their operations in order to prepare your own angle on the market.

To search for ISPs that may be servicing your area you can also refer to one of these online resources:

The List, a classic on the web   www.thelist.com
Boardwatch Magazine's ISP Directory   www.boardwatch.com

A check-list is included next; duplicate this for as many providers as you have in your local area plus one extra. Fill them out thoroughly and keep them nearby for reference. When you have filled one out for each ISP begin to think about what you would like to charge and fill in your own. Use pencil, not ink, on your own checklist. Like the old saying goes, only God writes in ink. You will be changing this pre-opening price list many times before you are ready for a public introduction.

Be sneaky when trying to root out this information! Call as a prospective customer who wants web services. Ask probing questions about their operation. Indicate that as a business customer you need to know how reliable their operation is, how it is connected, and how it is staffed and maintained. Call again on a different day as a customer who wants dial up access. Find out all of the stipulations, services and policies for dial up customers. Ask how they can take payment and if there are any hidden charges. See if you can visit their site! When calling you may want to even use the '*67' option, or whatever your local calling code is, from the phone company to block caller ID boxes. Basically you're on a reconnaissance mission in anticipation of a future search and destroy operation!

CHECKLIST FOR COMPETING ISPs

Competitor's name:_____

Voice number: _____ Data number: _____

Web address: _____

Address:

_____

Speed and provider of Internet Connection:

_____

Equipment utilized: _____

Hours of operation/support: _____

/ type of employees: _____

Providing Internet services for how many months / years:

_____

Subsidiary of / financial backing from:

_____

Marketing methods:
   Newspapers: _____

   Radio: _____

   TV: _____

   Other: _____

Strategic partners with: _____

DIAL UP ACCESS

Number of user home pages on the competitors web site: _____
(Note: This is not necessarily an indicator of their total membership)

Number of modem lines: _____ Modem Speed: _____

Number of ISDN lines: _____

User home pages, circle any that apply:

Text Only / Graphics are OK / Personal Only / Commercial Use OK

User home page fee: $_____ Megabytes included: _____

Other stipulations: _____

Price Plan #1   Hours included _____ $ per extra hours _____

                 Setup fee _____ Stipulations _____

Price Plan #2   Hours included _____ $ per extra hours _____

                 Setup fee _____ Stipulations _____

Price Plan #3   Hours included _____ $ per extra hours _____

                 Setup fee _____ Stipulations _____

Additional Email accounts cost: $_____

Usenet provided: Y / N   Number of groups carried: _____

Special plans / discounts: _____

Other comments on dial up access: _____

COMMERCIAL WEB PAGES

Is dial up access included with commercial accounts? Y / N

On a scale of 1 to 5, 1 being outstanding, how attractive is their web site: 1 2 3 4 5

How many commercial businesses have home pages listed on the competitor's web site: _____

Does the ISP have standard web packages? If so fill out the following two sections. If not, be sure to use the third area which may be a custom quote for the ISP. It will serve as an 'equalizer' for reference across all of your potential competitors.

Standard Plan #1:   Pages Included _____ Graphics Included ____

       Design and Layout Cost $_____ Hours Included _____

       Monthly fee: $_____ Monthly changes included? Y / N

       Amount of free time for changes monthly: _____

Standard Plan #2:   Pages Included _____ Graphics Included ____

       Design and Layout Cost $_____ Hours Included _____

       Monthly fee: $_____ Monthly changes included? Y / N

       Amount of free time for changes monthly: _____

Comparative web package. This may require a custom quote from the ISP. Five pages of text (8 ½ x 11, single spaced) including 10 graphics that you need scanned from photographs. An email 'form' will be required to ask questions of potential customers. No domain name service will be necessary.   You can use a woodworking company as a front, the photographs are of projects you have done in the past and products you currently sell.

Design and setup fee: $_____ Monthly fee: $_____

Are free changes included? Y / N   Allotted time: _____

Other comments: _____

DOMAIN NAME SERVICES

Will the company register a domain name for your web site? Y / N

What is the cost: _____

LEASED LINES

Get as much of this information as possible. Be sure to have them drop any equipment charges out and say that you will be providing your own equipment.

Line Type	Setup Fee	Monthly Fee
Dedicated 28.8		
ISDN 64k		
ISDN 128k		
Frac T1 256k		
Frac T1 512k		
Full T1		

What equipment is recommended for these line types?

Does price include cost of line at your site? Y / N

Does price include cost of line at their site? Y / N

Does price include IP addresses?   Y / N   How many? _____

Does price include domain name services? _____

Does the ISP have any stipulations on reselling Internet service. If so, what are they?

OTHER SERVICES
Are there any other notable services that this ISP provides at a cost?
What are they?

Are there any notable services that this ISP has available at no cost?
These may include a special service on their web site only for their
customers or perhaps a freebie they give to end users.

COMMENTS:

END OF CHECKLIST FOR COMPETING ISPs

Looking back over chapter two you can see that there are many
services available to prospective clients. You do not need to be a
master of all of them, though being familiar with them is important.
You may start your business with a given product mix and find that
as time goes on a service that you did not offer is becoming
increasingly popular in the marketplace. By listening to your client
base and reading periodicals like Boardwatch Magazine you should
begin to develop an intuitive feel for the direction of the Internet.
Changes are occurring very rapidly in this business, those who have

no knowledge of the industry at large are in jeopardy of being washed away. The time is quickly approaching where an Internet site and a handful of shareware software disks will not be enough to attract the new users. Be prepared! When you first open you should be prepared to offer all of the necessities. The niceties can be built upon from there. The necessities are things like a web site, even if it's only for information at first and not to resell web space. You must have voice support and a good marketing program in place. And finally, you must be prepared and capitalized for growth.

You never know when a surge of business will come your way that overloads your existing capacities. A local TV station could run a week long series on the Internet prompting not merely a stream but a raging tidal wave of new users to seek out Internet service. Perhaps a story in the local paper catches the interest of a large body of readers. It happened to me not once but twice, business snuck up on us en masse. We were so busy maintaining the customers that we had that we were unaware that the new influx of customers was about to wreck the entire system for everyone. How did this happen? Imagine that you're on a steady pace of adding 20 new customers per week. In your head you know you're going to need more modems and more phone lines within two months. The following month you begin to get 20 additional new customers per week. Overjoyed at what has happened and busy adding new customers your user to line ratio jumps far ahead of what it should be. New dial up customers are overwhelmed with the newness and neat features on the net. They will therefore use the net much more their first month or two than they will in following months. The busy signals on your system reach a critical mass in the evenings at peak hours until your existing client base, not counting the new masses pouring in, become extremely dissatisfied with your service.

Determining what type of service you will create will determine to a large extent how you are prepared to deal with problems like this. In addition to your own desires, your competition will shape your idea of a business as well. You will be constrained by the fact that there are already groups offering Internet access. What they have done before you entered the fray molds the mindset of your local customer base and your own possibilities within that market. Given that you have competition in your area you can choose one of three basic models of operation and positioning. I have never seen the first model in action but it intrigues me to no end. I am sure there are some out there already. The other two models are fairly distinct but in building your business you should keep in mind which group you are joining.

ISP Access Service Strategies

For your contemplation the following three access business strategies are explained. If you plan to offer dial up or other types of end-user access then these may provoke some ideas:

The Four Star Operation - 'Chez Nét'

This is the model I have not seen personally, though I have no doubt that there are people quite successfully running operations such as this. The four star ISP would offer uncompromising service and support to its user base, above and beyond the normal good quality service that most every company strives for. It would take a larger metropolitan city to support such an operation where there is a sufficiently large enough body of discriminating users. All of the products that other ISPs offer would be available from the four star operation. What you would not find at other ISPs is the large amount of value added services, support and quality. For instance, dial up customers may always get a site visit for one on one training or software installation. Users would be contacted by phone once every five to six weeks to find out if there were any concerns or problems they were facing. A basic user home page may even be created for them at no additional cost. The user to line ratios would be the lowest in the area because busy signals would not be a part of the high service ISPs operation. There would be quarterly mixers or get togethers that would be partially subsidized by the ISP for entertainment purposes only. Perhaps the ISP offers an ongoing and very high caliber training schedule. Each month a new class would be hosted on another aspect of the Internet, perhaps even programming and HTML creation would be offered in these seminars (for members only of course). The web site of the ISP would offer many functions and access to information that would not be generally available. Perhaps a very extensive file collection, schedule of local events, editorials on the direction and happenings of the net, and even discounts and special offers for local services (restaurants, stock accounts, the theater, etc). Voice support would be available from the wee hours of the morning to the wee hours of the night. Voice support would be available both Saturdays and Sundays as well, though perhaps for not as many hours as during the week. A monthly or bi-monthly newsletter would be printed and mailed to all of the customer base. Shareware would not be in the vocabulary of this ISP when offering software to its customer base. The best applications would be gathered together, site licensed from the software developer and offered at no additional cost to the user. What I've mentioned here are just suggestions for the dial up side of the business. What would be possible for the commercial web customers?

Such a high level of service would create a mind set that the users propagated when talking about their service provider to friends and associates. You would have to nurture the four star mentality not only in your offerings but to the public at large. The start up costs for such an operation would be much higher than the following two models so do keep that in mind as well. What could such an ISP command for this type of quality? Let's say that you have three other local providers in your area. One offers unlimited access for $20 monthly with a $10 setup fee. The other two offer unlimited access for $18 monthly with a $15 setup fee. Perhaps you would charge $30 monthly and have a startup cost of $30. Your pricing would depend of course on how many services you offered and what you could reasonably expect to get for the extra value. You would be trading volume for price in this scenario. Your rewards would be a smaller user base to support but generating more revenue than a user base 50% larger on the competing systems.

The Full Service Provider - 'Ye Olde Web Corner'
The full service provider is the type of ISP I personally ran. While unable to offer the type of support that the previous model gave to its

user base we did strive to offer as many features as possible with good service. We offered only a handful of value added features for the users as opposed to the barrels of value that a four star operation would include. We were neither the lowest nor the highest cost operation in our city. Differentiating yourself from the competition in this middle of the road model does not mean that you have to offer more and more features to the user body. How you package your existing services may be enough to give you a competitive advantage. Free user home pages were included with every account though there was little support offered on how to build one. On a busy Friday or Saturday night it might take a customer 5 minutes to get online though the rest of the time there were few problems.

A full service provider is like the a pleasant local neighborhood restaurant. You will not be able to order a lobster, but the meals are consistent and will not break the bank when you leave. A full service provider should develop cookie-cutter type packages, both for the end user and the commercial client. Web services should be quality work at a decent price. There are some services that these middle of the road providers may not be able to offer at all. You should specialize in one or two high quality options that you can become known for. You will not be charging the type of prices that will make all of your offerings best of breed, but your customers will understand this and appreciate the value. Perhaps you have an outstanding graphics artist that make your web pages stand out visually. Maybe you have access to a programmer that does outstanding data base work and you can offer niche services for your web customers, even though the pages do not look like a Hollywood movie company put them together. These companies, myself included, generally offer shareware to their client base. You could offer to sell users the real McCoy and you may even distribute your shareware on disk to those who request it. The majority of ISPs are full service providers.

The Cut Rate Provider - 'The Greasy Modem Pub'
The low end operation is a viable alternative for you if you find that you fall into one of two categories: 1. You have high levels of competition locally but none of the other providers are priced dirt

cheap. 2. You cannot afford to quit your day job or you are starting on an extremely low budget. The exception to rule #2 is if you are a monopoly provider to your local area. If you have a city that has NO local alternatives for Internet access then it is impossible to be a cut rate provider, at least in price! I'm not recommending that you should burn your bridges by offering crummy service and charging premium prices, but you will be able to get more revenue out of the local market than if you had competition. Keep this in mind, even if there is no local competition currently, there will be at some point. If you have an extremely over priced service with a large dissatisfied user base you will lose your business when a competitor comes to town.

The cut rate provider offers very little phone support, generally an answering machine is the greeting that a caller gets. The services you will offer as a cut rate provider will not nearly be complete, perhaps you do not even have an in house HTML guru (not even yourself!). You may recommend to users that they go to a local HTML artist to get their work done and then place it on your server. Busy signals may be encountered every evening with the occasional 10 minute wait to get online. This is not a necessity, but it does lower your operating budget. I think that providing access on a timely manner is the bare minimum that a provider should offer, even if there is little support for the services themselves. I have seen this operation first hand successfully work as a business. What you are trading to users is the bulk of services and support for absolutely rock bottom pricing. You will hope to achieve volume and low costs in return for price and high service. In a large area with a lot of competitors there are going to be more and more savvy users who need no hand holding as time goes on. Your high service competitors will train them! Once they know the ropes they may bale out and move to a cut rate provider to save the money. There are penny pinchers and budget minded individuals in every crowd, willing to take less if it costs less, but still wanting a piece of the pie. In a city where there is no local competition you will be limiting yourself to the technically oriented crowd. The novices will have nowhere to turn to get the basic knowledge they need so you will be unable to count on them to ever be able to successfully employ your low cost service.

What to Do?
Examine the competition, take a good critical look at your budget (chapter six), and make the right decision on what category you fall into. The worst mistake you can make is to pass yourself off for something that you are not. I've seen systems open up as full service providers which were really run like a cut-rate provider. Even if a customer has not paid you for service yet, your lack of availability on the phone or how you do business in general will tell them that you are not what you pretend to be. If they attempt to pursue business with you they will ultimately be dissatisfied with the service and results that you can give them. They will leave upset because you will have deceptively wasted their time which in any business is the same thing as cheating them out of their money.

Don't feel discouraged if the access business is totally saturated in your locale. There are many other opportunities for intrepid Internet endeavors. A number of companies are now offering email addresses for life. They basically host mail services on their domain and regardless of what provider you use you always have the same email address. Similar companies have arisen that cater to Usenet junkies, providing more archived messages and newsgroups than most companies can imagine. Other groups have left the end-user market to solely pursue dedicated commercial access and network integration. As you can see, there are many possibilities outside of a straight access provider. Above all else, you should love the business that you choose to participate in. Success is measured in many ways and the bottom line is only one of them.

CHAPTER IV

HARDWARE AND SOFTWARE

To reiterate the introduction, this book does not attempt to tell you how to specifically setup the particular hardware used to become an ISP. There are easily thousands of combinations of hardware and software that you can choose to provide the services listed in chapter two. This hardware, and ultimately the server(s), the heart of your ISP service, will have their own methodology, manuals and technical support channels. Some solutions do not offer any conventional support but rather rely on the users of the product alone to educate newbies in the nuances of its workings. Although these are not recommended to the new ISP with no prior UNIX knowledge, they are quite viable and with the proper know-how can create some dynamite ISPs. Your decision will ultimately be based on your existing knowledge and the resources and budget that is available to you. Your connection to the Internet will also dictate what type of hardware you will need. All of the hardware is discussed in this chapter and illustrations are provided to show you how it connects together. Refer to the next chapter before you decide how you will connect to the net yourself.

This next section really cuts right to the chase in discussing the different core methodologies for building an Internet service. The core of your service will be based around a software / hardware combination that handles the majority of your ISP needs. The core is where you will find the most notable differences in ISP systems. The other hardware used is often similar or identical from ISP to ISP. A discussion of those pieces will follow.

Servers and Connectivity Hardware

The heart of an ISP is the server or servers that perform the

---

VOCABULARY REFRESHER:

DNS   Domain Name Server (or services), converts domain names into IP addresses.

FTP   File Transfer Protocol, used to serve and retrieve files from repositories.

HTTP   Hyper Text Transfer Protocol. The language of the world wide web.

NNTP   Network News Transfer Protocol. Used to transport Usenet conferences from one computer to the next over the Internet.

POP3   Post Office Protocol. A service that allows intermittent connections, such as dial up users, to pickup stored email from a server.

PPP   Point to Point Protocol. Allows dial up connections to the Internet. Newer than and recommended over SLIP.

SLIP   Serial Line Interface/Internet Protocol. Used to establish dial up connections to the Internet.

SMTP   Simple Mail Transfer Protocol, moves email over the Internet from one server to the next

---

necessary functions to provide access and services to your clientele. The main server can be made up of standard hardware and a special operating system (OS) or a combination of special hardware and OS. This is one of the most important decisions you will make so take into consideration your prior knowledge and startup budget when making a decision. It may take one or more servers or other pieces of equipment to provide the following: DNS, SMTP and POP3, NNTP, FTP and dial up user access and control (RADIUS). Web servers may be impractical to run in a 'one box does it all' type of server due to the amount of work they may need to perform. The same is undeniably true for NNTP. The Usenet has become too popular to maintain all of its varied conference offerings on the same machine that services the rest of your network. Although it is possible to carry all of the Usenet and the rest of your services on one computer it had best be a high end server with LOTS of memory and drive space. If you're limited by budget you might consider carrying just a few thousand conferences on your main server as opposed to acquiring a dedicated machine to handle the 19,000+ conferences available today. News servers are discussed later in this chapter.

The Hobbyists Solution
For the ISP who is on a low budget and does not mind digging for answers you may want to opt for the no cost UNIX solution. Keep in mind, this is not the recommended way of running an ISP, but for the hobbyist it may be just what the doctor ordered. Linux, a popular collaborative effort of many individuals, is the ideal solution for those wishing to learn UNIX and run an ISP at little cost. Linux itself is entirely free though you will pay someone to acquire a nice copy of it with accompanying utilities. Linux runs on Intel platform PC's as well as a number of Motorola powered machines such as the Amiga. Higher end workstations such as computers utilizing the Dec Alpha CPU also support Linux. Linux is an open effort and is constantly undergoing changes and additions from not a 'team' but rather users of the Internet that participate in its development. It handles multi-user tasks quite well and features many niceties for running a high use system that will need to perform a lot of functions simultaneously. All of the hardware necessary for simultaneous dial up connections and your own connection to the Internet is documented (somewhere) and is available to anyone who wishes to root around a bit. Linux with some accompanying utilities will handle most every function an ISP needs.

Linux resources:

The LINUX HOW TO site is an excellent web based resource. Point your browser to this address to take a peek.

www.netlab.cs.rpi.edu/linux-doc-project/HOWTO/

FTP sites that carry Linux for download are available over the net but this is not the recommended way of attaining it. Linux is quite large and getting it in a prepared format on CD is the best route to go. For those who would like to taste it before they jump to a more complete distributed package:

FTP SITE	DIRECTORY
sunsite.unc.edu	/pub/linux
ftp.funet.fi	/pub/os/linux
ftp.uu.net	/systems/unix/linux

For a complete distribution set with a lot of nice utilities Walnut Creek offers the 'Slackware' collection on 2 CD-ROMs for $39.95. Contact them on the web at www.cdrom.com or by voice at (800) 786-9907.

The Linux users journal contains articles for any level of user:
The Linux Journal
POB 85867
Seattle, WA, 98145
(206) 782-7733

If you are in the market for a free operating system that will allow you to become an ISP be sure to also look into FreeBSD, another free version of a Unix look-alike available on the net and from Walnut Creek. Visit the home page for FreeBSD at www.freebsd.org

The Purist's Solution
For those who wish to learn a new operating system and become an Internet service provider you can delve into the world of proprietary

workstations and Unix. This is also a build-it-yourself solution, such as the Linux solution outlined earlier. As opposed to going with one of the two prior mentioned free solutions you can opt to acquire a professionally designed and packaged workstation and operating system and set off on the road to molding it into an Internet service. The main drawback is that this is a technically challenging feat and not an easy road to travel for the uninitiated. All of these solutions will take a good chunk of a budget but time is almost as precious when building a business. Your new business will have a certain 'window of opportunity' after which it can either fly or collapse. The budget will eventually run out, too many mistakes drive your customer base away, etc. If you're a UNIX guru you most likely are not reading this book. Building an ISP from scratch, especially when using this high-end hardware, is not for the faint of heart.

There are many such solutions available in the workstation market. Be careful not to tie yourself to a solution that has little support for it or a company that has not been around for a number of years. Sun Microsystems has one of the best reputations in the world in this particular market. Contact their web site at www.sun.com and take a look at their new Netra server line.

The Stubbornly Held 'Best' Solution Opinion - I personally did not desire to rebuild the wheel when entering into the Internet business. A number of people told me that I was foolish for prolonging the inevitable by not learning it all from scratch. We were also quite restricted as to our startup budget. I opted for turnkey solutions and never regretted it for a second. Our business began by first utilizing the eSoft Ipad. The growth of the Internet however demands quick and affordable responsiveness and as we evolved the need for more standardized solutions became apparent. The scope of our Internet service began in one city encompassing portions of four counties but grew rather quickly to encompass several counties in the state. The infrastructure management had to be maintained at good speeds and the hardware costs had to be kept low. This is where a turnkey can be an excellent solution for the entrepreneur.

MISnet Turnkey ISP Solutions

What is described next is an example of a professional answer for turnkey solutions, provided by MISnet. The hardware is only one key in this puzzle and the beauty of MISnet solutions is the flexibility in the strategies you can use to get a jump-start into this business. Additionally, MISnet is an access / connection provider with dual connections to the Net at large. This means you can get the hardware, services, *and* a data connection for your ISP business, all from one supplier. The reason this is so attractive is that many ISP's when they first begin are unable to perform all of the functions of the business. You could opt for a self contained pre-configured hardware solution and/or connection and provide all of the services yourself or you can choose the service package and strategy that MISnet offers to new ISPs. Additionally, you can have the services 'branded' under your own name or choose to become a true MISnet POP. The spectrum of offerings is a bit bewildering at first due to the flexibility of the

> **Strategy and your planning are more important than equipment.** (Always! Always! Always!) If your plans are solid and built upon a good understanding of the market your equipment choices become clear. Equipment and capital outlays MUST be secondary to your plans. Do not put this cart before your horse.

services you may opt for. A consultation is necessary to understand what type of market you are operating in and under what competitive constraints. This is key in the Internet business as well as any other endeavor you will ever enter into. Listed below is the basic spectrum of services for turnkey solutions:

Self supported turn-key solution:

In this scenario the proper tools are provided and the new ISP begins their business as a self-contained entity. A market analysis and your long range goals determine the type of hardware and software solutions you will need. Your turnkey provider helps coordinate a successful strategy for entrance into your market. A connection at whatever bandwidth is appropriate is planned as well. Hardware and software are pre-configured and shipped to your site. Initial technical support is provided for installation and on-site training is provided if necessary. All services, including support, HTML production, USENET, billing, etc. are the business owner's responsibility.

Sourced turn-key solution:

In this scenario the new ISP opts for the services listed above but instead of providing all of the hardware and staff necessary to run the full ISP they 'source' their services. 'Sourcing,' also known as branding, is a popular concept whereby a business undertakes key aspects of day to day work but contracts out peripheral portions of the work to other providers. In the ISP business you can source any portion of the business out which you are unable to adequately provide yourself: Usenet services, HTML design and layout, programming, help desk staff, engineering and billing & accounting services, etc. The users of these products do not necessarily know that services or products are being supplied by an outside vendor. A good example of 'branding' is whereby you purchase an appliance from a major retailer sold under their own name but the product is actually produced by one of the 'big four' appliance companies. This solution is ideal for the ISP that wishes to hyper-focus on a key element of their business, defined perhaps as sales, regional expansion or network integration.

'Sourcing' at Shiva Systems:

When we first began business as Shiva Systems we opted to source out Usenet services. The capital outlay and maintenance was simply too much for us to tackle on our own. In retrospect however, we would have grown much faster and provided much better service initially had we sourced additional services for our customer base. Help desk service, HTML design and accounting were all fumbled and slightly mangled at times. As such a small company it's a miracle that we persevered but if I were to do it all again I would not undertake these services on my own.

Partnered turn-key solution:

This is by far the most affordable solution for new ISPs. A partnered solution is whereby you wish to provide Internet service to your community but do not have the capital outlays and staff available to support the service. By partnering with a turnkey provider you purchase the hardware and connection for the site but all of the services are handled by your host. You are mainly responsible for promoting and marketing the service. Revenue is shared and everyone benefits.

Permission was obtained for providing the following white-paper on MIS turnkey solutions. This helps the new ISP in considering some of the issues at hand when building your business:

MISNet Turn-Key Network Solution
Professionally begin your Internet business
within just a few short weeks.

The Internet is the world's largest network of computers. These computers are connected via dedicated data pipes of fiber and copper wiring, satellite communications, cable network coax, cellular packets, microwave and even POTS (plain old telephone service). The *useful Internet* is made up of the services that are offered over these connections. Electronic mail, the World Wide Web, online discussion forums and video conferencing are examples of Internet services that are commonly sold to commercial clients.

The Internet service business is generally handled by a small, local organization with good ties into the community. The endeavor is usually begun by acquiring hardware and software and talented help to run the company and provide the technical expertise to keep the organization afloat. A common startup will have only a handful of individuals actively participating in the day-to-day affairs. This small group is expected to service what is to be presented to the outside world as a 'full service' organization, capable of handling any type of service and of any size. As the company grows, the need for additional manpower and hardware quickly outgrow the available resources and the group finds that working 14 hour days will not suffice. It's not a pretty picture.

The true 'full service' Internet organization requires a massive investment, of both time and capital. The initial startup costs can be staggering. To provide the full spectrum of Internet service an organization requires a multitude of servers and connectivity hardware that can easily amount to over $50,000 initially. These requirements pale in comparison to the manpower requirements; a full time engineer, helpdesk personnel available 10+ hours per day, programming support, accounting support and representatives, web and graphic design artists and a dedicated sales staff that is knowledgable on all aspects of Internet service. Once all of this is in place you must go through the initial two to three months of 'trial by fire,' working out all of the kinks in your online systems and personnel procedures. The new full service organization will incur massive losses during its first year of operation. The fight here is against time, striving to produce enough revenue to support all of your back room services.

Yet, to take full advantage of the market opportunities you must be a 'full service' organization. The largest accounts will only do business with the most reputable and well staffed providers. How do you escape this paradox? Mikrotec answers this by allowing the new ISP to make use of our network and to be up and running within 45 days or less. By utilizing our existing network, staff and systems, MISnet resells the difficult back-room services to our Internet affiliates.

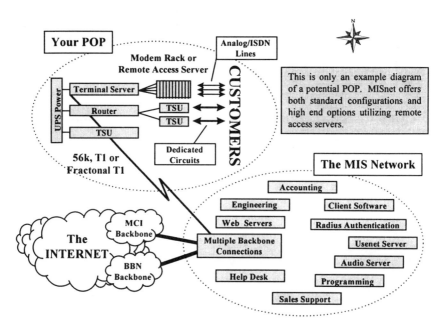

The ISP is then able to turn the standard Internet business model on its' ear. Your main focus is once again returned to the one element that makes you a profitable organization, **SALES AND MARKETING.** If you are one of the few groups that can begin a startup with a costly staff of ten or more individuals, then your resources will be all the better placed by hiring ten sales professionals who will be actively producing you new revenue on a daily basis. If you had intended to start your Internet business with just two or three full time staff then you can not afford to *not* have them producing new income in every working minute. The fight against time is over:

MISnet takes the small, local ISP, and turns them into a world class competitor literally overnight. The entire resources of 30 highly trained individuals with over 100 man years in Internet service experience is brought to your city. Cost is kept low and maintained as all of our advanced services are meant to be easily reproducable and scalable, available to any affiliate for any commercial client account.

Your organization focuses on selling the services and MISnet takes your new customers and provides them with premium care and support. Even the most difficult applications become easy when utilizing the MISnet affiliate program: Online database connectivity and applications become an easy proposition. MISnet RealAudio servers broadcast audio streams in real time from the MISnet NOC (network operations center) on a daily basis. Organizations who desire co-located Internet servers are offered A-to-Z solutions, from the building of the hardware platform to the monthly co-location and hosting. These are the types of advanced services that will set you apart from the competition.

Our goal is to make all of our affiliates the most competitive Internet providers in their respective markets. As the Internet service arena expands to encompass new technologies, MISnet will be there to embrace the technology and pass along the benefits to our affiliates.

We highly encourage you to call us for more information and a formal meeting where we can help you explore the possibilities further. The Internet, and your chosen market, is waiting for you...

Mikrotec Internet Services, Inc.
(800) 875-5095
www.mis.net

By building your new Internet service business in partnership with Mikrotec (MISnet) you assure your customers of the highest quality access and alleviate the majority of the daily burden on yourself. Duplicating all of the support functions of your competition only guarantees that you will spend more of your time fighting issues that are not directly related to producing new income. The MISnet plan allows you to focus on the true revenue producing portion of the Internet service business, marketing and sales generation. Back-end services such as user's software, POP hardware, technical support, Usenet, web hosting and markup, resold access and dedicated data circuits all become transparent and hassle free for the new provider. The vast majority of ISPs incur 80 to 90% of their cost structure from supporting these services. By creating a reproducable, stream-lined system and generating economies of scale for clients, MISnet is now successfully catering to over a dozen privately held ISPs.

Key advantages to a MISnet partnership

- Proven abilities: Mikrotec was founded in 1988 and is Kentucky's largest Internet provider. Coverage also covers portions of southern Indiana and parts of Tennessee, Virginia and West Virginia.

- Initial startup costs are kept low by sharing the MISnet NOC (network operations center) services (Ie. web, mail, Usenet, and Radius servers). In this way, POP hardware and investment is kept to a minimum. Your investment dollars are better spent marketing and building your client base. Both a standard and high-end POP implementation are available.

- By tying into the MISnet backbone you receive multiple high-speed points of entry to the Internet at large. Nowhere can a better connection value be purchased for the dollars.

- Backroom technical support and services are removed from your daily schedule allowing you to focus on the one universal element of all successful Internet service companies: **Marketing & Sales**

- Operational support elements such as software licensing, billing & collections and help desk support have all been streamlined by MISnet and may be taken advantage of immediately.

- Partners choose the level of support and features they desire from the service sheet. Optional services include billing and technical support. There is *no minimum* charge for service, we grow with you.

- Detailed services such as web design, dedicated access and programming projects are passed to the MISnet sales and engineering team allowing the partner to move quickly to the next potential customer.

- MISnet creates and maintains the partner's home page site. Our award winning New Media team will code an attractive and professional design with content and input from the partner. Advanced web services such as audio, video, forums and more are all available. As

MISnet adds new web services these automatically become available to the partner.

- Ongoing strategy and sales consultation available to you and your staff.

SERVICE & COST STRUCTURE

Hardware & Equipment

MISnet offers both a standard and 'high-end' solution for POPs (points of presence). You can choose the solution that is right for your area. All configuration and setup is handled onsite by MISnet staff and/or engineers.

Varies, See POP Options Sheet

Dedicated Access

- Full T1 pipeline
- Fractional T1 @ 512k

By quote

End user dial up accounts

- Radius authentication
- Usage / billing reports
- User mail accounts
- Home pages (5 meg)
- Dedicated Usenet server
- Provides licensed software at cost
- MISnet takes orders on behalf of partner
- Customers allowed 'roaming' access via any MISnet POP
- Technical phone support (Mon-Fri 8am-10pm, Sat 9am-5pm) 800# charge (approximately $200 - $500 per month)

$5.00 per account
up to 100 clients
$4.50 per account
100-250 clients
$4.00 per account
251+ clients

Billing & Collection

As opposed to the partner receiving a usage report, MISnet can optionally handle all aspects of billing and collections.

$1.00 per account

Dedicated Commercial Access (ISDN/T1) & Web Page Design / Hosting

The MISnet partner only needs to be responsible for initial sales inquiries and leads generation. MISnet's highly trained sales staff will then be

MISnet Affiliate
Receives 30% of the
recurring charges

able to take the client and walk them through the educational process for Internet services. Dedicated access up to T1 speeds, network integration, database connectivity and programming, and commercial high-end web services are all opportunities for increased revenue. Our sales team is dedicated to providing the best solutions for both the MISnet partner and the client. Partners may be required to give on site demonstrations.

Free services included in every partnership
• Total POP administration and remote / onsite maintenance
• Full web page design, hosting and updates for affiliates Home Page
    (Up to 25 pages and can include forums, calendars and Email forms)
• Training and support tools & access
• Ongoing strategy and sales consulting

POP Configuration Options

STANDARD POP
A fairly common configuration for an ISP's POP, utilizing standard hardware for connectivity. The standard POP configuration from Mikrotec includes the following hardware:

> • Standard 19" Equipment Rack
> • Shelving
> • 30 Port Terminal Server
> • 2 Port Cisco 2501 Router
> • Multitech Modem Rack w/Redundant power supplies
> • 8 MT2834 Cards, 3 modems each
> • APC 750 Rackmount UPS
> • Network hub and cabling
> • Adtran TSU
> • Fully configured and assembled
> • Onsite installation, travel & freight*
> • Professional home page for your ISP
> • Two hours of onsite training
> • All MISnet startup costs

Total cost: $29,800
(* Distant locales may have an addl. travel surcharge)

Mikrotec's standard POP utilizes industry recognized, 'tried and true' hardware. Additional options can include any number of analog or ISDN ports and an extra TSU for immediate support of dedicated access line customers.

ASCEND MAX POP

The MAX solution, an integrated Remote Access Server from Ascend Communications. Offers significant cost savings and flexibility. Ideal for metro areas and POPs expecting a large user base. The Ascend POP configuration from Mikrotec includes the following hardware:

- 19" Equipment Rack
- Shelving
- Ascend MAX 4004 Remote Access Server
- 2 digital modem cards, 12 modems each
  (Supports analog or ISDN calls)
- HDLC and ISDN MAX options
- APC 1000 Rackmount UPS
- Network hub and cabling
- Fully configured and assembled
- Onsite installation, travel & freight*
- Professional home page for your ISP
- Two hours of onsite training
- All MISnet startup costs

Total cost: $41,700
(* Distant locales may have an addl. travel surcharge)

Mikrotec's Ascend POP utilizes the state of the art MAX 4004 Remote Access Server. Advantages to the MAX solution include significant cost savings by utilizing ISDN PRI circuits to handle both your ISDN and analog modem calls via one leased line. Since analog calls are handled via ISDN PRI or channelized T1 circuits, the connections are digital the entire distance from your phone companies central office. Four entirely integrated WAN ports provide the ultimate in flexibility. There is no need for channel banks, CSUs or dedicated frame relay hardware for commercial client connections.

You can contact MISnet about these solutions by calling 1-800-875-5095 or emailing us at info@mis.net. Visit our Web site at www.mis.net.

MIKROTEC WORKS WITH AND IS CERTIFIED WITH THESE EQUIPMENT VENDORS TO PROVIDE THE BEST POSSIBLE SOLUTION WITH UNEQUALLED SUPPORT.

CiscoPro, AT&T, GTE, Farallon, Adtran and more...

END OF MISnet TURNKEY WHITE-PAPER

Another outline for a POP is shown next. The second showing here is a good performer but is entirely proprietary in nature. This means you are forever locked into this system and cannot hope to offer options that it does not internally support. This inflexibility in the architecture and the high cost of regional expansion is the main disadvantage to this solution. This proprietary nature is also what gives it strength, as almost anyone could setup this system for some basic, but solid, dial-in capabilities. Ideal uses would be dial up access for small to medium organizations that also need basic functionality for web services. Let's take a look...

ESoft Inc. is based in Aurora, Colorado. The driving force of the company is Phil Becker, an ex-NASA programmer. Their most widely known product is the TBBS bulletin board system, The Bread Board System. TBBS is a text based dial up system that serves up files, message bases, online polls and more. A companion product to TBBS is TDBS, The Data Base System, that gives TBBS an xBase type programming language and compiler. xBase is an industry standard database language that is also widely used by the government. Utilizing TBBS you can hook up to 96 lines to just one computer and allow dial up callers to access all of the functions of the system. Companies such as Intel and Creative Labs utilize the

TBBS system to support their customers with drivers, information, and software patches. Microsoft even ordered a custom version to support their own software distribution system. Using the same programming techniques that created TBBS, eSoft has built a new dedicated Internet server which handles many of an ISPs service needs.

The IPAD, or Internet Protocol Adapter, handles the following functions:

V.35 Interface   Utilizing a built in Niwot Network card the IPAD takes a feed directly from the CSU/DSU to support high speed connections such as 56k, Frac T1, and full T1s. A two port version is optional.

Router   The IPAD features an internal 'software' router with configuration information stored in text files on the system.

DNS server   Domain Name services are all handled internally by editing control files and creating new control files as you add more names under your system.

Terminal server The IPAD utilizes Digi International 'Digi-Board' multi-port serial cards. Cables from the Digi-Board connect directly to your modems serial interface.

SMTP/POP3 mail services - SMTP services are handled for as many domains as you carry. Users connect and using POP3 services can receive stored email and send new mail.

Basic FTP and HTML servers are also included. They are not as powerful as most organizations will desire but are supplied for basic functionality.

The hardware is made up of both standard off the shelf computer components and proprietary hardware. The mini tower unit sports a 486/66 (or higher) motherboard. The Niwot interface handles the connection and routing of Internet traffic with a built in microprocessor, and the drive sub-system is on a fast two megabyte caching controller. The software that powers the whole system is 32bit proprietary code. The DOS operating system that it boots from is effectively gone once the system loads. It may not sound powerful enough to support a POP but it does an amazingly good job for its niche. You can contact eSoft, Inc. at www.esoft.com.

For your own perusal a suggested low end implementation utilizing the IPAD is shown next. This does not take into account your leased line access, staffing for services or the need for additional workstations. It also leaves out many of the extras such as list servers and Usenet access that you will need to provide. Due to this the 'total cost' portion of this diagram is actually understated. For ISPs that intend to expand and may need more flexible options on services you will do best by consulting with a total solution provider.

An initial ISP implementation utilizing the IPAD server:

Ipad server with two 16 port Digi-boards for up to 32 simultaneous dial up connections, NIC card and software. Dual Niwot card, one port for accepting 56k, Frac or a T1 feed to the Internet, second port used to resell a leased line connection at a later date.	$8,750 plus shipping (approximately $110).
Web server: Pentium 166 with 32 megs of RAM, Windows NT server, NIC card, 2 gigabyte SCSI II drive, 17 inch monitor, quad speed CD-ROM and 16 bit sound card, mouse and keyboard.	$3,100
Workstation: Pentium 133 with 32 megs of RAM, Windows 95, 1 gig IDE drive, NIC card, Quad speed CD ROM drive, 17 inch monitor, 32 bit sound system, mouse and keyboard.	$2,400
Text Based BBS: Low end 486/100 with eight megs of RAM, 500 meg hard drive, NIC card, and 14 inch monitor, two 16550 COM ports, and keyboard.	$1,000
TBBS bulletin board software	$300
Boca ethernet hub	$130
32 Courier Modems utilizing one of the discount packages listed.	$8,000
HP Scanjet 4C desktop scanner	$500
Conner Tape Stor 4000	$400
Data line surge supressor package	$300
(3) APC SurgeArrest strips	$135
APC Backups 1200 UPS	$600
HP Deskjet 1600 Color Printer	$1,179
Adtran CSU/DSU	$1,200
O'Reilly and Associates Website Server	$300

TOTAL: **$28,404**

TSX BBS

TSX is another proprietary server solution that may be worthy of your consideration. TSX has most every Internet capability built into it that the aspiring ISP could desire. The entire system runs on a proprietary multi-tasking 32 bit operating system which is reported to have very good performance. SMTP, WEB, SLIP/PPP, and NNTP are all built into the system. It acts as both a BBS and an Internet server in one box so you can give your users text based Internet access as well as graphical Internet access. I've logged onto their home system as well as a number of other TSX systems and the software is indeed very powerful. As well as seeing the successful systems I have heard of a number of problems that some owners have encountered as well. The most prominent is a tale in Boardwatch Magazine from the gentleman who eventually gave up on the software. Your mileage may vary. As with most integrated solutions, running NNTP on the same box with the rest of your system can hurt your performance. S&H Computers, the company that makes TSX, can be reached on the web at www.sandh.com.

Multitasking (v): Screwing up several things at once...

What About Windows NT?

Many people have asked me about running an entirely Windows NT based Internet business. There are a number of groups that have successfully done this and are currently using Windows NT for all of their connectivity and service offerings. The biggest drawback to this currently is that NT is new to this game. Since the release of 4.0 Microsoft has been trying to compensate for this in a large way. The inherent abilities of NT 4.0 show that Microsoft wants to go head-to-head with the Unix server market for Internet providers. Let's take a look at some of the built-in capabilities of NT 4.0:

- Built-in TCP/IP
- Integrated software router
- Audit capabilities and usage logs
- Domain Name Services (DNS)

- Remote Access Services, for handling serial card and terminal server functionality
- The Internet Information Server for Web services
- File Transfer Protocol (FTP) and Gopher servers
- Integrated utilities such as Ping, Telnet & Traceroute

Many of these options will not be the performance leader in their category. For instance, a software-based router in the OS will never give you the performance or flexibility of their hardware-based kin. However, for the new startup they may be just the ticket.

Because of the relative youth of NT in this market one of the biggest hurdles to running an NT based ISP is the integration difficulties. There are many fine server applications for NT available, and we'll discuss some of them shortly, but they do not currently talk with each other easily (if at all). Does the prospect of having to access your web server, mail server, FTP server and authentication server individually for each user account sound appetizing to you? Probably not. Because so many of the applications available for NT use their own proprietary authentication schemes it's very difficult (if not impossible) to get them to work in tandem.

Microsoft's (MS) end-all answer to this is their own suite of ISP tools dubbed Normandy. Normandy was the project name for Microsoft's own endeavors into the commercial online-access market and has since been named the 'Microsoft Commercial Internet System.' The Microsoft Network (MSN) utilizes Normandy and since MS's decision to move their network solely to Internet based access and technology, Normandy has become all the more important as a strategic beach-head for their strategy. UUNet (partly owned by MS) is moving to Normandy technology and Compuserve has made public their intentions of using Normandy for their shift to an Internet based network.

At the heart of Normandy is a suite of server components built upon the existing structure of the NT server operating system and its inherent network management tools and Internet Information Server (web server). You will also need the SQL Back-Office database server which these components rely upon to store and manipulate data. Below this foundational server platform resides all of your remote access equipment such as hubs, routers, modems, ISDN and WAN access equipment. On top of the server platform the component servers of Normandy do their job. Let's look at the different pieces:

- Membership System
  The user authentication and access control system for Normandy. Handles all user access privileges and billing events.

- Commercial Internet Mail Server
  Handles all Email functionality for your user base

- Commercial Internet News Server
  An NNTP server for NT. Provides for both public and private newsgroups and moderated conferences.

- Conference Server
  Real time conferencing, groupware and document manipulation (white-boarding) server.

- Information Retrieval Server
  The search engine used for querying all of your web content, newsgroups and even MS Office documents. This server plays a key role in making the Normandy system capable of advanced operations.

- Content Replication System
  Provides for multiple mirrored web sites as well as production staging of HTML documents to a distributed set of servers. A very advanced staging system and replication system when you are doing high-end web production and site hosting. Also allows you to distribute privileges across multiple servers for distributed processing and user's service handling.

- Personalization Server
  Allows for personalizing of web content for users based on user's input or administrator's control options. An add-on for the IIS web server.

- Merchant Server
  Microsoft's answer to the shopping-cart experience. Used for building virtual storefronts and handling transactions.

Microsoft has created a complete Internet Service Provider's package in all of these components and it is a compelling story.

The downside to this is that not all of these components are available currently (as of this writing) and the ones that are only exist in beta. So, in the words of Clint Eastwood, "Do you feel lucky punk? Well, do ya?" By the end of '97 Microsoft will probably have this system down pat and be releasing updates for all the world to see (and use). For now I believe it's still a risky proposition.

With that said however, Microsoft is not the only player in the NT ISP server game. There are many other organizations that have built upon the NT server to create very functional solutions for ISPs. Web servers are a prime example. MS's IIS web server is still playing catch-up to a great degree with other web servers (for NT) that have been on the market for far longer. Web servers such as O'Reilly's WebSite and Purveyor from Process Software are far more functional in their current iterations than the IIS is alone. For that matter, I wouldn't consider running a web server on anything but NT because it's simply too easy to use and administrate for this particular function. You can't imagine the amount of grief I'll catch for saying that.

Some additional resources for you to investigate:

Internet Shopper (http://www.net-shopper.co.uk/)
Here you can find NTmail, our Best of Breed winner for NT based mail servers. With low site licensing costs and more bells and whistles than you can imagine, this one is definitely worth looking into. The performance is stellar and the powerful administration functions will make you water at the mouth. Remote user administration, such as holiday messages and password changes, via an automated mail responder manager is just one of the features you

have to look forward to. The NTmail software also makes a fine compliment to an existing NT based web server for your clients. In this way you can package a single-box solution that does Web, Mail and FTP services, and all at a particularly attractive price. Internet Shopper also sells a RADIUS implementation for NT, NTlist (an attractive add-on list server for NTmail) and Dnews, an NT based NNTP Usenet server.

More Options: See Software.Com's (http://www.software.com/) Post.Office product and Netscape's mail server for NT. Seattle Lab (http://www.seattlelab.com/) produces a very nice Telnet server and has recently added a mail server to its lineup for NT.

Putting the Pieces Together

We're going to now look at how your ISP infrastructure is built. The following outlines the way this would be done with an IPAD because it was the first turn-key solution we used. If you are using a more powerful site system, such as one of the MISnet solutions discussed prior to this, the diagrams would be very similar with the exception of the connections being made to Cisco and Livingston products. An example is shown in the comparison section concerning Ascend equipment. If you are planning for growth you will need to utilize the more standardized equipment as the costs will be much lower in the long run.

Let's take a look at a simplified outline of an ISP's network. The next diagram outlines the way connections are made. My own link to the Internet at large was made by plugging a CSU/DSU directly into the Niwot router via a V.35 cable. The CSU/DSU is fed with a full

> **CSU/DSU:**
> Customer Service Unit / Digital Service Unit. A device that provides a digital connection to high speed leased lines. Although it functions differently, the best analogy is that this is the equivalent of a modem for a leased line.

T1 link from my own provider. Likewise, because I ordered a dual port Niwot I had yet another port to spare. Utilizing the Niwot's (or Cisco's) built-in routing, this second V.35 port and another CSU/DSU, I had a fractional T1 ported to another customer who desired to have their business network connected. If you wish to connect your Internet server via a 56k, Fractional T1, or a full T1 you will need to have a CSU/DSU to let it communicate with your network. How would this type of configuration appear without using the IPAD's built in system? The diagram below shows this:

The Internet

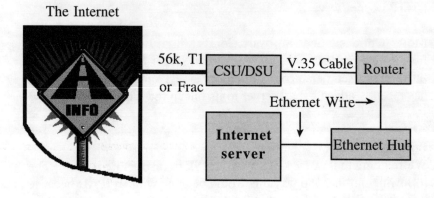

My network configuration utilizing the IPAD:

My original (proprietary solution) network configuration utilizing the IPAD is shown next.

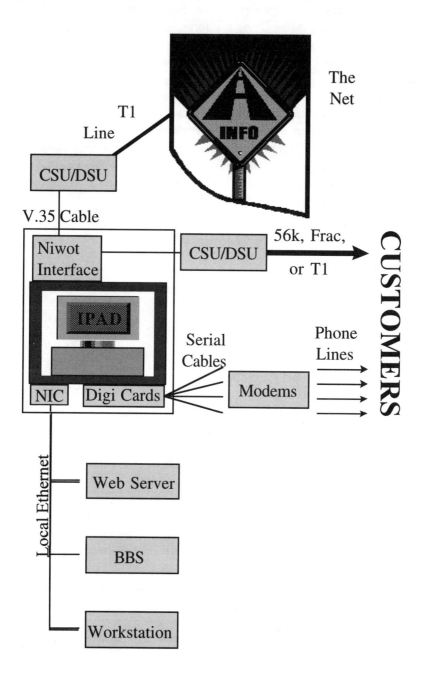

Note that my own network shows all of the computers tied together in a line, which would be the situation when you use 'thin-net' or thin coax wiring. The picture prior to this shows that the server is tied to an ethernet hub. Using a hub and 10Base-T connections are much preferable over the thin-net (10 Base-2 with BNC connections) solution. The reason for this is that in a thin-net network, one broken link can separate the two halves of your network. In a hubbed network if a wire goes bad or is broken then the rest of the network continues to function normally. Boca Research (www.boca.org) makes a nice line of inexpensive and reliable ethernet hubs. Why did I run thin-net you ask? It was a leftover from a long time ago when I knew no better. You know better now so when you design your own local network be sure to use a hub and a 10 Base-T topology.

Ethernet(n): something used to catch the etherbunny.

CSU/DSU units - These digital adapters allow you to interface to real speed. Even if you are starting your ISP on a 56k feed (see the chapter on location and connections) a CSU/DSU can grow with you to support fractional T1 and all the way up to a full T1 feed. A good unit and one that we incorporate into our own network and all of our customer's quotes

The Adtran TSU

is the Adtran TSU. The Adtran TSU can start as a 56k CSU/DSU if you like and then grow into T1 service which uses multiple 56k/64k channels. The unit features a single V.35 interface which is used to connect to your router port. Its configuration is performed through the front LED and button panel. A whole slew of alarms and error conditions are recorded by the unit which can be called up on the display and subsequently cleared as well. The Adtran unit can be purchased for about $1,000 on the street; maybe you could even find a better deal if you shop around. We've also heard very good things about the Tylink CSU/DSU product family. Tylink is frowned upon in some circles due to its low price but their equipment is in place at a number of ISPs I have spoken with and humming along without a problem. The bad reputation might be due to 'hardware elitists', of which there is no lack of in the Unix community. My recommendation is that if you can get a good deal on one go with it. Contact Adtran on the web at www.adtran.com or by voice at (800) 332-6945. To save some money be sure to buy the actual product from a reseller who will always sell these below the list price. Tylink can be reached on the web at www.tylink.com or by voice at (800) 828-2785.

Routers

Routers are the post offices of the Internet. They switch data back and forth and move it in the proper direction. If your router goes down neither incoming requests for data nor outgoing packets of data will be serviced. Nothing will work! The router is therefore a crucial piece of equipment. For every leased line that you have, incoming or outgoing, you are going to need a router port. That is, you will need to have either a number of stand alone units that each service a single port or a unit that can service multiple ports to the CSU/DSUs. If you were to use a stand alone dedicated router you would have to find a reliable choice for the new ISP and one that would not break the bank. I highly recommend the Cisco series of routers for this purpose. Cisco has been making routers since before there was dirt. The Cisco 1005 or one of the 2000 series routers will serve you well for a long time to come. The 2501 model can be purchased for $2,200 on the street and supports dual v.35 ports. Once you decide on your router, shopping around can save you a lot of money. Don't be hesitant to keep calling. Every $100 you save is more that you have to spend on marketing later!

Terminal Servers and Dial Up Customers

Let's examine the way dial up customers get access to an ISP now. In my own network I initially utilized two 16 port Digi serial cards tied to the IPAD. This was not the most expandable solution as the IPAD was limited to a total of 32 ports. Other servers that support internal serial cards will vary in the number of ports they can support. Digi cards are dependable and served us well for our first year of operation. The cards sport 16550 chips that buffer the communications stream so they are able to handle the fastest modems on the market. They can also handle low end ISDN serial based terminal adapters, the type of ISDN equipment that you normally plug into a no frills COM port. The Digis plug directly into the server and the server software handles the dial up security access. Not all server solutions that you find will support serial cards. If they do support serial cards their recommended solution will be different from one platform to the next so be sure to check with your equipment provider before rushing out and buying any. What other types of equipment provide this service? Terminal Servers. Dedicated terminal servers are the preferred method of supplying incoming ports for dial up users. Terminal servers can be of a software based nature, such as that found in the IPAD and Windows NT RAS (Remote Access Service) that is built into NT. This type of solution can handle a few dial up customers but does not have the type of power to really move a lot of data. The other option is hardware based (dedicated) terminal servers. These devices connect directly to your local ethernet based network and have cables that plug into the serial ports of your modems. If your server has no integrated management system available that you can use to configure the terminal servers then you will be forced to mucking with them individually for configuring such things as modem initialization strings, user names and passwords, etc. Be careful, this type of solution can turn into a nightmare if you can not manage them properly from your management system! What does this type of solution look like?

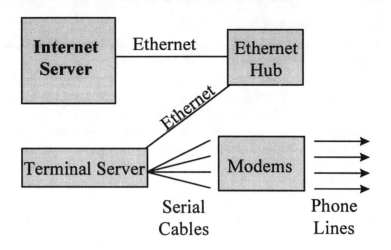

A leader in the terminal server market is Livingston Enterprises. Their Portmaster series are used worldwide for Internet and other networking needs. The Livingston Portmaster 2E-30 is a 30

Livingston Portmaster Series

asynchronous port unit which will service 30 modems at top speeds. The list price is $3,750, but you will not pay this much on the street. As with all of the hardware listed here, shopping around will save you a bundle.

Modems

Modems are the gatekeepers to your end user market. Until ISDN takes the lead as the most requested access service modems are your main entry way. Do not even bother with 14.4 modems. The rest of the world is moving too fast and the Internet is too slow over such connections. The money you save will be lost to disgruntled high speed users who complain that you do not have enough lines for them.

Modems - Speed

The most recent standard in high speed is the V.34 specification that allows for 28.8kbps over a POTS line. The newest addition to the V.34 standard makes a minor leap to 33.6k speeds. Brand new specifications are being hammered out for 56k speeds, known as X2 technology, and these should be available en masse by mid '97. I will tell you now that you will want to support this speed. Even if it is impractical for most people to make a clean enough connection to your service much less to their neighbor at those speeds, they will want to know if you support 56k. It's a psychological edge even if it perceptually offers nothing more to the users. The problem is that many users can not connect at 33.6 today! The top speeds listed are only achievable under ideal circumstances. Given that the lines are as clean as possible, the phone companies switching equipment is in good shape, the tides are in, Capricorn is in your moon, etc. etc. you may get a perfect connection. Some users will be able to consistently get a perfect connection to your site, other will not. I myself can not connect to my own system at better than 26.4, which is one of the many baby steps outlined in the V.34 specification as a fallback rate under non-ideal line conditions. One of my programmers gets a perfect 28.8 on every single call. Go figure. You will constantly be answering to your users on why this is, it's not a lot of fun. Nevertheless, ours is not to question why but to explain the problems to the user base. The 56k spec should give us all a little better connection than we enjoyed previously. If you were connecting at 26.4kbps with two 33.6 modems, the theory goes that you should be able to connect at something better than 33.6kbps given two 56k modems.

Modems - Expandability

Some modems are shipping with 'Flash ROM' chips. These are modems that allow you to update their internal code with software. Once the new revision of the code has been patched into the chip it stays there! This is a terrific idea and one which a number of companies who will go unmentioned should incorporate into their own products. If you have a Flash ROM capable modem today you should be able to download the software revision after the new protocol addendum has been added and upgrade them to a 56k modem painlessly. Since you are probably buying your modems new you can be sure to purchase a stack of them that do have Flash ROM capabilities.

Modems - Rack Mount or Stand Alone Units

Computer racks make for some very attractive and organized computer rooms. There is a lot of equipment that comes in rack-mount format and all you have to do is bolt them into the rack and hook up the accompanying wires. Modems can be ordered stand alone or rack mounted as well. Rack mount modems present a very clean environment with a minimum of wiring. Rack mount modems also have the benefit that they are remotely manageable. Many major vendors have software for managing their rack mount modules which allow you to 'connect' to the rack mount over the network. This is very advantageous for remote POPs and tweaking hardware when you're away from the office. In the early days we used stand alone models. This can make for a lot of mess, but if you design your shelving properly it's actually not unattractive. Additionally, if a power supply goes bad you don't have to worry about the entire rack grinding to a quick halt. What is the major drawback to rack-mount modules? You usually pay a premium for them.

Modems - Best of Breed

I firmly believe that the best modem in the world is produced by U.S. Robotics (www.usr.com). Their Courier V.Everything modem is the Cadillac of the industry. In review after review you'll see that

The Courier V.Everything

the Courier is tops in performance characteristics such as speed, noise reduction, and the lowest number of disconnects under adverse line conditions. The Courier features a Flash ROM upgrade path that makes it easy to stay current on the latest and greatest standards as well. Due to the Flash ROM we were offering 33.6k on our system a full three months before any of our competitors; they had all been 28.8 modems prior to applying the software patch. The warranty is a five year factory fix or replacement. In addition to its stellar performance the V.Everything is named such because it can talk with just about every protocol ever conceived, even the old standards that were intermittent steps to the 28.8 V.34 standard are supported. Personal testimonial time; I had a user who had one of these older modems that had a top connect speed of 19.2kbps. The particular modem was a piece of junk and had been identified as such in a number of modem reviews. His company purchased four of these monstrosities and was unable to get them to connect to each other at 19.2 speeds! The highest connection they could get was 14.4k when talking with their kin. However, when calling in to our system from any of them they received a perfect 19.2 connection when hooking to our Couriers. Now that's a sad situation but the Couriers saved the day. The customer called desiring to know what type of modem supported the junk he knew he was in possession of. When we ended the conversation he left with an impression of our company that was outstanding. That's the type of experience that makes a believer out of one. The Courier lists for something awful at around $400+ apiece. Don't panic however. The U.S. Robotics company offers an internal discount plan to ISPs that was listing them at $250 when last I checked. For the very best deal possible, check to see if the AOP (see the chapter on resources) is still offering the member's discount that drops this price to about $215 plus shipping. You can't beat that type of deep discount with a stick. U.S. Robotics also offers the 'Total Control' rack mounted solution that is quite out of reach of many budgets but you can find all the details on their web site.

For a lower cost rack mount solution try the new Hayes 'Century' series. Available in either eight or sixteen modem configurations these units are Flash ROM upgradable and have some very nice management  The Hayes Century 16 features built into them. Hayes also offers an ISP discount so be sure to take advantage of this when making a purchase. The ISP pricing on the 16 modem model is $4144. If you are intent on buying other modems check for ISP discounts. Boardwatch

Magazine occasionally runs a sysops / ISP discount price list for modems so you might check their pages for the latest and greatest deals. One last alternative, another rack mount solution that comes high recommended is the Microcom product line. They have a line of high capacity rack mount solutions that hold a lot of modems in just a small amount of space. Be sure to check with your equipment provider for their own recommended solution.

ISDN

As an ISP you can use ISDN as your main connection to your own host Internet provider for supporting just a few dial up users. You can also offer ISDN dial up and dedicated service as mentioned previously. There are two basic ways to hook ISDN equipment to your network, one involves utilizing an ISDN terminal adapter which will plug into a COM port or free serial communications port somewhere on your server or your network. The second method uses an ISDN / router combo package that hooks into your ethernet network.

ISDN - Routers

The right way to hook to your own provider (or your customers to you) would be to use an ethernet connected ISDN router. This type of equipment plugs directly into your ethernet hub and communicates TCP/IP directly across the wire. The very best product in this category is made by Ascend Communications. You can reach them

at www.ascend.com. Their Pipeline 50 product family is an outstanding choice for this type of application. The Pipeline 50 is not hindered by 115kbps limitation inherent in most ISDN terminal adapters due to the fact that it does not hook to a communications (COM) port. It can travel at the full 128k that ISDN gives when multiplexing both 'B' bearer channels together. This type of solution is simply more robust and flexible than the COM port attached adapters. As opposed to terminal adapters, ISDN routers can handle multiple IP addresses and thus connect many users to one

ISDN connection. These products should be used when designing a quote for a business customer whose needs outpace the terminal adapters. With an ethernet connected ISDN router you simply point computers to the internally configured IP address and they communicate seamlessly with the connection at the other end. It's clean, it's reliable, and it's fast. What are the drawbacks? Price and setup. The price on ISDN routers is quite a bit higher than ISDN terminal adapters. The Pipeline 50 that includes the built in NT1 terminator (remember those from our discussion of ISDN technology?) can be had for $1,000. The list price is a bit higher. The difficult configuration of the Pipeline product can be intimidating but technical support is just a phone call away. If you need a rock solid high end ISDN connection this is the product for you. Ascend also makes a line of 'dense' ISDN servers that can accept multiple BRIs.

Another option for ISDN router combos is Farallon's Netopia line of products. They are very affordable and seem to have many of the high end functions down pat. Point your browser to www.farallon.com.

ISDN - Terminal Adapters

ISDN adapters that connect to a COM or serial port are generally used by the end user. They are limited to 115k transmission and receive speeds even when both 64k channels are multiplexed together. Perhaps this particular drawback will be fixed when internal adapters are tweaked to take advantage of the full 128k limit. You can use such a device for your own Internet connection to your provider but it is  not nearly as viable a solution as using the high end router combo adapters. End users love these products because they are inexpensive (comparatively) and fairly easy to install. You do not need a NIC (network interface or ethernet card) to hook one to your personal computer either. Plug one into a 16550 equipped or other buffered serial port, configure it with the included software, dial and connect. These are definitely the type of adapters you will want to offer to your dial up ISDN user base. The product we standardized on when offering these to our clients was the Motorola Bitsurfer Pro series (www.mot.com). These devices can be had on the street for a low $300. We use them quite successfully when doing product demonstrations and technology and expo shows as well. One of our Bitsurfers serviced the Wired Magazine presentation when ISDN connectivity was requested on short notice. Although we had never used one on a Macintosh before it was as easy as setting up a modem.

Be aware that many terminal adapters do not allow you as the ISP to service separate calls from two clients on a single BRI. This is another strong reason to use the ISDN routers in house, regardless of what your customers use.

The Path of the Integrated Way - Best of Breed

You have already noticed that we like to recommend the 'best of breed' in product categories. Some products simply shine brighter than all the rest and access equipment is no different. We've looked at all of the individual pieces that place the ISP squarely between the Internet at large and their customer base. On the customer side you have POTS lines, ISDN circuits, T1 and frame relay pipes. These circuits connect to racks of modems, ISDN routers, and CSUs. These in turn connect to your terminal servers, ethernet hubs, and routers. Your authentication server (Radius) sits in the middle allowing authorized users to access your network. On the back end you connect to the Internet via a T1/frame relay connection.

A trend that is readily apparent within the industry is the aggregation of these components into one extremely compact and manageable package. Making separate components perform advanced functions, such as bandwidth on demand, is often difficult if not outright impossible. These types of advanced functions are another benefit of integrated solutions, as they are far easier to implement if you're dealing with a single vendor's solution. We will bring onto the stage now Ascend Communications. You will remember their name from our earlier discussion of the Pipeline 50 product for ISDN routing.

Ascend Communications (www.ascend.com) manufactures a broad range of high-speed network access products that enable ISPs to construct extremely flexible wide area networks for Internet access. Their products universally provide "bandwidth on demand" because they establish switched digital connections whose bandwidth, duration and destination can be adjusted automatically based on rules provided to the equipment. Outside of their ISDN and Ethernet routers, Ascend makes a line of highly integrated 'Remote Access Servers,' dubbed the MAX. The two flavors of the MAX we'll deal with are the 4004 and the 4002 model. The differences lie in the number of WAN (wide area network) ports and ISDN BRI ports that they offer. The 4002 supports two WAN interfaces and up to 48 ISDN B channels while the 4004 supports four WAN interfaces and 96 ISDN B channels. This will be made more clear in diagrams that follow.

As we will see, the MAX is particularly well suited for an ISP's needs. In all fairness, their remote access servers are modular units that are also utilized for services such as video conferencing, combined voice & data communications and standard WAN connectivity. We are only concerned however with their Internet access service qualities.

The MAX utilizes a chassis and back-plane architecture similar to that of a common PC. The chassis serves as the foundation and modular expansion cards are used in slots on the back-plane. In this way you can mix and match  expansion cards to get any mix of services that you so desire. Most ISPs would stock these expansion slots with digital modem cards for ISDN and analog modem access. Before we get too deep into the discussion of the MAX, let us compare a diagram of a standard POP and an Ascend POP. A picture in this case *is* worth a thousand words:

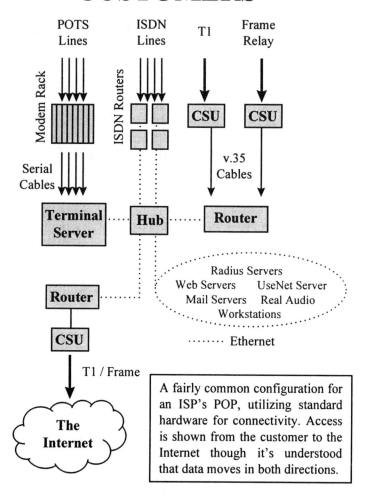

A fairly common configuration for an ISP's POP, utilizing standard hardware for connectivity. Access is shown from the customer to the Internet though it's understood that data moves in both directions.

THE ASCEND MAX POP CONFIGURATION

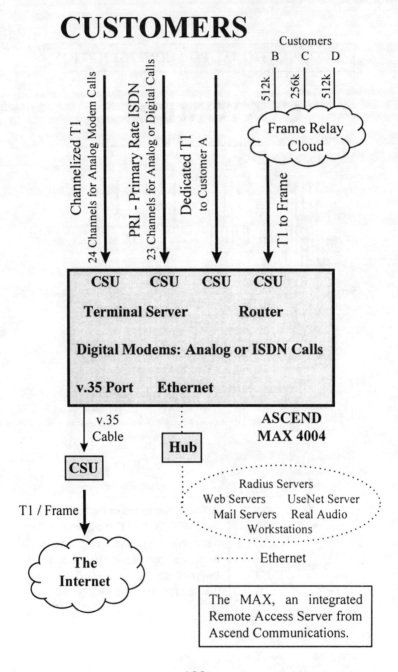

CUSTOMERS

The most apparent difference in these two POPs is the stark lack of wires in the Ascend solution. Always a plus with integrated hardware, there are fewer messes and fewer pieces of equipment to manage separately. This becomes increasingly important as your number of POPs grow. Let's try to dissect our diagram of the Ascend POP beginning in the top left-hand corner.

WAN PORTS
In the conventional POP an ISP must have a free CSU and router port available for each type of WAN connection. If you have two dedicated customers with fractional T1 service then you must have two CSUs and two available router ports. If you add a connection to a frame cloud then you must add another CSU and router port. The MAX integrates four CSUs with the router and handles the entire process internally. The only CSU you may need will be the one for the v.35 port which is used to tie you back to the Internet. If you have not used all of the available WAN ports on your MAX then you can dispense with even your own CSU (utilizing one of the internal ports) until such time that you need the additional port for a customer.

CHANNELIZED T1 ACCESS
We have discussed channel banks previously as a way to conserve copper pairs and to reduce the wiring mess within your site. A channelized T1 brings 24 channels over two pair of copper into your site and terminates into the channel bank. The channel bank then breaks these channels out into individual analog / voice circuits. These circuits are in turn ported to your modem rack where calls may be answered. The MAX does away with the need for a channel bank and can take one or more channelized T1s directly into one of the four available WAN ports on the back of the unit. These circuits are then ported to the digital modem cards which accept incoming calls.

PRI ACCESS
Any of the MAX's four WAN ports can accept PRI circuits which consist of 23 B channels each (compared to the two B channels of a BRI circuit). The MAX makes full use of ISDN's ability to carry voice or digital traffic. Incoming calls are identified by the MAX as

either analog or digital and routed automatically to either a digital modem or to an HDLC (for ISDN) processor. In this way you could use a single PRI to handle all of your dial up customers. If you run multiple PRI into the MAX you increase your total dial-up capacity, both for modem and ISDN calls. This eliminates all of the management difficulties associated with forecasting how many ISDN and analog circuits you will need in a given month since both analog and ISDN subscribers are assigned the same access number. This also simplifies your marketing, management, and support functions. The total capacity of your MAX dictates the number of simultaneous callers you can service. If you can imagine the time and headaches saved from this feature alone you are starting to get a feel for the power of this box.

DEDICATED T1
Any of the four WAN ports can route a full or fractional T1 to another location.

FRAME RELAY
Any of the four WAN ports can route a full T1 connection to a frame cloud. By tying into a frame cloud you are then able to sell frame connections back to your network (and the Internet via your network) in any incremental size you may choose. By utilizing frame, where available, you expand the total number of customers that may tie into your network with no further investment in hardware. Imagine the cost of setting up 5 dedicated 256k connections, with a CSU and router port for each, and the cost savings of frame relay become readily apparent.

DIGITAL MODEM CARDS
We have already mentioned the ability of the Ascend MAX to accept either ISDN or analog modem traffic. Another advantage to bringing analog calls over digital lines is the increase in the noise immunity of the circuits. This means less packet loss and fewer prematurely terminated calls for your customers. The MAX 4004 will accept up four WAN connections and up to six 12-port modem cards. This configuration will allow a total of 96 simultaneous connections including up to 72 simultaneous modem-based customers.

Other advantages include:

BANDWIDTH ON DEMAND
Ascend equipment can manage your bandwidth and thus make full use of your resources. If a customer requests a large amount of data via their Ascend Pipeline connection, the MAX and Pipeline can negotiate to automatically engage the second B channel on the BRI. Once the data requested has been successfully sent the second B channel can be 'torn down' and made available for another customer. This is far more advantageous than leaving both B channels nailed up constantly for what may only be a trickle of data. Likewise, it is worlds above using a terminal adapter on your end where one of the two BRI channels are wasted if a customer has made a 64k connection. From the ISP's perspective, dynamic bandwidth allocation based on actual bandwidth usage can free valuable dial-in ports for use by additional subscribers.

EASY MANAGEMENT
Since your entire realm of access equipment resides in one package, total management is available via a single interface. All of the internal functions of the MAX can be handled utilizing SNMP (simple network management protocol), Telnet or through a VT-100 terminal or standard PC.

CALL DETAIL REPORTING
Each call to and from your site produces a record in the MAX which includes the date and time, the duration of the call, the called and calling number and information on the port and usage. This can then be used to create detailed reports that help you understand your bandwidth needs and further manage your resources.

USAGE CAPPING
If you offer a per-hour charge on any of your accounts you will invariably have the customer who calls up and wants to know why they received an $80 bill. Usage capping allows you to set a pre-determined amount of time after which a connection will cease to

function. This can help you prevent the stray user from running up their bill and then chastising you for their mistake. C'est la vie.

INTEGRATED FIREWALL
For network security, an internal firewall has been included with the MAX.

Ascend MAX - What's The Downside?
PRI circuits are not universally available. It's not uncommon to be in an area where BRI is offered and PRI has not yet been tariffed. In this case you can still handle both analog and ISDN subscribers by bringing a channelized T1 into your site. Because there is no D channel signalling, each of the 24 T1 channels must be preconfigured for either analog or ISDN service. Also, each ISDN B channel will support only 56k instead of 64k. Fortunately, CAPs are entering many parts of the United States and forcing the local telco to be more competitive on their ISDN PRI tariffing.

It is often heard that the pricing is a downside to the MAX but I've worked the numbers and this just does not pan out. If you want to handle a lot of ISDN, analog and large data circuits the MAX is ideally suited. Any premium paid once you've duplicated the functionality of the MAX is minuscule. This difference is more than canceled out by the cost savings associated with carrying ISDN and analog circuits over the same pipe, the ease of management and the lack of channel bank fees from your RBOC (if applicable). This is perhaps where the confusion arises, as most groups piece their POPs together one bit at a time. Comparing their first baby step to the total cost of the Ascend solution is flawed logic. If you are under capitalized than piecing together a POP may well be the proper choice for you in the short run but the long term solution still remains in an integrated access server with functionality similar to that of the MAX.

The MAX 4004 chassis can be had for about $12,000 and the 4002 comes in at about $9,000. The only additions you will want to make to this are digital modem cards (12 modems each, analog & ISDN capable) for about $5,000 each up to a maximum of 6 cards. For the

ISDN capability you will add the HDLC and ISDN software options which should come in under $2,000. xDSL technology is also available in the form of expansion cards.

It would not be right to end the conversation without showing you the numbers. The MAX is in good company it would appear. 27 of the 30 largest ISPs (PSI, UUNet, Microsoft, and so on) utilize MAXs for Internet services. Additionally, Ascend commands an 84% market share in the ISDN PRI server market. Not too shabby....

Web Servers
The web server supplies one of your main revenue streams. It can potentially dwarf your user base as a money maker within a matter of months if you market the services correctly.

Web Servers - OS Platform
Although there are many proprietary servers which have built in web servers my recommendation is that you find a nice, new, fast moving web server that will grow with you as time marches on. Outside of the high end workstation market (which I am not going to recommend) there is only one platform really worthy of consideration for housing your web server. Windows NT, the network operating system of champions! Almost every web server you can imagine is now available on the NT platform where you will have the familiar windows based interface. Windows NT is fully 32 bit with true multi-tasking capabilities. It has many built in Unix-like services which make it the perfect complement to any web server it may host. Windows NT features a built in FTP server so that you can assign permissions for both yourself, your dial up users and your commercial clients to get into their own respective directory while not bothering anyone else's work. It also features a plethora of other tools that are useful to have on any machine in your network: Traceroute, or 'tracert' as the command on NT is used, is a program for tracking the route to a particular server from your own connection. Ping is a utility that tests the connection speed between your own computer and that of another on the Internet. A basic telnet client, explained prior to this chapter, is also included.

Windows NT has full support for TCP/IP networking built into the operating system so you will have no difficulty attaching it to any network that walks and talks Internet. Not only is NT stable but it's just bloody fast. NT comes in two flavors, workstation and server. Check with your specific web server software vendor, if it will run on workstation equally as well as it will on server you can save about four megs of memory and $400 by utilizing the workstation version. Workstation requires 12 megs just for the OS (operating system) and server requires 16 megabytes. Workstation will cost about $300 while server is considerably more. Shop around for your best deals.

Web Servers - Hardware
We ran our own server in the beginning on NT workstation powered with a 486/100 with 20 megs of memory. We eventually upgraded to a Pentium 100 with 64 megs of memory. Web servers can really chew up memory depending on what type of workload they have and how many 'extras' you are running with them. NT takes full advantage of the SCSI drive system which can make quite a considerable speed difference on any 32bit processor/memory configuration. Be sure to get a PC with the new PCI bus if starting from scratch. If using an older PC try to utilize the VESA local bus for your drive interface if it is available.

Web Server Software - Website
O'Reilly and Associates, publishers of a very popular line of books concerning Unix and Internet topics, released its first software product in the form of Website. The Website server software is what we utilized at our own operation as our main web server. It has tremendous ease of use and capabilities built into it such as: easy setup of multi-homing sites (multi-domain web sites on the same machine), easy mapping of directories for resources such as CGI programs for enhancements to your site, terrific performance, proprietary and open image mapping capabilities and a busy third party market. Website has already had two commercial add-on enhancements released by O'Reilly. Polyforms, the first, allows you to configure very easy to use forms for your web site which send the completed information to an email box or flat file database (or both). Webboard, the second add-on, is a full featured message conferencing system. Webboard features loose or tight security,

moderated conferences, full featured message retrieval, 'follow features' and a bevy of other niceties. Website is inexpensive too! The street price is currently around $200 for the standard edition. If you will be using secured services and need a web server which can handle credit card transactions and other sensitive data transfers you can order their high end Website Pro (list price of $350).

Website Pro supports the two current protocol leaders in web based cryptography, Secure Socket Layers (SSL) and Secure Hyper Text Transfer Protocol (S-HTTP).

Additionally, Website incorporates the latest PERL 5 scripting language for Windows NT. This allows you to draw upon the hundreds, if not thousands, of publicly available PERL CGI scripts. Simply drop them into your mapped CGI directory and call them via HTML. Voila, you have a number of nice add-ons to your web server with no pain. Some common Perl CGI scripts include such applications as guest books, conference systems, hit counters and more. A good repository of freeware and shareware CGI applications can be had at Selena Sol's repository, point to http://www.eff.org/~erict/Scripts/ for more information.

One of the downsides to secured servers is the need for a digital ID or 'certificate.' Once acquired, the ID is entered into your server and allows it to communicate with web browsers using encrypted protocols. ID's are currently assigned by Verisign (http://www.verisign.com) and cost $290 per year for the first web server and $95 per year for each additional server. It is rumored that the U.S. Postal Office will be entering this arena and providing secure certificates. Any competition is sure to be a good thing for the buyer and will no doubt lower the cost over time. Figure the additional cost into your business plan if you intend on running a tight ship.

Website is a winner in my book and thousands of sites around the world are currently using it. It will not break the bank and is actively being developed and extended. The recent release of version 1.1 will be followed later this year by another upgrade. O'Reilly and Associates can be reached on the web at www.ora.com.

Web Server Software - Internet Information Server (IIS)
For the low budget ISP, Microsoft has begun shipping their Internet Information Server (IIS) at the low low cost of nothing. That's right, it's absolutely free and included with all new versions of Windows NT server. You have already figured out the catch, you must have Windows NT Server to run IIS, it will not function on the workstation version of NT. For those with NT 3.51 you can download the server software at no cost from the Microsoft home page at www.microsoft.com. Although the features do not stack up against Website it does include a few niceties that are not yet available in the O'Reilly product. Multi-homing and limited CGI capabilities are included. ODBC is included as well, this is database connectivity that generally only the higher end web servers offer. Utilizing ODBC you can connect web pages to databases and users from the web can search, edit and maintain data in this fashion. Keep a close eye on this one, Microsoft may be ringing the funeral bell for other web servers if they expand on the work they have done so far.

Web Server Software - Apache
For friends of Unix we can unconditionally recommend the Apache secure server. In the spirit of the net it seems appropriate that the most common web server in use today is absolutely free. Apache is run on over 100,000 web servers as of this writing. The disadvantage is that there is no formal support system for this software so you must rely on what is available on the Web and Usenet if any problems arise. Click over to http://www.apache.org/ for the entire scoop and the latest version of the source code.

News Servers
As mentioned before, if you want to offer a full Usenet feed to your customers you are advised to run a separate news server. Usenet server are generally in the Unix flavor so in this area you will have to learn about the operating system. Be prepared for a major investment in hardware as news servers require a lot of memory and need some very large and very fast drive systems. Many ISPs are

now offering 15,000 to 19,000 conferences on their Usenet servers. This takes a lot of space and horsepower and can eat a 56k line for lunch at peak load.   BSD Unix is one of the best for handling Usenet.   For an NT implementation you can try Net Shopper at www.net-shopper.co.uk.   Microsoft will be releasing their own product for Usenet service shortly.

Initially, the Usenet was a bit too much for me to tackle on my own. I did not have the time nor the resources to do the job correctly. Additionally, I didn't want any of the liability that might come with running a public message system on the Internet that transports pornography and pirated software, which is not coincidentally two of the biggest draws to this service. An alternative to running your own news server is to contract the service out with another provider. The costs can be very low, especially if you consider the amount of time and money that a good Usenet server requires for upkeep. When contacting your potential Usenet server contractor ask them for a trial run. Try their server out and make sure the performance is up to par, especially in the evenings when all of the other users of this server will be hitting it simultaneously. This is the true test of how well the system holds up. If the performance is good than you should be able to have full Usenet services for your users within 48 hours. Generally the costs are low and the prices are based on the number of IP addresses or simultaneous users that could access the server at one time. If you would like to contract out this service you can try MISnet or any number of ISP service providers. Write to info@mis.net for details.

RADIUS

Remote Authentication Dial-In User Service. RADIUS is an open and quite standard authentication protocol that was originally developed by Livingston Enterprises. The simplified picture is as such: The RADIUS server holds the User Ids and passwords for your dial up users. RADIUS clients such as terminal servers or remote access servers will prompt a user for their login ID and password and then pass this back to the server. The server in turns either allows or denies access to the network. Additionally, the server can send information to the client that instructs it on how to handle the call and what services are available to that dial up user. The third function of RADIUS is to do extensive tracking and logging of activities. This information is then used for security and billing purposes. Usage is computed from the RADIUS log files and a customer can be billed appropriately for any usage overages for their account type. Since the RADIUS standard is open, third party developers have actively ported the system to all sorts of hardware and software platforms. RADIUS systems now exist for high end workstations and Intel boxes as well as a myriad of UNIX flavors and Windows NT. A RADIUS system has even been developed for Galacticomm's Worldgroup hybrid BBS/Internet access system. This should give you some idea of how widely available RADIUS currently is. Since there are so many variations of RADIUS you should check with your main hardware and software vendor to find what they recommend for your particular configuration. Some RADIUS systems are available at no cost and some are available free (such as Livingston's) when you purchase equipment from a manufacturer. Other flavors may have many bells and whistles and as such, you pay for the privilege. Net Shopper, mentioned earlier, offers a RADIUS solution for NT boxes. (www.net-shopper.co.uk)

Other Needed Equipment

The heart of your future ISP network has been described above. There are still a number of bits you will not want to be without. Let's talk about the peripheral side of your computer network now.

Text-Based Interface
If you choose to not go with a Unix system you will need to provide some sort of text based access option for your dial up customers. By 'text-based' we mean that users can connect with this type of system using a simple terminal software package and their modem. Unix can support this internally and provide many Internet services through this interface as well. It's a major advantage for the Unix camp. Most modems today include a software package to hook to text based services. Potential customers can use what they already have, no further software needed, all the manuals are included, to

connect to you and get some basic services and even software for accessing your PPP network. All of this will be automated as well since your text based service runs night and day without intervention from you. Note that this type of service is not required for you to become a successful ISP, but it is highly recommended. With a standard low end PC and a modem or two you can provide all of the functionality you need for this in the form of BBS software. The basic functions you want your text based service to provide are as follows:

- Information on your service in the form of text files, multimedia executables, and question and answer format databases.

- A subscription system that takes credit card orders for new subscribers.

- Software to connect to your Internet server and other miscellaneous software. This is just plain service, you need to provide instructions on how to setup this software as well as all of the goods. This also saves you disk costs, postage and time for those users savvy enough to already use their modem. If you will not be distributing a pre-packaged all in one solution than be sure to use the PKZIP utility (Use the NET SEARCH button in your browser to learn all about this utility) to create self-extracting compressed ZIP files out of the software packages. This will save the users time when downloading the software and make it easier for them to extract it from this compressed format.

- Email services to communicate with users who have not yet made the 'net connection' on problems they may be having.

- A conference where your users can communicate with each other and therefore help each other. This turns into a huge net gain for you as they tend to educate each other when given a forum where they can communicate their concerns to each other.

Keep in mind that this text based server will not need to be huge. However, given the time it takes to download many megabytes of software and read all of your help files, you may do well to start with two phone lines into this system. If not running Unix, I can highly recommend the TBBS bulletin board system from eSoft (www.esoft.com). TBBS can be had in a four line configuration for a list price of $295. Utilizing two 16550 equipped com ports you can plug two modems into an old 486 and get an outstanding text based service up and running quickly. If you find that you need more lines to support your customer base you can purchase a special serial card to add two additional lines with no upgrades to your software.

Surge Suppression
Stray electricity is one of your worst nightmares as an ISP. You rely on your network as a business just as your customers rely on your network as a service. Lightning storms and brownouts can nix not only your server but your modems, your workstations, routers, CSU/DSU and any and all other components hooked to your system. Often a surge coming through the electricity to your site will kill not one but MANY components at once. Electricity can travel over phone lines just as easily as it can over the electrical lines as well. One of my programmers experienced first hand a surge that came over his phone line. A summer storm ruined his phone, his answering machine and his internal modem all in the blink of an eye. He was lucky that the surge didn't spread further and take the entire PC as well. The RBOCs usually install gas tube type suppressers at their demark (demarcation) point on a building where the wires enter the premises. Do not be fooled into a false sense of security by this, these are highly ineffective against serious surges coming through the lines. They clamp the voltage far too slowly, by the time their protection kicks in the damage has been done.

Both of these entry points to your network, data lines and electrical lines, need to be protected! Do not start an ISP or any other such computer intense operation without making certain that the expensive equipment you are installing is fully protected.

Data Line & Coax Protection

Contact Citel on the web for a complete catalog of data protection equipment. They carry a line of high density multi-line protector blocks that work great for ISPs. Their address is www.citelprotection.com. There are too many options to list prices and the cost will depend on your particular needs. APC, mentioned next, also carries a line of products for data circuits.

Electrical Protection

At each and every workstation you will need a surge protector. APC, American Power Conversion, makes a line of products called the 'SurgeArrest' series that will do the job for you. These products come in both personal and network versions so be sure to get the

The APC Net-7 w/phone protection

network version for the most reliability. Many models also include a single telephone circuit port for those workstations that may have one modem attached to them. The APC series also features up to $25,000 in insurance for computers that are damaged by surges that get through their equipment. You will have to read the product literature for all the details. An additional benefit of many surge supressors is that they have a site wiring fault light. This will indicate if the electricity is badly wired up to the point of the wall outlet. Problems such as bad grounding will be apparent if this light comes on. Be sure to not ignore this warning and have a certified electrician look into any problems. Do not attempt to use these individual units to protect all of your phone circuits, buy a dedicated data line module to service your main bank of dial up lines. APC can be reached at www.apcc.com on the web.

UPS, Uninterruptible Power Supply

Imagine all those short black-outs that happen when the spring storms come rolling in, tearing your network to the ground. The main servers as well as the CSU/DSU or ISDN equipment and modems that your business uses must be supplied with a steady stream of clean electricity, whether the electric company is providing it or not. The price on this type of equipment has decreased

An APC UPS

dramatically in recent years. You can now pick up a single unit that will power a huge stack of modems, your main two servers, and all of the necessary peripherals through a 20 minute outage of power. Add more to extend your protection time. I can not tell you how many times in April and May, our own thunderstorm season in Kentucky, that I've heard a crack of lightning and all of the lights in the office go out. The entire world seems to shut down when this happens. All of those familiar whirs and buzzes of electrical equipment in your office suddenly go dead, with the notable exception of a loud intermittent beeping coming from your UPS backups. The computer room continues to buzz along happily being powered from your battery systems! Ah, the world is good and your business is still operating. You hear the next day of one of your less prepared competitors having a major system crash due to the outage that took them a day and a night to recover from. Seem far-fetched? Don't bet on it, this has happened more than once in my term as an ISP. Even if you do not lose all of the electricity a brown out can be extremely damaging to your system's health. Brownouts can introduce subtle corruption into your operating systems and the code they are running. Things can purr along for another few hours but end in a catastrophic system crash with the drive being totally corrupted by a process gone wild. You will have plenty of other tasks to keep you busy; protect yourself now with the proper sized UPS for your network. APC, makers of the recommended surge protector discussed previously, also make a complete product line of UPS systems. Check their website at www.apcc.com.

A quick note on electrical connections for all of this: It is easy to make some mistakes that are not entirely intuitive at first. The first is to use an under-powered UPS for your particular job. Be sure to read the product literature to determine the proper sized UPS to purchase. If the electricity goes out and the UPS shuts down immediately you've done nothing to save yourself work. What do you plug into your UPS? Anything that is critical to the continued functioning of your network in the event of a power outage. Do NOT plug printers into these as printers can drain a lot of power very quickly. Do not plug any unnecessary monitors into the UPS. Plug your main server into it and the server's monitor so you can control the system even when the lights go out. Plug your dial up ISDN and modems into the UPS so your customers are not disconnected. Plug any equipment you use for your Internet connection into the UPS. The web server can do without if absolutely necessary but I recommend getting a small UPS to service it directly. Additionally, do not plug your surge supressor strips into the UPS, they do not like the square waveform output that most UPSs generate. They will buzz loudly and you will eventually damage their circuitry as they attempt to 'cope' with this odd electrical output. When most UPSs contain a surge supressor, why install one anyway? Because the surge supressors in most UPSs are only good for one shot! Meaning, they take a strike and then they are unable to perform their job anymore. The next surge kills the UPS or worse, passes through to kill your other equipment. Surge bars are much less expensive than UPSs so it only makes sense to protect your UPS investment. Additionally, you will not want to plug every component into a UPS so having the extra ports on a surge bar allow you to protect this equipment as well, even though it's not powered by standby electricity.

How to effectively protect your most valuable equipment

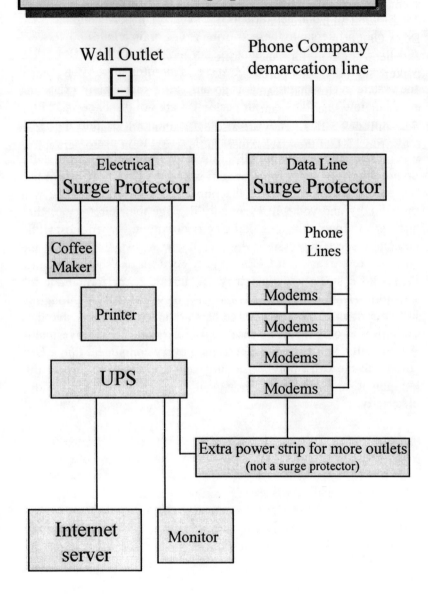

Coffee Maker

Coffee is as necessary as HTML to the aspiring ISP. Nothing ever seems to get done properly without coffee. I highly recommend the Bunn-Omatic corporation for excellent high performance coffee makers. You can purchase the  model you desire that features the capacities you need. There are many models that constantly keep a hot water supply on hand for 'just-in-time' coffee. They are also offered in both white and a sleek black finish. Get the black finish and impress your customers! The really intrepid ISP will hook their Bunn-O-Matic up to the water supply so that it refills itself. Check their web page out at www.bunnomatic.com.

Good programming is 99% sweat and 1% coffee.

Printers

You know already that you will need a printer to handle basic reports and other letters. However, where many ISPs fall short is that they begin their business with a 300dpi (dots per inch) model. Purchasing a low resolution printer is a cost saver in the beginning but can cost you much more over the long term. Business customers will want to see example home pages, graphics, and other samples of your work. Printing these type of documents out on a 300dpi printer leaves a lot to be desired. The best printers in the world are made by Hewlett Packard (www.hp.com). For an outstanding high speed black and white laser printer check into their Laserjet-6 series. If you want to trade a bit of speed and really want to make an impression on your customers, produce color output using one of the high-end Deskjet models. HP also manufacturers one of the most popular lines of desktop scanners on the market. You should have a scanner if you intend to offer HTML design and layout to your customers.

How do I set my laser printer to "Stun"?

Credit Card Terminal

If you hope to process credit cards yourself you will need a merchant account and a credit card processing terminal (or software). And let's say this up front, if you want to be a successful ISP you MUST be able to process credit cards. Obtaining a merchant account is like getting candy from a baby (for those of you that have tried this). The banks are babies, they do not believe that Internet companies, especially without store fronts, are capable of running a responsible merchant account. The merchant account is what actually allows you to take credit card orders and have the money transferred directly into your bank account. The problem with merchant accounts is that the business is responsible for credit card 'chargebacks' for a period of six months! This means that if any customer within the first six months of his purchase with you wishes to contest the charge they can have the money credited back to their account, especially if you do not have a sales slip with their signature. Well, how often will an Internet company be getting a signature? Not that often. When the customer requests this chargeback it comes right out of your bank account, usually with a handling charge, and goes back on to their card. If you do not have the money in the bank account to cover these you will be penalized and could find that you lose your account. To obtain a merchant account you should play from a position of power. Approach the bank in the beginning with your startup money in hand to deposit in a new account. Explain to them that you will not be starting a checking account unless a merchant account is given to you! You may have to approach a lot of banks but you will eventually find one that will play ball with you. Try the local banks, credit unions and any credit authorization companies first. They tend to be more receptive to small local business needs. If this fails, attempt to contact companies that do nothing but the authorizing of credit card charges. Such organizations are often called processing agencies. You may have to look in a nearby city to find one if you're not in a larger metropolitan area.

The terminal is the piece of equipment that lets you 'swipe' (now that's ironic, isn't it?) a credit card through it and get the money deposited to your account. If the card is not in hand, have no fears, you can punch in the credit card number manually and this works just as well. The terminal will run you between $200 and $400 dollars depending on how fancy you want to get. You may opt to also lease this equipment at a hefty premium from the bank as well.

For the smallest ISPs, manually processing card payments may not be too burdensome. However, most companies will want to acquire a credit card processing package. This generally comes in the form of programs that work with desktop PCs and use a modem to communicate with the head office. Once you have to process over a hundred card payments a month the value of one of these packages will become readily apparent. You should check with your merchant service provider to find out what solution they recommend for their system.

Which cards should you accept? Mastercard and Visa! Many of the other card companies require a yearly payment from you to accept their cards! They require you to pay them so they can make money off of your customers, now that's taking the money from both ends. If you choose not to accept anything but Mastercard and Visa you will find that there is little business or revenue lost because of your decision, especially when you figure in the yearly fees to the other card companies. If you wish to delve into other cards American Express should be your third option as it tends to be the corporate card of choice.

If all else fails and you are still unable to get a merchant account you can contact a merchant account 'middle man.' You will have to pay a bit more for your transactions, but this is far better than not accepting credit cards at all. Try Electronic Merchant Systems at (503) 691-6364, email at emsglobal@aol.com or on the web at http://webmall.net/emsinfo.htm.

Tape Backups
Backing up your system is a process that should be performed at a minimum of once per week. The ideal solution is to put into place a nightly backup routine that is automated. Your user accounting system, web pages, and setup and configuration files will be changing on an almost daily basis after your first couple of weeks of

marketing. Do not be burned by a catastrophic data loss! In my personal experience I knew a gentleman that ran an online system for 2 ½ years before he was bitten. It was a reputable system in a city just outside of our local calling area. I had watched as his system grew to over 20 incoming lines (this was back in the days when that was BIG). The operation was professional and the features and pricing very attractive. It appeared to all outsiders as a professional organization. Installing a new version of disk compression software on his main server one day he lost the entire hard drive. It was a common foul up with compression technology: an incompatibility here, a software error there, and everything is wiped out before your very eyes. In 2 ½ years he had not made one backup. I called and spoke with him to find out what had happened and I couldn't believe what he told me. How could such a quality operation not have anticipated an eventual hardware or software failure? It's not a matter of 'if' it will happen, only 'when' it will occur. Nevertheless, he learned the hard way and never re-opened. How could you duplicate 2+ years of work overnight? Do not make the same mistake. Get a good tape backup drive and keep current copies of your system stored safely on tape for the eventual mishap. A common tape backup procedure which is normally NOT followed, at your own peril, is keeping an off-site backup. A full backup of your system, the more current the better, should be stored in an entirely different location than your system. Why? Fire, floods, lightning strike, you can take your pick. I knew a company that did an excellent job of keeping backups of their system, over a million product records and 5,000+ customers all stored on their system and on tape. However, when the building housing the computer system sustained a direct lightning strike they found to their everlasting dismay that the tapes which stored the data, kept in a stack next to the main server, were hopelessly garbled with none of their data recoverable. The down time lasted over a month even with emergency help called in to rebuild their computer network. Without a large cash reserve this could have been the end of this company. Make backups regularly and keep at least one set of tapes off-site. For your tape backup needs I can highly recommend the Conner Tape-Stor series of backup products (www.conner.com). There are too many to list and the actual capacities you need will vary from one ISP to the next. Additionally, you will need to determine whether you want an internal or external model and whether or not it truly needs to be a portable system. My best advice is to get a large, fast tape backup system. A minimum capacity of 1 gig per tape is highly recommended. If you want to make your backup schedule much less of a burden get a 2 to 4 gig DAT tape system that will hold most all of your computers important data on one tape. In this way you can set the tape backup software to do a full backup of your system on a nightly basis totally unattended. Another common mistake in backup operations is that a total of two or three tapes are relied upon all the time. Cycling two tapes a couple of times a week can wear them out over the period of a year. Get a small stack of tapes and add fresh ones occasionally. All you have to do is remember to switch the tapes AND KEEP ONE (or more) OFF-SITE!

Switch Box

There may come a time when you have quite a few machines in your main computer room that are not utilized on a day to day basis. These machine may well perform valuable services for you but no one actually sits down at them daily to do lots of work. A tremendous cost savings can be had by using a switch box with all of these computers and replacing all of the keyboards, mice and monitors with just one main console. If you anticipate this need at the beginning you can save a lot of money on monitors immediately! You can purchase a switch box that has five inputs for VGA, Serial (Mouse) and keyboard cables. The box has one output set of connections which go to your main console area. You should be able to purchase all of the proper cabling to accommodate five computers and the box itself for approximately $120. If you do utilize this as a solution be sure to configure each computer attached to the switch box so that it does not do a 'keyboard check' on startup. This way if you lose power and some of these auxiliary machines are not on standby batteries they will be able to restart themselves without locking up at the boot process. Just be sure to have the computers configured so as to automatically restart any services they perform. The 'keyboard check' option can usually be found in the BIOS settings that is accessible when the computer is first turned on. Check your manuals for more information.

In Summary

Choose your platform and hardware carefully! Good hardware means reliable service, high performance, and expandability. Bad hardware means poor performance, no reliability, a bad business reputation and a poor revenue machine. Do not settle for list price on *anything* listed above. There are very few times when you will ever need to pay the premium price for your equipment. ISP and sysop discounts can be found in abundance. Contact discount mail order warehouses and Internet-based resellers as well.

CHAPTER V

CHOOSING A LOCATION & CONNECTION

Many budget-minded ISPs begin their business in their own house. I would not discourage this route if it's the only direction you can take when getting started. I ran our BBS & ISP based business part-time out of my basement for over four years before I moved to a real office. For ISPs who are going to move ahead full-steam you should consider a professional looking office somewhere in the business sector of your city. Remember, this is an online communications business. Almost all of your computer resources can be managed from home when you are *not* at the office! When choosing a location there are a number of considerations you should be sure to take into mind, outside of the obvious cost of rent. These considerations are discussed in this chapter.

We also want to discuss your connection to the Internet. Your pipeline to the net is most often a nailed up connection that is time consuming and expensive to relocate. Additionally, the phone lines and ISDN circuits you use for your business all involve a setup fee for installation and these are considered part of your 'site' as well. Getting your connection can be one of the most frustrating ordeals you go through. This task can be even more involved than choosing and purchasing your equipment. Leased lines involve a lot of technical jargon that is difficult to decipher for the novice. You also must decide what type of circuit your connection is going to require. The size of your pipeline to the net affects your overall speed, as well as the traffic on the particular network that you connect to.

Choosing a site for your ISP

If you are unable to afford an office location and must work at home, your decision on a site has become a lot less complicated. There are both pros and cons to running an ISP out of your house:

The Good:
- Working at home is easy and very informal. Wake up, get coffee, go to work.
- You are with your system night and day so if something goes wrong in the wee hours of the morning you don't have far to go to fix it.
- You can provide technical voice support at any given hour you choose from a much more comfortable location than an office.
- You don't pay any additional rent for a second location.

The Bad:
- You don't make much of an impression on business customers who will want to see your site before doing business with you. Unless you live in gorgeous mansion do not invite them over, you rarely will get their business.

- Working at home can be less productive, lulling you into a false sense that you are getting more done than you think.
- There can be a lot of distractions at home.
- There may not be enough room for employees at your house.
- County business licenses may restrict the number of employees in a home-based business.
- There is no escape from the office!
- Loneliness

The Ugly:

- Leased lines may cost you much more because urban neighborhoods tend to be farther away from telco POPs than business sectors.
- Business lines or leased lines may not even be available in your neighborhood due to zoning or tariffs!
- Neighborhoods tend to get the new phone services and options only after they have been installed at the telco POPs nearest the business heart of your city.

Outside of the poor appearance of a company that is run from a home, the leased lines may be considerably more expensive depending on how far you are from a telephone office switch, or POP. If you're in the business sector you will not be too far from one of these buildings. This distance between you and the POP is called the 'local loop' portion of a leased line bill. If you are more than a mile from a POP your costs tend to rise very rapidly. If you're under a quarter of a mile from a POP then you are considered to be in the 'zero mileage' zone and your local loop portion of leased line bills will be much smaller. Keep this in mind and check with your local RBOC to find the distance from your house to the POP that services it. Also, be certain that there are no restrictions or zoning problems with business lines and leased lines being run into your home.

When choosing your location there are a number of factors that must be taken into consideration.

- The rental cost for your budget

- The distance to the POP which affects leased line costs (the closer the better.)

- The security of the location and alarm systems. You will be placing a lot of small, expensive equipment in this location. Do not underestimate how fast someone could steal your hardware.

- If you will be on the ground floor or the basement level, what are the chances that flooding could hit the site? Water and computer equipment do not mix.

- Will you have any storefront area or advertising opportunities? Many small store-fronts can put large billboards out front.

- Does the area have above or below ground wires for electricity and phone service? Areas with above ground wiring is much more prone to lightning strikes (and subsequent damage) than areas with wiring below ground. Since below ground wiring is relatively new in a lot of areas the equipment used to service it is newer and of a better quality.

- Will the site cost a fortune to air condition? Humidity and heat in some parts of North America are too much for standard computer equipment to go without good A/C. A computer room with as few as eight machines and a stack of modems can raise the temperature quite substantially depending on the size of the room and the ventilation that it has.

- The rental agreement must have a **60 day clause** if the renter wishes to not renew your contract (and preferably longer!). One month is not enough time to find a new location, move the phone lines, move the leased lines, and get settled in. If you only have a 30 day clause you will get burned at some point in the future if the owner wishes to get you out.

What type of Internet Connection Do You Need

Choosing your own connection to the net is of the utmost importance. You are an Internet provider. In turn, you must connect to another Internet provider. This is what the Internet is, many millions of computers and definitely millions of individuals all linked together through one means or another. As has been discussed previously, there is no one group that is *the* Internet. If you choose a connection too small or badly connected your customer base will know it, they will feel it when using your service. The outline below shows approximately how many dial-up customers you can service simultaneously given a particular size of a connection.

What happens when you exceed these numbers? Well, the Internet is a packet-based network. Data moves in packets that are all lined up and sent down a pipe of a particular size. When you have more data than you have bandwidth, the data traffic at the other end of your pipe tends to grow. Data waits patiently (usually) for its turn at transportation as servers resend any lost packets and continue to retry connections. Your users experience a lag or slowing down of their services but everything continues to operate otherwise. We refer to your own connection to another Internet provider as your 'pipeline' in this chart.

Your pipeline size	Approx. # of simultaneous dial up users
28.8k modem connection	2
56k DS0 leased line	6
64k ISDN connection	7
128k ISDN connection	15
256k Fractional T1	40
512k Fractional T1	100+
Full T1	300+

These figures do not take into account the fact that there are other bandwidth demands upon an ISP. For instance, if you have 10 simultaneous remote users pulling HTML files and graphics off of your web server your bandwidth demands are different than those listed in this chart. At the high end it makes much less of a difference because a large pipeline can support many more simultaneous users than you would imagine. Why is this? From a practical standpoint, in the evenings I could find times when all 50 of our dial up connections were busy with users, both text based users of the BBS and Internet users. When looking over all of the modems at once it was difficult to find a time when more than ten of them were sending or receiving data. Lots of time on the net is consumed with users just reading information on their screens or typing a message that involves no data transfer until it is actually sent. This is a very good thing indeed for the ISP who is connected with a good Fractional or Full T1 connection. As you grow your bandwidth you begin to experience economies of scale that are not present on the low end. Let's look at all of your connection options one by one.

28.8 Connections
28.8 modem connected ISPs are not practical. This is a hobbyist's solution for only the smallest of sites that wish to host a very minor number of dial up customers. Although I've seen people dip their toes into the Internet by starting with this type of connection, you can outgrow it so quickly that it tends to just make it a waste of time.

56k Connections
56k connections (not to be confused with the new 56k modems) used to be the standard way of starting an ISP. They were the low end of the scale and cost a great deal less than T1 wires did. Since that time T1 wires have fallen in price and bandwidth needs have increased making them a much less attractive alternative. With the advent of ISDN available to 85% of America or more, they have become even less popular. For a 56k leased line you will need to have some type of CSU/DSU interface. If you use the Adtran suggested in the chapter on equipment you will be able to 'grow' it to a full T1 later as you expand. Do not purchase a dedicated CSU/DSU that can not outgrow the 56k limit. They are expensive to start with and when you do upgrade your line you will find that you just need more equipment.

64k ISDN Connections

For those ISPs on a budget ISDN offers a very attractive alternative to the fractional T1. Although half of an ISDN line at 64k is a bit restrictive, if you purchase the right equipment in the beginning you will be able to expand to a full 128k with only an upgrade from your provider. The down side to ISDN is that when you do approach the limits of your bandwidth you will need to make an additional investment in a CSU/DSU and an interface for it. This is not entirely bad however as you will be able to use your ISDN equipment to resell a line to a business customer. Make certain that your local RBOC or CAP, competitive access provider, has a flat rate plan for ISDN. If your only option is metered service you may find that it costs you as much as a frac T1 each month to keep the connection up. When purchasing ISDN be certain to check into compression options with your provider. Some ISDN equipment offers 2:1 compression schemes and the Ascend product on our recommended equipment list offers even more compression. Your mileage of course may vary.

128k ISDN Connections

This is simply ISDN service utilizing both 'B' channels to effectively double your bandwidth. Although most ISDN adapters will communicate with each other at 64k very few of them currently will be able to 'inverse multiplex' both lines together. Be certain to check with your own provider concerning their ISDN equipment and the possibilities for 128k bandwidth. Using a COM or serial port connected adapter as opposed to the ethernet variety here will come back to haunt you. Adapters such as the Motorola Bitsurfer can only communicate at a maximum of 115kbps which is a limitation of most serial buffers.

Fractional / Full T1 Connections

'Frac' T1 as it is often called is bandwidth that travels over a T1 wire utilizing only a percentage of the available data channels. There are 24 channels of 64k or 56k each, depending on how the equipment is configured. Utilizing 4 of these channels gives you 256k worth of bandwidth. Eight of these channels gives you 512k bandwidth, and so on. The TSU (CSU/DSU) is a determining factor in what size channels you can use as well as if fractional service is allowed or not. 256k is a terrific starting point for new ISPs. This is enough bandwidth to service a large stack of simultaneous dial in connections while leaving plenty left over for remote users to view your web sites and your own workstations to suck files from the net at a good pace. However, what you will find with fractional T1 service is that most of the cost is 'front loaded' on the bill. What I mean to say is that you will pay a lot of money initially just to establish the 256k connection and the jump to 512k or a full T1 will not be nearly as expensive as you might imagine, as a percentage of the entire bill. This is due to the fact that the physical wire from your site to your provider's site contains a large amount of your overall cost. The wire charges generally do not change as you graduate up to higher speeds, only your Internet service fees.

Fractional / Full T3 Connections
A T3 is also known as a data service 3 (DS3) in the RBOC infrastructure. It is simply the combination of 24 T1 lines utilizing a special type of CSU/DSU and router that can handle this type of traffic. Generally T3 wires are 'backbones' of large Internet networks. If you hear of a provider getting a T3 it generally means that they purchased a fractional T3, with perhaps three or four T1 lines of capacity, as opposed to truly buying 24 T1 lines worth of bandwidth. T3 lines are only mentioned to fill out your leased lines vocabulary as most new ISPs will never start with more than a T1 pipe.

xDSL, ADSL, HDSL Connections
These are all variations of the same technology that is under development today. By late 1997 the use of this technology should be in full swing. ADSL is what we are seeing most often today. ADSL stands for Asymmetric Digital Subscriber Line whereas xDSL can stand for any variation on the basic theme. The technology offers a tremendous amount of potential due to the large bandwidth that it offers. xDSL technology utilizes standard phone lines, like ISDN before it, to pump massive amounts of data back and forth. Another variation is to use 'dry pairs' for the wires. These are copper circuits such as that used by alarm companies that connect two points directly together but with little or no management function on the telco's side. The odd thing about xDSL technology

is that the upstream bandwidth is generally less than the downstream bandwidth. A common figure you might see is 640kbps upstream capacity and 6mbps downstream capacity. Compare this to a standard T1 circuit that can move 1.54mbps in either direction (though not at the same time) when at its' theoretical maximum capacity. ADSL is positioned to be the phone companies answer to the speed of cable companies broadband hybrid fiber/coax networks, the potential successor to ISDN. Although intended for end-users, there is probably little stopping the new ISP from utilizing this (when available) as their main connection to the net at large. The majority of ISPs 'receive' much more information than they 'transmit.' This is mainly due to users continuously making requests on the pipe for web pages, files, etc. where small upstream requests bring avalanches of data coming back down the pipe. Keep you eye on this one.

Bandwidth Costs: The Wire & The Service
When you are discussing leased line Internet services there are two major portions of the bill that need to be identified. The first is the cost of the wire itself. This is determined mainly by three factors: The distance from you to the telco POP, the distance from your provider to their telco POP, and the distance in between the two POPs. With fractional T1 service there is not always a discount from your carrier, the one providing the wire, for choosing fractional over full T1 service. This may be because they are not 'tariffed' for it, meaning that it is not in their pricing structure according to the public utility or tariff commissions pricing scheme. There is a good reason for this as well, the wire that actually carries the data is the same regardless of whether or not you're utilizing the full bandwidth. Remember, fractional T1 bandwidth is achieved by using x channels of a T1 connection.

The second portion of your bill is the service charge for Internet access. This is where you can get a discount because if you purchase 256k of bandwidth from your provider that is the maximum that you will be able to use. They will lock their equipment at x channels, you will do the same, and 64k times x is the maximum bandwidth you will have.

What about frame relay?

Frame relay might allow you to get a discount on the service and/or wire portion of your charge. Frame relay works by creating a communal 'cloud' of bandwidth that data can travel over. This is opposed to actually 'nailing up' a dedicated wire from every customer to a provider's central site. The RBOCs and long distance carriers are the ones to turn to if you wish to hook into 'frame clouds.' There are small regional clouds as well as nationwide clouds available to you.

Take a peek at the following diagram:

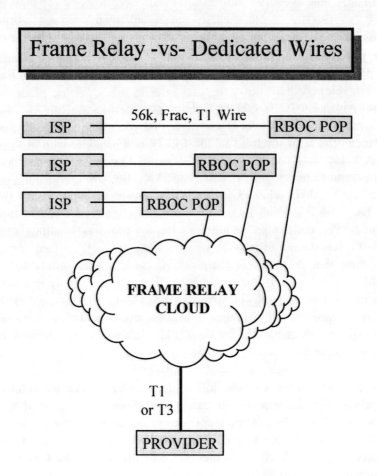

Although you may not have actual frame relay equipment at your site, you may still be going over a frame relay cloud to access your Internet host provider. You will run a normal wire to the nearest frame relay POP which then transports the data over the cloud back to their central site. Many of the largest national providers are using this strategy so that they do not have to incur the high costs of running equipment and lines everywhere. Their equipment can be maintained in one central location and using frame relay technology they can hook up ISPs and businesses all over the nation. In all actuality, where Frame Relay is alive, dedicated wire service is dying. It's that good!

What should your concerns be with frame relay technology? For one, you are sharing the total bandwidth of the frame relay cloud and the providers connection to it with other customers. A standard has been developed that allows the users of the service some peace of mind however. The CIR, Committed Information Rate, is the amount of bandwidth over frame relay that you are guaranteed. For instance, you may purchase a 512k frac from a provider who utilizes frame relay, and your CIR would be set at 128k. This means that you may not always get 512k of bandwidth, but you are guaranteed (in theory) 128k. When traffic is low on the frame relay cloud you can burst up to the full speed of your connection for short amounts of time. You could also get a frac 512k over frame relay with a CIR of 512k, which should guarantee you all of the bandwidth all of the time but you would pay a premium for it.

One of the major advantages of frame relay is the cost savings. The 'sharing' nature is the drawback to frame relay, the up side is that it can cost a lot less to get connected to providers who utilize this. After all, a provider who moves data through a frame cloud does not need a router for each individual connection. One router tied to a frame cloud at T1 speeds can feed a number of T1 connections from this single piece of equipment. Keep this in mind when providing connections to your own clientele.

When discussing your connection, especially to the largest national providers, be certain to find out if it travels over frame relay. If it does, find out what the CIR is and see if for a small extra cost you can up the CIR as well. Some providers will allow you to do this while others will not. For the most part, where frame relay is alive, dedicated wires are dead. The cost savings are just too good to ignore for most organizations (and customers).

How to shop for a connection
When you begin to price your connections there are a number of issues that you want to delve into. Remember, you will be paying a lot of money for this connection and your users will rely on it. Do the homework up front! You will need to know your site location and the phone number for pricing leased lines. This is because the prefix to your phone number is what tells the carrier the distance to your site from their nearest POP.

- How oversold (if at all) is their own connection? It's not uncommon to find a T1 connected provider that has sold 20 T1's off of their original. While I would consider this an awful gouging, it does happen quite often. For your own reselling a ratio of 6:1 or 7:1 is probably more realistic. Of course the type of companies you sell to affects your ultimate ratio as well. If you connect a video conferencing company that uses a lot of bandwidth all of the time this ratio will need to be lower.

- Does the company utilize frame relay to connect you to their central site? If so, what is the CIR on your given choices of bandwidth. Can you pay a surcharge for a higher CIR?

- Will your provider supply you with a newsfeed if you intend to run an NNTP Usenet server. At what cost? How many newsgroups do they carry? Do they carry the whole line of coveted alt.binary.whatever groups?

- What are the installation and monthly charges? Are there any other charges for the initial setup not included in this pricing?

- Is there a particular type of equipment that their systems will only work with?

- Are there any surcharges or limitations on reselling service? If so, what are they?

- How many Class-C addresses will the provider give you? What will extra ones cost?

- If you are discussing an ISDN connection, is compression possible? What ratio of compression does the equipment they use provide?

- What are the standard charges for upgrades to higher levels of bandwidth?

- Approximately how quickly can the line be dropped and installed?

- What are the hours of operation for technical support? If the wire goes down in the middle of the night, who can you contact to fix it?

- If they are a smaller local provider ask where their own Internet connection is fed from.

- Ask for references and contact them! Ask them what their own experiences have been like with lag or down time over the network. Ask if the service has been up to par.

Haggling - That Age Old Art

Once you have all of the above information for your preferred pipe size from your potential providers you should organize it on a sheet and do some comparisons. Make your top two picks the focus of your haggling efforts. You should go to your top pick first and ask them for the following terms and conditions: free newsfeed if you so desire it. Some companies will charge $50 a month or so for a newsfeed. See if they will offer it at no cost if you choose their service. One free bandwidth upgrade. Many providers will charge you $200 or more to simply change the number of channels on their

CSU/DSU that feeds you, this is in addition of course to their new higher monthly fee for the expanded service. See if you can't get your first bandwidth upgrade at no cost. If the provider is using frame relay haggle over the CIR or try to whittle them down based on the fact that it IS frame relay and not a dedicated wire. Once you have all of the concessions from the first provider go to the second, haggle the same issues AND the price based on your first providers figures. Finally, approach the high cost player and see if they will not undercut the other provider. In my own negotiations I was only concerned with two providers, Sprint and MCI. They were the only two providers I could get service from!! How times change... There were no second tier players feeding our city during that time. If there was I would have gone to them first. Finally, when you do sign a contract be sure to get EVERYTHING in writing. Contracts keep honest people honest and details can easily be forgotten. Again, **GET ABSOLUTELY EVERY DETAIL IN WRITING!** If you do not you may be sorry later.

Who Provides You With Internet Service

You have a lot of alternatives today so your options are a bit more wide open. There are three main sources of connections to the net. These companies will generally price the wire and the service and handle the whole shebang in one shot: The long distance carriers, the large national networks, and other local providers.

The Long Distance Carriers
Sprint and MCI have been providing Internet connections for some time now. Sprint offered this type of access nationwide before MCI did and therefore ended up with more customers earlier on. In my own ISP we eventually owned two T1 connections, one from Sprint and one from MCI. The reasons for this were varied but I will say right off the bat, the MCI connection seemed to respond faster and the data appeared to move quicker when connecting through their leased line. Additionally, the MCI network experienced far fewer

outages than the Sprint network did during our six months of Sprint service.

These top-tier type of connections tend to cost quite a bit more than the tier-two providers (shown next). For the money you get good performance, a professionally run network, and they tend to contact you in the event of problems, even if the problems are on your side of the connection. Overall MCI tends to be much more willing to wheel and deal than Sprint. This may be due to their coming to the game late. Contact your local MCI Network and Sprint Link offices for price quotes:

> www.mci.com
> www.sprintlink.net

The Large National Networks

There are many large providers of Internet access lines that are not really carriers. They have arrangements with other carriers to handle their network traffic but other than small spans of wire they don't truly own the infrastructure over which the data travels. You should be able to find some of the most outstanding deals in this second-tier provider group. Not all of these companies have true nationwide coverage like the long distance carriers listed above. However, they are heart-and-soul Internet providers who have much more experience in the area you wish to be focused upon. A carrier will not help you with your business strategy and probably doesn't care if you succeed or not. This is the area I would shop first as a new ISP. Many reputable providers are listed here in no particular order:

www.mis.net	Mikrotec Internet Services. A complete access and ISP solution provider based in Lexington, Kentucky. (MISnet)
www.agis.net	Apex Global Information Services (AGIS)
www.psi.net	Performance Systems International (PSInet)
www.uu.net	One of the oldest (and possibly

	most trafficed) Internet access providers. Merged in 1996 with MFS Communications but still retains their own name. (UUnet)
www.bbn.com	BBN Planet, the original ARPANET constructor.
www.crl.com	CRL Network Services. A 45mbs backbone provider based in San Francisco, Ca.
www.ans.net	ANS, Advanced Network and Services. Acquired in 1995 by America Online (AOL).
www.ibm.com/globalnetwork	IBM Global Network

Local Providers

If there is a sufficiently large presence in your area currently you can opt to get your connection through another local provider; if they allow reselling of their service. This has a couple of disadvantages to it compared to the prior two methods. Local providers rarely offer the 24/7 technical support and problem centers that the companies listed above do. By connecting to another local provider you are also further down the line than you would be by connecting to a tier two provider, meaning that you connect to your provider, who in turn connects to another provider, and so on and so forth. How far down the line do you really want to be? When you go to resell connections will you receive the support you need? How do you explain your connection to potential business customers who could utilize this other provider? And finally, what if you become more successful than your provider likes? Could they cause you trouble on the connection side? There are a lot of 'ifs' to this scenario. With that said, if you do have a reputable local provider with a good connection to the net there is no reason that you couldn't start off with a connection from them and graduate to another provider later. No reason except for potential down time, re-propagation of your domain through the routing tables on the net, and the general pain of moving. Try to do the connection right the first time!

Advanced Topology Issues

A note on NAPs and why they MAE be good for you

Let us step back a moment to the topic of Internet topology. It was decided in 1993 that Internet traffic, which was increasingly commercial in nature, would be turned over from the National Science Foundation (NSF) backbone and placed in the hands of commercial organizations. The plan outlined the creation of three major cross-connection points where private networks could attach to each other. These were to be in effect the cross-roads of the Internet. Any organization could create national or regional networks and tie in to the other networks on the Internet via these points of access. The three NAPs were subsequently built and are located in and operated by:

1. San Francisco   PacBell
2. Chicago   Ameritech
3. New York   SprintLink

This cross-connection idea was not new at the time this was put into action. Even before the NSF began the process to move the capitalist traffic from its wires, Metropolitan Fiber Systems (MFS) was running an informal cross-connection point in Washington, D.C. Their network connection point was named the Metropolitan Area Ethernet-East (MAE-East). Over time this abbreviation has evolved to become known as 'Metropolitan Area Exchange,' due to the large number of networks exchanging data at this hub. MFS now runs a number of MAEs with more on the way.

1. Washington, D.C.   MAE East
2. Washington, D.C.   MAE East+ (Faster than MAE East)
3. San Jose   MAE West
4. Chicago   MAE Chicago
5. Los Angeles   MAE LA
6. Dallas   MAE Dallas

NAPs and MAEs are important to make note of as they are so central to Internet topology. If the Internet was a tree, the trunk of the tree would be the closest analogy that we would have for these exchange points. While we are doing analogies, if the Internet was an airplane would you take a trip on it? Forgive me and don't answer that, I digress. These exchange points are valuable because they are the closest point of contact with all sorts of Internet backbones. Backbones hosted by ANS, MCI, Sprint, AT&T, BBN and more all connect at one or more of these junctions. In some cases they connect to *all* of them. Now, if you were building a distribution hub for packages, would you prefer to build it in BFE (this is *not* a technical acronym) out on a long stretch of road or would you prefer it to be at a major metropolitan nexus of traffic. Likewise, a connection to, or close to, one of these junctions will give you a shorter (and we would hope faster) connection to other networks. Your users who are accessing data on a backbone that you are not directly connected to should be able to access that network faster if you are close to a cross-connection point. Remote users attached to other backbones should be able to get to your web site through fewer connections if you are connected close to a MAE or NAP.

Local Peering
Now that all of this is said let me point out that this discussion is highly academic and does not always prove to be true in practice. There are more exchange points for data than just the NAPs or MAEs. The largest players connect to some or all of the NAPs and MAEs. We find increasingly that regionals and even local ISPs connect not only to more than one NAP or MAE but to each other directly. This concept is known as regional or local peering. Let us say that you were an ISP in Dallas and you found that much of your traffic was directed at other local sites in your area. Under this condition you may opt to connect to other local providers so that you may all move traffic directly between yourselves. This is much more attractive to sending a request to Los Angeles only to have it come back to a building down the street from you.

This is exactly what happened to the Commercial Internet Exchange (CIX), which you may or may not have heard of, albeit on a much grander scale. The CIX was, and to a much lesser degree still is, a junction on the Internet. The largest players (including Sprint and MCI) used the CIX as a cross-connection point where their IP networks exchanged data. At the CIX's insistence of a $10,000 fee to move data traffic through their plumbing so that it could reach other networks, inter-connections between these other networks sprung up literally over night. In this way the CIX junction was bypassed and data continued to move to its destination. The CIX group was rather shocked to find that few would play their game nor would anyone need to in order to be a viable provider.

Redundancy

In addition to dispersing pockets of power, as was the case with the CIX, multiple inter-connections can also serve to protect ISPs in times of outages. Multiple connections to the Internet allow an ISP to tout redundancy to large clients with mission-critical applications. These clients want to be assured that there is more than one direction for their Internet traffic to travel in the event that a circuit or other piece of equipment fails. Redundant connections to the same host are far less valuable than two or more connections to different backbones (Ie. ISP A ties a T1 to backbone B and an ISDN backup connection to backbone B). In this way you can spread the risk for both yourself and your dedicated line clients. Although it's quite common to have a backbone outage, it is far less common to have two major backbones fail at the same time. Redundancy is rather expensive due to having the stand-by procedures in place with your backup provider. For your redundant connection to be automated in the event of an outage it also requires equipment, circuits and systems that in times of good weather do nothing but collect dust and cost money. How can you achieve redundancy with some other advantages that might make it more attractive to implement?

Regional Hubbing

Full time multiple connections to the Internet allow you to become a regional junction (or 'hub') for traffic. In addition to the reliability issues being dampened you can exploit these multiple connections for faster service. For instance, if you have a connection to the BBN backbone and a connection to the MCI backbone you could intelligently route your traffic. This might allow you to shuffle data packets out the particular pipeline (BBN or MCI) that will get them to their destination with the shortest possible travel time. Obviously this scenario requires more than one connection to the Internet and these are rather costly to begin with. You will also need a more sophisticated router and a bit of know-how in your engineering department, but you get three distinct advantages for your trouble.

- Redundancy - In the event of an outage on one backbone your data traffic can traverse the alternate backbone and still find its way home, given that the destination is not on the network with the outage.

- More Bandwidth - If you have many dedicated connections or high traffic web sites you may find that you need more bandwidth to service them all simultaneously. Additional bandwidth is also a selling point to corporations that desire to hook to 'the big provider.'

- Speed - Intelligently routing your data allows you to potentially claim a speed advantage that your competitors do not possess.

In the interest of efficiency we'll ask the following question again. How could we lower the costs of implementation and squeeze more advantages out of this scenario so that it is more attractive?

Local Hubbing between ISPs

We have discussed local peering, a situation whereby two Internet providers connect to each other to make local data traffic stay local and not travel the NAPs or MAEs to flow back and forth between neighbors. This type of arrangement says nothing about passing your neighbors Internet traffic out your main connection to the net. We have also discussed regional hubbing, where one ISP connects directly to two backbones. It is attractive and offers many advantages but it is also expensive due to the added service cost of the second connection.

We're going to get convoluted here so stay tight. Let's subtract the additional service cost for a second full time net connection in regional hubbing and add in the benefits of local peering to cut down on long distance data travel. What would we have? Let's call it local hubbing between ISPs. We could even call it 'local NAPping' but the connotation leaves something to be desired. Whatever you want to call it, it is happening right now, and it is pushing the interconnection advantages and power down to the local level. After all, why should the big boys have all the fun?

Let's put together a hypothetical situation. We have two ISPs who have a bit of overlap in their service areas. Perhaps both serve five or more counties in a state and in one county they both have a POP. We'll call them SERIOUS ISP and FUN ISP. SERIOUS uses ANS as their main connection to the net at large while FUN uses MCI. In the county that they both service they could run a T1 wire between their two POPs and share the monthly circuit bill. Note that no service costs are incurred. Their engineering teams get to work on configuring their routers so that the magic can be allowed to happen. Once configured correctly your data traffic moves out not only your own connection to the net but your neighbors main connection, depending on which one is the most efficient for the job. The same applies to them. Once this shared routing is up and running we have almost every advantage that we've discussed in this advanced topology section minus the additional service cost of a second full time Net connection.

+ Redundancy
+ Additional Bandwidth
+ Intelligent (faster) Data Flow
+ Local Peering
- Additional service cost for second Net connection

People could argue that you do not get additional bandwidth through this scenario but I would say that you do. Internet pipes such as T1s are not measured in what you will always get but in what the theoretical maximum 'burstable' capacity is. It all works akin to statistical multiplexing, in that you can really burst out a lot of traffic when others are not pumping data quite so hard through the pipes.

What are the downsides to this? You have to cooperate with the competition to make this happen. However, you both stand to benefit if it's implemented correctly. The pessimist protests, 'But this will never happen in real life.' It already is happening, it is just happening on a level much further up the pipeline then you are familiar with. This cooperation on the high end is what created the NAPs and MAEs. It only benefits the largest players if 'cooperation' is not in your vocabulary.

At the risk of breaking the camel's back and driving you insane with yet another possibility, let's ask our question again. How can we make this more efficient. Do not purchase a dedicated wire, use wireless technology to tie the two POPs together. It's more expensive up front but far more cost effective over time. Refer to wireless in the index for further discussion on this topic.

More Resources
All of the different aspects of getting an Internet connection would be a topic that could engulf an entire book by itself. Luckily, just such a book has been written. For a detailed discussion on connection issues please pick up a copy of GETTING CONNECTED, (The Internet at 56k and Up), by Kevin Dowd and published by O'Reilly and Associates. Your Internet connection really is of the utmost importance and it deserves your full attention when it's time to lay some wire.

Detailed information on a number of the largest national providers and their backbones can be found in Boardwatch Magazine's directory of Internet Service Providers. This guide includes graphical network diagrams and associated service pricing. Additionally, you'll have a handy desk reference to all of the known ISPs in North America with associated pricing and contact info.

CHAPTER VI

FINANCING AND BUDGETS

You still want to be an ISP after reading all of the previous chapters, assessing your competition and analyzing your leased line costs? Well, good for you. The market is booming and with the proper planning and budgeting you will enter the hottest new business of the 90's prepared to do battle.

How do you get the money you need? Well, the obvious places to start are as follows. These may seem intuitive but are listed just in case one doesn't pop to mind immediately.

Your own pocket!
Do you have any savings or reserves of cash to pour into this venture? What about mortgaging your home for a startup budget? Early retirement? Regardless of whatever other means you use to finance your endeavor you should try to collect all of the personal

sources of money you can and list them individually. You will probably need to contribute something personally to this business even if you do find venture capitalists or get a loan from the banks.

Friends and Relatives
Do you have any friends or relatives with deep pockets that would like to get involved in this with you? Keep in mind that personal partnerships can be one of the worst endeavors you ever become involved in. More partnerships have ruined family and friend relationships than possibly any other contractual arrangement.

Venture Capitalists
Are there any firms or groups in your city that fund new business? Once again, be careful, venture capitalists are often referred to as the vultures of the industry. They can end up taking a larger share than what they provided in the beginning if you are not careful.

Strategic Partners
This may be one of your best resources. If you can locate a strategic partner that will help you market the business or provide you with some sort of benefit in addition to capital then you are that much more likely to succeed! Firms that specialize in computer networking, telephone systems, and advertising or print publishing are all excellent resources! They either have a built up customer base that trusts them or they can provide you with a lot of marketing muscle. These types of partnerships are just naturals for a potential ISP.

The Government? (Yikes!)
An initiative from the U.S. government that may be of use to you (depending upon your circumstances) is the Telecommunications Information Infrastructure Assistance Program (TIIAP). This program provides matching funds to schools, libraries and other non-profit groups that raise money from private sources to access the Internet. If your project falls into the parameters for this program a grant may be forthcoming. Rural and 'universal' access to the Internet is a hot topic with the government today! Check your local government office for details on grants and how you can apply for one.

Partnering

You can opt to partner with another provider such as one of the MISnet solutions suggested earlier in the book. This type of arrangement is very attractive because you will be associated with a much more experienced group than what you will have in-house. You still bring Internet access to your community but without having to fund and provide all of the services. This type of solution is often more affordable than a 'from scratch' approach and is seen more and more now as the market matures.

The Banks and the Small Business Association (SBA)

These may be your only alternative if all else fails. If it comes to this be prepared to work for it. The SBA will require a very detailed business plan and you will need this to present to potential investors regardless of whether you go to the bank or not.

Included next in this chapter are some example sections from a business plan that you can use when formulating your own. There are a number of pieces left out, this book is not meant to show you how to write a business plan. The highlights for an ISP are shown in the hopes that you will be able to convey your message better. For an excellent resource for online business planning contact the AOP, the Association of Online Professionals, at www.aop.org.

Example Sections of an ISPs Business Plan

SUPER SYSTEMS

Internet Service Provider

Project Summary

The mission of Super Systems is to build upon an existing need for online access and computer networking (Internet) services in the Kentuckiana area business community.

THE INTERNET
The new medium of the Internet is the most powerful and far reaching computer network in the world. It is a global computer network connecting schools, libraries, businesses, government agencies, and individual home computer users giving access to the exchange of ideas and information. The Internet is not merely text based information but a new medium filled with vivid color-rich graphics, photos, voice and even video. The Internet will be the main venue of communication in the future for a world growing smaller by the day. The Internet allows for not only more information to be transmitted than traditional outlets, but at a far lower cost, doing away with high material, printing and postage costs. Instantaneous, world wide, and at a low monthly flat rate, a business owner's dream has come to the market place.

WHO BUYS INTERNET SERVICES? Business organizations, charitable groups, individuals, religious organizations and even government institutions. Almost everyone is a good candidate for one Internet service or another. Once the use of one Internet service is utilized these customers often find that they are unable to live without -all- of the Internet services.

WHAT INTERNET SERVICES ARE AVAILABLE?

Web Services
The 'Web' is a world wide distributed collection of millions of documents that companies, individuals, educational institutions, and government bodies

maintain. Web pages are made up of textual information, pictures, audio, and even video files that a user accesses from their computer. Web 'space' costs very little compared to conventional advertising mediums. Institutions who create a Web presence generally provide massive amounts of information through them, far more than through other conventional means. Web pages are generally linked to Email (see below) services for interaction with potential customers and other interested parties. Web documents are not like conventional advertising either, in that a user must actively choose to 'go to' the web pages that interest them. If I were looking for information on truck parts I would choose to 'search' the Web by using what basically amounts to an online yellow pages. By typing in the words 'truck' and 'parts' I would be able to locate relevant web pages of interest to me. No one group owns the Web. Some examples of the uses of Web pages include:

- Jimsim, a Chicago based Diesel company, distributes financial information to its shareholders through the Web as opposed to printing and mailing reports every quarter.
- The Laughable Spot, a local comedy club, posts its schedule of shows and upcoming events for users to access.
- Froley Truck Parts, a local truck parts manufacturing and distribution company, actively solicits business from distant customers by advertising their product line through the Web.
- Joe Doe, who is looking for a new career move, advertises his resume on the Web.
- Jane Doe, who is a huge fan of Saddlebred horse riding, posts pages concerning the sport so as to network with others in her area of interest.

Email

Email allows company personnel to keep in touch with remote offices and business contacts without spending a fortune on long distance. Email also provides an excellent distribution system as companies may distribute information or a new product offering to all of its distributors at once. Email also allows for the 'attachment' of computer documents to messages. In this way, a graphical presentation or a spreadsheet can be distributed to many individuals instantaneously. Email is the fax of the future. Some current examples of Email usage:

- The Ludgate Library uses Email to stay in touch with other libraries all over the world for quick and inexpensive communication.
- Nuro Enterprises uses Email to stay in touch with its worldwide chain of distributors and inform them of changes in policy, new product offerings, and price reductions.
- Jane User uses Email to communicate with her daughter at the University of Illinois.

FTP

FTP is the File Transport Protocol. FTP is used to move large documents and other information through the Internet to parties who choose to receive them. FTP is used to transport medical images, financial information, catalogs, and other large items.

- Friendly Hospitals use FTP to transport medical images to far away specialty centers.
- Magic Streams uses FTP to distribute updates to its line of engineering CAD software to its many customers nationwide.

Leased Lines

Companies use leased data lines from an Internet service provider to provide 'bulk' Internet services to its many in-house employees. A firm utilizing email as a standard world wide communications link to other offices might need to allow 20+ simultaneous users to access this service. For this high use purpose 'dial up' access (see below), over a standard phone line, is too cumbersome. A leased line, run into the company and integrated into their existing computer network, provides many users the ability to simultaneously access all of the above Internet services. Some examples of leased line usage:

- Grimwald Llc. , located in Louisville, needs to allow 60+ employees in their heavy manufacturing division access to government Internet sites and Email. In order to accomplish this they have installed a T1 line.
- The Louisville association of Carpenters needs to allow 20+ employees access to Internet Email and wishes to run their own Web area 'in house' without contracting this service to outsiders. They are in need of an ISDN link to the Internet.

Dial up or 'Modem' Services

Dial up access allows a user, whether company based or not, to access the Internet and its vast resources from a home or office. A customer purchases an account, generally at a flat rate for unlimited use, and connects by having their computer modem contact a modem at the Internet Service Provider's site. Dial up access to the Internet has become wildly popular and the business is literally banging on the door without being solicited.

THE CURRENT MARKET

The Louisville market currently consists of the major national service providers and three privately owned providers of any consequence outside of Super Systems (Big Fun Internet Services, Serious ISP, and Tastes Great Service Center). The national providers are finding that their proprietary systems with closed content and high hourly costs are now dwarfed by the rest of the Internet at large. Once the only players in the market, their user base now is outnumbered by other Internet businesses and end user accounts by 5 to 1. They will be struggling for many years to deal with this new paradigm shift to a totally open and fully connected computer community, not reliant upon their private content any longer. Of the three privately owned service providers outside of Super Systems, not one unburdened with a history of poor service and customer dissatisfaction. Additionally, their strategies are hampered by a narrow view and knowledge base of the workings of the Internet and lack the vision to foretell the future paradigm shifts in computer networking. Due to the hyper-paced changes in the online world the largest markets will be shifting quickly from one area to the next. The current trend is to provide connectivity (through dial up modems, ISDN, leased lines, etc.) and World Wide Web page design and hosting. However, this area is only viable as a business target for the next 24 to 36 months. After this the next paradigm shift will be to provide custom programming and 'project based' Internet services. Only a company operating from a position of insight and experience in this market, 'lean' and quickly, can hope to survive and profit in the long term.

SUPER SYSTEMS HISTORY

Super Systems was born out of the market desire for clean well serviced Internet Providers to focus on the local business market. The need for such services is at an all time high and the current providers are unable to fulfill this need in a timely and cost-effective manner. Super Systems identified this void in the local marketplace and set in place a plan to service these customers effectively. Please see the attached testimonial letters.

Joe Entrepreneur has a long history of (business, computer networking, entrepreneurial endeavors?) that will guide Super Systems successfully through its startup phase and later through expansion and growth. Please see the attached resume.

CURRENT POSITIVE POSITIONING

Super currently has x number of businesses which wish to sign up for web accounts. (Try to line up at least five and get a testimonial letter)

Super currently has testimonials from x (preferably 10 or 20) local users who would like to use our Internet services on a dial up basis.

The Louisville District High School has agreed to help promote Super Systems Internet services in return for a trade of services. (Try to line up more than one of these such agreements and include letters from the organizations!)

An agreement between Super Systems and the Lithgow Wood Workers Club will create our first special interest area on the web. They have agreed to provide information and graphics to create this special interest area in return for advertising on the web site information about their club. We hope to use this area as a draw for other local wood manufacturing companies to host their web sites.

A strategic alliance with Super Telephone Systems, an RBOC authorized re-seller, allows us to move faster on new leased line contracts than the competition. They will additionally be referring all Internet inquiries they get to our offices in return for a Web site.

Super has the most complete service bundle for new businesses wishing to gain an Internet presence at the lowest cost of any of our competitors. (See SERVICES OFFERED; Web Packages)

Super has plans to utilize advanced server technology produced by Big Systems, Inc. While other competitors opted to use high priced general purpose Unix machines for their connectivity to the Internet Super has opted to use proven performance leaders in online access communications. This combined with the speed of our backbone connection (see below) makes for a noticeably faster system than the competitors. (NOTE: Big Systems, Inc. produced the dial in server for Big Company A that supports 200+ simultaneous dial in connections as well as the dial in server for Big Company B).

Super Systems is in possession of the most direct Internet access in the Kentuckiana area. Other local providers opted to go through older connections to access the Internet. Super opted to connect directly to the 'backbone' Network Access Point (NAP) to provide superior speed to and from the system. An analogy makes this most clear; the NAP can be considered the Interstate of the Internet. Other providers connect to neighborhoods (which exist in multitude) that are in turn connected to the Interstate. Rules of traffic apply, if you start on an Interstate that goes in five separate directions you can immediately choose the best direction to go to get to your destination (a neighborhood). If you start in a neighborhood and need to get to another neighborhood you must first travel out of the one you live in, jump onto the interstate, and then exit to another neighborhood. What our backbone connection translates into is the fastest and most direct Internet access point available.

Super's current assets are $XX,000 in equipment and software, outside of the needed equipment we hope to purchase.

Super is spearheaded with the most experienced and thorough knowledge base of any of the online access providers in the Kentuckiana area. With our strategic partnerships, lean management, and experience, we wish to become a major influence in the local Information community.

CAPITAL INVESTMENT

A capital investment of $60,000 is needed to fund the expansion of Super Systems, Inc. over the initial 12 months. $30,000 is needed for new equipment purchases and $30,000 is needed for operating expenses.

Details for capitalization of the first twelve (12) months is included in this project plan with cash flow extrapolations through the 2nd and 3rd years of operation.

There are currently no liens or debts on Super Systems.

The ultimate goal is to build the company over the next 24 to 36 months into a powerhouse in the local community. The Internet has yet to become truly a -highly- competitive industry. With the massive media attention it is gaining every day and the millions of new customers wishing to hop on board this will change over the next two to three years. The absorption of the smaller Internet providers into larger companies has yet to become a standard business strategy in the market, yet that time is coming. The company needs to be positioned properly for when this begins to occur.

Although not necessary, if an investor is able to contribute sales leads from their existing base of associates it will lead to the bottom line.

The **recurring** monthly revenue is the heart of Internet services. The projected growth of $1,500 new recurring monthly dollars must be achieved for the desired goals. The cumulative effects of this type of subscription business is staggering, as can be seen in areas such as long distance providers and cable companies. Costs will be controlled and capital used wisely. The best salesperson for the Internet is one who understands all the technology and the costs associated with it. To this ends Joe Entrepreneur will be the #1 salesperson for Super Systems once adequate support and in house help is acquired.

The potential profitability for this type of business is immense. Currently, there are no regulatory boundaries for an Internet provider. Should regulation become affected, those providers already online will have the advantage over any new competition.

The computer industry is the "New Frontier" for investors and entrepreneurs alike. It is perhaps the final frontier as well, since industries of the future will spring from an entirely computer literate society. The Internet is a $10 billion global market; with the services it provides and those who provide it. Super Systems aims to provide access to this new frontier.

Products & Services

World Wide Web Services

The World Wide Web (also Web or WWW) is a relatively new medium that exists on the Internet that allows you to combine visual and interactive pages of information. Rich graphics and photos are combined with text to create the 'pages' and a user maneuvers through the Web utilizing 'links'. Links allow a user to jump to another topic or area of 'pages' immediately. Interactive forms are combined with pages to allow users to request more information, order a product, email the company with a question, etc. These capabilities allow a company to proactively market products and services like no other medium available today. Because the Web is contained on the Internet access to its vast store of information is available at any computer with an Internet connection, whether from home when dialing up through a modem, or at your place of work if the company has opted to install a full time connection (see leased lines).

FEATURES AND THE LANGUAGE OF THE WORLD WIDE WEB:

* Home Pages

     A home page is the beginning of a companies, individuals or other groups online presentation.

* Full Color Graphics

     Existing graphics, company logos, or pictures can be scanned into a digital format or placed directly on a home page if they are delivered to Super digitally.

* Interactive Links

     Links can be either text or graphics that a user selects on their computers which takes them to either another area of the same home page or another location on the Internet entirely.

* Hits

     Hits are how many times a home page has been viewed, a hit is one viewing. Hits are usually monitored and a counter placed at the bottom of home pages for companies to use.

* Email Access

     Email is a standard type of 'link' that allows anyone viewing a home page document to immediately call up a window and write mail directed to a company.

* Forms

     Forms look like standard paper forms but are filled in while a user is online. The input to a form can then be mailed to a company or can interact with a database to perform some function, ie. purchase a product, search a catalog, locate another home page area.

* Domain Names

Domain names are unique addresses for a companies home page presence.

Super Systems World Wide Web Services

Super Systems bundles more services into our World Wide Web packages at less cost than any of the competition. All web services include the following:

Design and layout of your content (business flyers, presentations, etc.) into HTML, the language of the Web. Graphics are scanned if needed, text is imported or typed into the Web pages and all links are established. Color schemes are selected by the company or we can custom design the look and feel of a home page area.

One email 'form' is included with all Web accounts. This allows a company to dictate the type of responses they will receive when a user wishes to contact them as opposed to a user simply choosing to type whatever they wish into an email reply. This is a tremendous time saver for the company as they should be able to get a feel for the type of potential customer they are dealing with before they ever reply to the users mail. Standard form questions are *FULL NAME, ADDRESS, PHONE NUMBER,SIZE OF COMPANY*, etc.

One Email account is included with all Web accounts. Without Email the company is unable to interact with potential customers and other business associates.

Unlimited Internet access is included with every web presence. After the design and layout has been completed a site visit is made to the companies or users site and all the software needed to access the Internet is installed and demonstrated. Now that the customer has full access to the Internet they can view their Web area online and make any revisions to the content before we go any further with the process. Without Internet access a Web presence is just like an ad in a magazine, very dull and lifeless, and it throws away all the advantages of this interactive medium.

Propagation of the Web address is begun after the final revisions are made to the Web area. Super submits information on the Web area to 18 of the largest search engines, or 'Yellow Pages', on the

Internet so that potential customers and interested parties can find the Web area by searching on key words. Ie. If I were looking for a local telephone system provider I might search the 'Yellow Pages' for keywords such as *business, telephone, systems, Louisville, Kentucky* to locate one. A Web presence is useless if no one can find it.

LEVEL ONE - The 'Homepage'
An entry level service for the business customer. Includes all of the above services with up to 2 pages of content and 1 graphic or logo. SETUP FEE: $75.00 MONTHLY RECURRING: $45.00

LEVEL TWO - The 'Web Presence'
A larger presence which includes all of the above services with up to 5 pages of content, 5 graphics or logos, and 5 links. SETUP FEE: $225.00 MONTHLY RECURRING: $99.00

Other Options: multiple dial up accounts, multiple email addresses, additional content

By special quote: searchable databases, secured areas, special programming

Super Systems Dial Up Internet Access

Dial up Internet access is a service whereby a customer connects to our internal network, and thereby connects to the Internet at large through our dedicated backbone connection. Dial up Internet access allows a customer to access the World Wide Web, private email (one email address included), Usenet message forums where millions of people interact with each other on topics of interest to them, real time chat, and many more new services appearing daily. All of this access is billed at a flat monthly rate for usage.

Internet access is the hottest end-user service to ever come to computing. It is estimated that there are currently 35 million individuals world-wide who have access to the Internet. By comparison, the large national services such as Compuserve, America Online, Prodigy, etc. only have about 7 million members collectively. The Internet is the hot spot for growth and it will be mainly local companies that will be providing this access. Super Systems is currently signing up an average of 20 new customers a week to our dial up access services. With the proper advertising and manpower we should be able to double or triple this number.

All dial up accounts include the following services and costs:
- A one time $10 setup fee for new accounts
- One email address
- Up to 5 megabytes of disk space for a user if they wish to develop their own home page
- Ninety minutes per day free access to the Dance of Super BBS, a huge local resource of computer files, online games, and other services included as a value added feature.

DIAL UP ACCOUNTS LEVELS

Level One - The 'Trial' Account
This account allows 10 hours per month of graphical Internet access with additional hours being billed at 65 cents each.
MONTHLY FEE: $10.00

Level Two - The 'Super' Account
This account allows unlimited Internet access with no additional hourly billing, by far the most popular account. Note: Not to be used for 24/7 services (see leased lines)
MONTHLY FEE: $20.00

Level Three - Extended Discount Plan
Six months of unlimited Internet access at a cost break.
FEE: $135.00

DIAL UP OPTIONS

Additional Email addresses: $5 each per month
Email 'form' for personal Web areas: $5 each per month

Super Systems Leased Line Internet Access

Leased lines are dedicated data pipes that are installed at the customers premise and at the Super network site. Once the lines are run the customers computer system is networked into the Internet so that all of their employees may have Internet email, Web browsing capabilities, and more. Companies with this type of connection to the Internet can also manage their own in house Internet services, perhaps putting their own web server online or some other type of service for the users of the Internet to access, day or night. Leased lines are becoming more popular as the Internet is expanding at a terrific pace.

JARGON

DEDICATED 28.8 - This is the same type of connection Super offers in our dial up access except that the connection is allowed for full time services such as Internet access.

ISDN - Integrated Services Digital Network, an inexpensive option for companies not needing a tremendous amount of bandwidth. ISDN offers either 64k or 128k worth of bandwidth depending on whether one or both channels are utilized for data connections.

T1 / FRAC T1 - T1 lines are large data connections used primarily for companies that need to connect a lot of users to the Internet or who intend to run their own service and need a lot of Internet users to be able to access it simultaneously.

PRICES

SERVICES	SETUP	MONTHLY $
Dedicated 28.8	$150	$125
ISDN - 64k	$250	$175
ISDN - 128k	$250	$250
T1 / FRAC T1	$500	$500+

Needed Equipment List

Internet server with two 16 port Digi-boards for up to 32 simultaneous dial up connections, NIC card and software. Cisco 1005 router.	$8,250 plus shipping (approximately $110).
Web server: Pentium 166 with 64 megs of RAM, Windows NT server, NIC card, 2 gigabyte SCSI II drive, 15 inch monitor, 8X speed CD-ROM and 16 bit sound card, mouse and keyboard.	$3,100 (street price)
Workstation: Pentium 133 with 24 megs of RAM, Windows 95, 1 gig IDE drive, NIC card, Quad speed CD ROM drive, 14 inch monitor, 16 bit sound system, mouse and keyboard.	$2,400
Text Based BBS: Low end 486/25 with four megs of RAM, 500 meg hard drive, NIC card, and 14 inch monitor, two 16550 COM ports, and keyboard.	$800
TBBS bulletin board software	$300
Boca ethernet hub	$130
32 Courier Modems utilizing one of the discount packages listed.	$8,000
Conner Tape Stor 4000	$400
Data line surge supressor package	$300
(3) APC SurgeArrest strips	$135
APC Backups 2400 UPS	$1,600
HP Deskjet 1600 Color Printer	$1,179
Adtran CSU/DSU	$1,200
Racks and Furniture	$1,200
Miscellaneous	$800
TOTAL:	**$30,104**

Assumptions

1. Salaries
    A. <u>President</u> - $15,000 Salary
    B. <u>Technical Support Operations</u> - $7.00 hourly
    C. <u>HTML Web Master</u> - $8.00 hourly

(Note that your salary is set low with the intention that you will be taking dividends or other sorts of payments once the company is profitable. You could also show the two support positions as part time if you will man the office during the mornings.)

2. Phone Service
    A. Voice Lines - 2 lines @ $55.00   Monthly: $110.00
    B. Dial in - 20 modem lines @ $35.00   Monthly: $700.00
    C. Long distance charges   Monthly: $100.00

3. Network Costs - Fractional T1 leased line: $1600 monthly
4. Merchant Account Status @ 3% of charged sales
5. Advertising - Monthly: $600.00 (Preferably more!)
6. Office Supplies Monthly: $50.00
7. Service Fees Monthly: $50.00
8. Postage Monthly: $60.00
9. Printing Monthly: $100.00
10. Miscellaneous Monthly: $50.00

Corporate Structure

Super Systems - Organization Chart
Month, Year

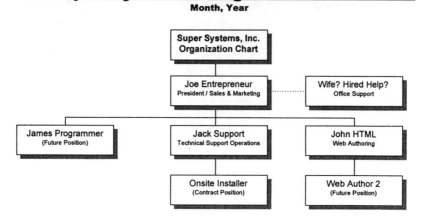

(Be certain to include a few future positions as it shows you are thinking about the long term.)

Network Design

(Here you should design something like the network diagram that is seen in chapter four. Be sure to include where the revenue streams are as well, similar to the diagram in chapter two.)

Cash Flow

(In your cash flow diagram you should show three years of projected income and costs. Design this using your favorite spreadsheet. Be realistic here! Investors do not want to see pie-in-the-sky, only a good return on their money. Be sure to show when items such as phone lines are increasing or new employees are hired, new leased lines sold and equipment purchased, etc. This affects your overall budget. If you have a three year projection and do not show any new employees what does this say about your plan?)

Super Systems Corp.

Business Plan Projections / Cash Flow: 1996 - 1998
1st Year

Months	Jul-96 1	Aug-96 2	Sep-96 3	Oct-96 4		Year end TOTAL
Salaries	1,900	1,900	1,900	1,900	(etc.)	
Payroll Taxes	229	229	229	229	(etc.)	
Contract Fees	50	150	150	150	(etc.)	
Phone Service	910	960	1,010	1,060	(etc.)	
Network Connection	800	800	800	800	(etc.)	
Hard/Software	200	200	200	200	(etc.)	
Advertising	600	600	600	600	(etc.)	
Office Supplies	50	50	50	50	(etc.)	
Service Fees	50	50	50	50	(etc.)	
Accounting	20	20	20	20	(etc.)	
Postage	60	60	60	60	(etc.)	
Printing	100	100	100	100	(etc.)	
Miscellaneous	50	50	50	50	(etc.)	
Operating Costs:	5,019	5,169	5,219	5,269	(etc.)	

Revenues:

	Jul-96	Aug-96	Sep-96	Oct-96		
Modem Cust.	40	55	70	85	(etc.)	
Modem Rev.	800	1,100	1,400	1,700	(etc.)	
ISDN Cust.	-	-	1	1	(etc.)	
ISDN Rev.	-	-	250	250	(etc.)	
T1 Connects	-	-	-	-	(etc.)	
T1 Revenue	-	-	-	-	(etc.)	
Web Customers	5	10	15	20	(etc.)	
Web Revenue	350	700	1,050	1,400	(etc.)	
Setup Fees		525	775	525	(etc.)	
Programming Fees	-	-	-	-	(etc.)	
Total Revenue	1,150	2,325	3,475	3,875		
	Jul-96	Aug-96	Sep-96	Oct-96		
Cash Flow 96-97	(3,869)	(2,844)	(1,744)	(1,394)		

END OF EXAMPLE ISP BUSINESS PLAN SECTIONS

The previous pages of example sections are only meant to show you the highlights for an ISPs business plan. Not all of the required sections for a business plan are involved here, as there are more than 100 inexpensive books that will explain this in excruciating detail for you. I highly recommend you go to your local bookstore and pick one up. What this is meant to show you is that you must describe in layman's terms what your business is going to do. Many of the people you will be approaching have no concept of what the net is about nor what products and services it offers. Keep this in mind when designing any correspondence that will be seen by potential investors / partners.

Other items you should include that are not shown above:

- A resume of yourself
- Testimonial letters from business and end users desiring your service
- Letters from any strategic partners or barter partners who you will be trading services with in order to get recommendations and access to their customer base
- A couple of choice articles from major business magazines and the local paper that reinforce the need for ISPs
- Sample advertising you have worked up in advance
- A marketing plan that details where and how you will acquire new customers. Be sure it corresponds with your advertising budget

When creating your budget for the cash flow don't leave anything out! You have initial startup costs which will be very expensive and include installation charges for phones, leased lines, equipment, etc. Your monthly costs however can eat you alive if you do not go into the business fully informed. Create a couple of cost sheets that show you exactly what you will be spending from month to month. Include insurance and other quarterly or yearly payments broken down into months on this. By doing this you will have a better feel for what your average costs will be like. Be sure to include some 'fudge factor' miscellaneous in here to take care of the unknowns, everyone has unexpected expenses.

When you have finally put your plan together have it printed on a high end printer and then get 15 or 20 copies reproduced and bound at a local copy center. Begin to distribute them to all of your potential partners and investors TODAY! The more you get out there the more interest you will generate. Be sure to look sharp when presenting the business plan.

When you finally get to the point where you are debating a contract be certain that you have a good lawyer with a lot of business contract experience. Absolutely every detail should be mapped out, including a very thorough discussion of what is to happen in the event of a divorce, dissolution, etc. Contracts are not used when times are good, only when things turn bad. Be certain you're prepared for the worst, even while you hope for the best. Your contract should reflect this attitude.

A NOTE ON BUSINESS STRUCTURES

You should consult your CPA or lawyer about the form that your business will take. A sole proprietorship has many advantages to it but you are also personally liable for anything that is brought up in court against the company! A Subchapter-S corporation is a terrific way to shield yourself from some of this liability and also has a number of tax breaks built in that you may be able to take advantage of. However, for a Subchapter-S corporation to be truly effective in shielding you from personal liability there must be two or more true stock holders. Discuss your alternatives with a professional.

CHAPTER VII

ALPHA PREPARATIONS & MARKETING

You are on your way to being an Internet guru and a mover and shaker in your community as well. The following chapter is an assortment of issues that you should take care of before opening up for service. You should also time the installation of your dial up phone lines and leased line connection so that they fall somewhere in the middle of these preparations. There is no sense in paying for these pricey lines before you need them! You will however need about two weeks to thoroughly beta-test the system and work out the kinks before your advertising kicks in. Take your time and make sure the following issues are either resolved or are close to resolution before you begin the day to day operations of your business.

Press Releases
Be sure to have one or two short and sweet press releases prepared for your big day. Make them no longer than one page, newspapers are not in the business of advertising your business for free, only reporting what's new and happening in their community. Be sure to have the mailing addresses, fax numbers and preferably a contact

name for the following: all of your local papers, any computer group newsletters, local entertainment and business weeklies and radio stations (especially the talk radio in your town).

User Policies
Are your price plans in place? However, have you designed a policy for users and payments? Are you going to charge extra for those you have to bill by mail? What about late payments and users who are expired? Do they pay the setup fee again? How about abuse policies for users who are undesirable? Have you laid out the law concerning what is and what is not allowed on your system? What about acceptable usage, do you outline that dial up accounts are not to be used for 24/7 servers that are being run on the user's machines? How about acceptable usage and limitations on user home pages? Are you going to have users sign a waiver of liability for 'naughty' Usenet access? What about a user contract that is universal? Some ISPs require this.

Write all of this down and be sure it is prominently posted on both your web server and your text based system if you have one. Be certain it is included with any user pricing information or literature that is sent through the mail.

Product Literature
Have you designed attractive literature to send out? You will get many requests to send information through the mail. Be sure that all of this information is on your web page and text based system as well! Make it as easy to get to as possible. Get a stack of plastic trays and make up about 50 copies of each of the following. The reason you don't want to make more is that even with the best laid plans you will end up changing these over time.

- Dial Up User Information / Pricing / Sign up sheet
- Commercial Web Customer's pricing, policies and sign up sheet
- Generic information sheet outlining all of your servers details such as phone number, DNS IP address and domain name, news server name, SMTP/POP3 mail server name, etc. This is for customers who do not wish to use your recommended software
- Leased line pricing sheet

- An 'all products' pricing sheet
- Agreement contracts with generic blanks so you can fill them in when you have a new web or leased line customer.
- A 'site-visit' check list for any site visits that you or preferably contract employees will perform.

Flyers

Flyers are a generic advertisement for your services that you can leave in 'friendly' computer stores, grocery stores, car windows, user group meetings, etc. Do not underestimate how valuable inexpensive flyers can be. We distributed over 2,000 one month by hand with incredible results! Your flyer can even be a blown up copy of your newspaper ad if you like. To save money do your flyers on just half a sheet of paper, put two to a page and have the copiers cut them in half for you!

Recommended Software

Do you have your recommended software list made up? If not refer back to chapter one. All of the client software should be picked out at this time. You should also have a choice of dialers, the software that actually dials into your system and makes the TCP/IP connection to your server. Trumpet Winsock is the choice for Windows 3.x but what about Windows 95? You should use the internal dialer with this operating system, the same for Windows NT. Walk through the process of installing a shortcut for your service and document ALL of it in excruciating detail. This will be the instruction file for users of that operating system. Likewise, you should have a basic instruction file for all of the software you recommend. Include this with the software when you make it available to your users. Be sure that this software and the accompanying instructions are included on your web server and your text based system if you host one. Have printouts ready if you need to fax these instructions to someone.

To Disk Or Not To Disk?

Will you send your recommended software out on disk to users? You could, if it is allowed by the software companies licensing agreements. It would usually take about three disks to distribute a complete suite of Internet utilities, perhaps even four. There are

alternatives though. If you do have a text based system from which you distribute your software you could just mail out one disk with an excellent terminal package that connected to your text based system. In this way you would save a lot on disk and postage charges. Additionally, your customers could have access to quite a bit more software than you could ever distribute on floppy. You could force them to read news about the system at login and there are many other advantages as well. A company called Banana Programming creates just such a package called Bananacom. It installs seamlessly into either Dos, Windows 3.x or Windows 95 and icons are installed for those running Windows. The com ports and speed of the modem is auto-sensed and configured automatically for you taking all of the pain out of it. This may be something you want to look into. You will get requests for software by mail so you'll need to be prepared to provide the users something.
You can contact Banana Programming at www.split.com.

Web Search Engines
What about when that first commercial customer is ready to have his/her web pages listed in the search engines? Do you know the best way to get them listed in all of them quickly? What you want to do is point your web browser at www.submit-it.com and then bookmark the site. The service is free and within 20 minutes you can have your customer's site information submitted to all of the major search engines. Potential customers will appreciate the value added service and your existing customers will thank you for all of the time and effort you went through to get them listed! Note that the search engines will not list your site information immediately, sometimes it takes as long as a week for the information to show up.

News Server
Are you prepared to offer Usenet news to your users? Sending them to a public server will not cut it anymore. You will either have to send them to your own server or to the server you contract with.

Home Page
Is your home page complete? Is it attractive and professional at the same time? Are you able to showcase any of your more technically

demanding abilities on your home page? Be sure that the following are included in your web site in an organized manner:

Users Area:
- User policies
- User pricing (and possibly online signup?)
- Client software and instructions
- Email support options, support contacts, voice numbers, etc.
- User home pages (Seed this area with your own home page and those of friends and associates. Work them up at no cost. By doing this you do not appear to be a ghost town on the Internet. Seeding is one of the most valuable tools you have when just opening up for business.)
- Links to other areas of the net with HTML instructions
- Late breaking news, planned down time (This area will be a main communications channel between your users and you.)

Business area:
- Business web pricing and policies
- Business web pages (Again, seed this area with some web pages that you have pre-made, at least five. What organization would want to do business with you if they see that no one else has web pages on your server.)

Services area:
- A history of your company and mission
- Voice / fax numbers and address
- User policies
- User dial up pricing
- Web services pricing
- Leased line pricing

BBS or Text Based System
Is your text based system online (if you're going to run one)? Has it been thoroughly bug tested. Do you include instructions and software on it? Can users sign up online? Is there email support available?

Voice Mail

Has a good voice mail system been installed? If not, contact your RBOC and see if they offer voice mail on the phone lines. This way, when a line is busy it still goes to the messaging system. You just have to pick up the message later. Do you want to offer fax back services through this with information and pricing plans? What about frequently asked questions, can you create a voice 'menu' with your system so users can find the answers they want at all hours? Check into the latest voice mail modems as well, many include some pretty spectacular services.

FAQ

Create a frequently asked questions list and fill in the answers in detail. If you are including so many details that the process is truly painful for you then you know you are doing a good job. These questions will be asked again and again of you. Be sure it is on your web server, your text based service, voice mail if possible, and give a copy to all of your help, spouse, relatives, pet, etc. Be sure that everyone knows the answers to these questions. Include the following on your FAQ; you will add to it as time goes on:

- What size connection do you have?
- Where do you hook up to?
- What speed do your modems support?
- How many dial up lines do you have?
- What software do you recommend?
- How can I get the software?
- Does your web server support CGI?
- Do I get a free home page with my dial up account?
- What are you commercial web services and prices?
- What are you dial up accounts and pricing? (Include setup fee, site visit pricing if you offer it and any other details!)

And the doozy, give this one a lot of thought:
- Why should I choose you over (insert competitor)?

Do not bash the competitors, it makes you appear 'cheap' and is not a good business policy. Stress your strengths and commitment.

Insurance

Is all of this valuable equipment you've invested in insured properly? Most business and home insurance policies need special qualifiers and premiums in order to protect computer equipment. It can also be quite expensive going this route. The most comprehensive computer insurance I've ever found is offered by Safeware Insurance. The costs are low and the coverage is astronomical! Computer equipment is covered for accidents, theft, fire, floods, etc. Take a look at their home page at www.safeware-ins.com.

Recommendations

Do you have a policy in place to reward those who will be sending members your way? Perhaps you give them a free week or two or a gift certificate of some type? Publicize this loudly so that people know they will be rewarded for talking you up. Word of mouth is potentially, and if done properly can be, your best source of new customers.

Company Image and Selling

Why would I put marketing in the same chapter with your alpha preparations? Your marketing plan needs to be well thought out *before* you begin incurring those large monthly bills. Why? Because once the clock starts ticking you need to be bringing in customers immediately, not a month from then when you have your marketing ideas ready to go.

Creating and maintaining a company image is very important. It will be with you for the duration of your business so put some good thought into it before you begin. The first part of business image is your **mission statement**. This should be a short statement of your purpose, goals, and commitments. Be sure that it is as timeless as possible because your mission statement should be with you for a long time.

One of the most important image makers is your **company name**. Your company name should be professional or have a particular ring to it. I highly recommend something very unique. A unique name stands out from the crowd when people have ISPs on their mind. If you have a hum-drum name no one will remember it. My own particular company name was inherited so I didn't give it much thought at the time. This was back in the labor of love 80's when most online services were done for the fun of it, no one at the time had much ambition for running them as a business. However, the name of 'Dance of Shiva' certainly stood out. Perhaps more than we would have liked at the time. It became abbreviated quite often to just Shiva Systems in the later years which lent it an air of professionalism. At least it didn't raise as many eyebrows. I encourage you to NOT use acronyms, they are overused in the computer industry as it is. CRP, AMPX, BRTS and other such acronyms have no ring to them (any similarities to existing companies are purely coincidental, my lawyer made me say that). It just so happened that 'Dance of Shiva' was abbreviated by the users quite often as DOS in the early days, which may or may not have been a good thing. (The prior stated acronym has no relationship to any operating systems and similarities are entirely coincidental, my lawyer made me say that too). Pick a name that can be both professional and memorable. I'm particularly partial to these two names, both of which did not show up with a web server. Perhaps they are not taken yet. What do you think about 'Floodgate' or 'Tsunami Internet Servies'? I think they're quite catchy myself. If someone does own these sites my most sincere apologies. Avoid names that have a high tech ring to them, they are a dime a dozen.

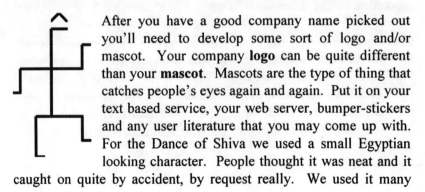

After you have a good company name picked out you'll need to develop some sort of logo and/or mascot. Your company **logo** can be quite different than your **mascot**. Mascots are the type of thing that catches people's eyes again and again. Put it on your text based service, your web server, bumper-stickers and any user literature that you may come up with. For the Dance of Shiva we used a small Egyptian looking character. People thought it was neat and it caught on quite by accident, by request really. We used it many times throughout the years and people did recognize it as something very distinctly ours. Your company logo can be something entirely different that you will use on your stationary or other commercial services literature. Perhaps something a bit less cute and more professional.

When you start to consider all of the literature that you will be passing out you realize that you have quite a bit of graphic design and layout work to be done as well! Your first month will probably see changes in your literature as small additions and updates are added. After you believe you have solidified your literature you should approach a graphic artist and design person. Try to find someone that does layout on their home PC in their spare time and **trade services** with them! If you can get them to design your brochures and business cards in return for services on your system you have saved a lot of money. This barter type arrangement should extend into all areas of your business as it is a very cost effective way of getting things done.

Print advertising should be prepared and ready to go for your opening day. Your ads should not try to explain everything, just catch the viewer's eye and get them to seek out more information. Again, if you do not have any experience with Corel Draw or another very nice graphics package you should barter or contract with a desktop layout guru. The large firms will charge you a fortune but the smaller firms will play ball on a more affordable level. The smaller firms are also much more likely to trade services. I located an outstanding freelance artist who did this work in his spare time. The work was top-notch and the price was definitely right: services plus a little extra was traded for most of our work. Be certain that your ads stand out, you want them to be able to catch a viewer's eye when it is jumbled in a page with a lot of other ads. Take a look at the following:

This ad was worked up by myself in Corel Draw with the help of some licensed art work. I'm no graphic designer so it wasn't easy, but it was free, aside from the time. (You're not sleeping are you? New business owners should shun sleep as a rule of thumb.) The portions of the ad that really stand out are the 'Internet Access' title and the price of the service. We show all of the numbers here (changed to protect the innocent) and the web address as well. The extra portion of the black globe on the right of the ad makes it appear as though the ad is 'breaking out' of the space allotted for it. In actuality it fits perfectly with our local news print ad sizes. The white space to the right that is unused, yet paid for, is sacrificed for effect and I think the trade off has worked well for us. I have seen ads that actually turn a prospective buyer off because they were done so poorly. Do not fall into that trap.

Where should you place your ads? You could opt for the most expensive daily newspaper, and possibly be seen on page C-45. You could also try your other local papers. How about computer club newsletters? They're generally very inexpensive to advertise in. You could also go with a local business magazine, church newsletters, and a coupon type mailing system where someone receives 20 coupons stuffed into one envelope. I've tried all of these and generally the first two months you will get a good response from them as the "hungry" come to find you. Not all of them however will be a long term good investment of your marketing dollars. Newsletters in particular seem to have a useful life of three months a year unless they are available to the general public in stores or other outlets. Wherever you advertise, you should track as closely as possible where your respondents are coming from. If you ask them where they heard about you when they call in you should be able to get a good feel for this. You could keep a score sheet as well and have anyone who answers the phone follow through with it.

There are other outlets for advertising as well. You might want to try the text advertisements on your local cable system. Most cable companies now offer what they call a community bulletin board for text ads. They tend to stay on the screen for 15 or 30 seconds and then it flips to another screen. These are very inexpensive and you'd be surprised how many people read them. The best time for advertising in this outlet is late evenings. If you start your ads at 8 or 9pm and show a few every hour until 1am you should be able to catch the majority of people who would be watching. The night owls make terrific customers too. If they have nothing better to do than watch ads on TV late at night then you can believe they are in the market for something fun and intriguing to do.

A sure fire method of building a professional image and bringing in new customers is to write a regular article for a local paper. Many papers are itching for more content about the Internet and you can provide it to them for free! In return, you get the status and free marketing for being the one to cover the hottest technology of the nineties. Of course, you need to be able to communicate in your writing. However, with the state of most news print publications even this may not even be a requirement. Contact some of your local print publications today and see if they are receptive to the idea.

A good method for gaining some inexpensive publicity is to allow your local public radio or TV station to auction off memberships to your system during pledge week. Provide them with a few memberships each year and a long description of your service! When they announce this on the air they will be publicizing your services to all of their local patrons. If there are other large fund raisers in your area consider these too for publicity and inexpensive advertising.

As you can probably tell from my marketing advice, I am not geared towards a lot of traditional marketing. I have been a lean low-budget advertiser most of my life. Since I have not had the tremendous marketing budgets that others may be privy to I had to make every bit of it count. The very best books on marketing that I ever read are the Guerrilla Marketing series from Jay Conrad Levinson. These books are must-read material for any new business. His latest, Guerrilla Marketing Online covers the gamut of online marketing and should be highly recommended to your customer base. If you really want to make your efforts effective and have every dollar count go out and grab these books today. You can reach the Guerrilla Marketing HQ at 800-748-6444 or on the web at: www.gmarketing.com.

CHAPTER VIII

RESOURCES, TIPS & TRICKS

Resources

Established ISPs will be in a better position than new ISPs to cope with the onslaught of legislation the government is sure to enact. In addition to future legislation the successful ISP will need to keep up with the most current developments on the Internet. For now there are five resources you should become familiar with to help you deal with current and future issues that will affect your well being.

The first is a book by Lance Rose called Netlaw, the online legal guide. This is an excellent resource for all the various legal issues you may encounter in running an online service. It is an indispensable guide for those who wish to run any type of online system.

The second is the Association of Online Professionals (the AOP). The AOP is an association, with low membership fees, that has many advantages for members. They will keep you informed of upcoming legislation, offer members many very advantageous deals on hardware and software from participating corporate sponsors and even field complaints about companies if it comes to that. The privileges that come with being an AOP member are too many to list; I highly recommend you look into it today. The online industry needs a professionally run industry advocate association and that association is the AOP.

Finally, you will need a way of staying on top of current happenings on the Internet. Hardware developments, new features and news will all need to be part of your weekly fare of knowledge you ingest so as to continually reposition yourself for the paradigm shifts that this industry is going through. The most valuable publication to ISPs or people interested in online communications is Boardwatch Magazine. Boardwatch and its faithful editor, Jack Rickard, have led the online industry for a decade. From the birth of the BBS industry to the current explosion of business on the Internet, Boardwatch has been there. Also, be sure to check the Internet Access FAQ and the Inet-Access mailing list for a current discussion on the industry.

Netlaw, by Lance Rose
Web: www.boardwatch.com/mag/writers/ROSE.HTM
Email: elrose@well.com

Association of Online Professionals
Web: www.aop.org
Email: info@aop.org
Voice: (703) 924-9692

Boardwatch Magazine
Web: www.boardwatch.com
Voice: (800) 933-6038

The Internet Access FAQ List
Web: www.amazing.com/internet

The Inet-Access Mailing List
Web: www.scomm.net/inet-access/

PERSONAL TESTIMONIAL: In my dealings with the AOP we had a situation where a shipment for a particular hardware product had been delayed by TWO MONTHS. I wanted the hardware, not an alternative, and the great demand for this particular product made it in short supply for everyone. I had purchased the product directly from the manufacturer to take advantage of their low cost system operator/ISP offer. I was unable to get any amount of satisfaction from repeated calls to the manufacturer. I eventually went to the AOP and they called the company on my behalf. Within the week the product had been delivered to us. This was an amazing show of force to me and more than justified my membership fee many times over.

Timeouts
There are two tools you can use to make your dial up offerings as fair as possible on a busy system. Your system will have these two options, though the wording may be a bit different. Look for a 'maximum idle timeout' and the maximum connect duration variables. The maximum idle timeout refers to how long a user can sit idle on the connection before your server hangs up on them. The maximum connect time refers to how long a caller can stay online in one continuous sitting before the server hangs up on them. If you have a very busy system setting these values lower can open up windows for other users who wish to get online. Consider it heavily though as you don't want to cause your users too much hardship. I recommend a minimum idle timeout of no less than 12 minutes. For a maximum connection limit you should probably not go below two to three hours.

Call Forward No Answer
At times you may experience difficulties with modems hanging on you, not answering the calls after a certain duration of time. This can be for a number of reasons but it is a fairly common problem in the ISP business. If you find you are getting bitten by this, for whatever reason, check with your RBOC to see if they offer 'call forward no answer'. This is a feature that will send a call to another

line after a designated number of rings have occurred. By applying this to all of your dial in lines in daisy chain style you can avoid any difficulties. If a modem refuses to answer, goes dead, etc. the call will simply be transferred to the next available line and there doesn't appear to be any interruption of service.

WhatsUp! (Formerly WsWatch)

WhatsUp is a small program that does a big task. It allows you to build a map of a network and log the downtime and performance of the machines you have mapped in it. The program will automatically verify that the machines and destinations you have mapped are pinged or telnetted to on a regular schedule that you specify. If the lag time is long the colors of the destinations on the map changes. If the machines are unreachable this is also noted by color. This program is a beauty! Not only do you get a graphical representation of your network but it will also log to a text file the down times of any of your sites. It also has an option that allows you to be paged if a site goes down! Now, outside of the obvious reason of monitoring your own network through a pager 24 hours a day, you can also track your competition! If you start to see their performance lag or downtimes increasing you know they are having difficulties. Although WsWatch takes a bit of tweaking to get configured I highly recommend you obtain a copy and install it on your workstation. Place it in the startup group so that it automatically runs every time you reboot your machine. The workstation will need a modem to utilize the paging functionality but this can be tied to your last voice line if you so desire. The web address for WhatsUp is www.ipswitch.com.

Hunt Simulators

Some areas are still strapped with outdated rollover charges from the local RBOC. Rollover is what allows a person dialing a phone number to reach the next unused phone line in a chain. Generally the RBOCs will offer this service for a couple of dollars per phone line. This is how it should be as it is nothing more than a bit of software in their computers that handles this service. In the best of all possible worlds this service would be priced like call waiting: inexpensive and just another option on a give phone circuit. If you find that your RBOC is behind the times and wishes to charge more than $10 per line for this service (Yes, some of them still do) you may still have an alternative. There is a little known feature that some RBOCs offer called 'call transfer' that is generally in their premier business services. You will have to have business lines to make use of this feature. It was designed primarily for boiler room operations such as telemarketing where an incoming call to phone line A could be transferred to phone line B by picking up line B and dialing a code on the keypad. This way if your coworker was out of the office and you heard their phone ringing you could 'pull' the call to your own phone line. There is a company called Connlab in Tennessee that makes equipment that utilizes this feature to simulate rollover service. The actual boxes are called Hunt Simulators and come in five, seven and nine line configurations. You can chain them together to get more circuits utilizing this simulated rollover service. The call transfer feature is generally only about $1 per line so you can imagine the cost savings if you were to be using 20+ lines each month and saving $9+ dollars on each one. To utilize the equipment you will need to have touch tone as opposed to pulse capabilities on your lines as well as the call transfer feature. Your savings will vary according to what these features cost in your area. Connlab does not distribute directly to anyone but utilizes distributorships to sell their equipment. To find out more about these little gems contact Business Telephone Systems at (502) 266-0880 or at www.bustel.com.

Bad Phone Lines
Your own phone lines should be as clean as possible for your patrons to get uninterrupted and speedy access to your dial up modems. If you are ordering business lines be sure to have the installer computer test each line after they have been terminated in the 'demarcation' point at your site. Insist on this! When we switched locations in 1995 and had 50 lines installed at our new office the installer found to his surprise that there were SIX lines that had bad grounding or unacceptable levels of static on them. If we had not had him test each one, insisting on the importance of our 'clean' business lines, these would have gone unnoticed by him. The amount of trouble we saved ourselves was immeasurable.

There will be times when you encounter customers that have terrible line noise and poor connections. Many times this can be due to a cheap modem or a bad setup or initialization string in their dialing software. More than one of our customers has fixed all of their problems by swapping out their el cheapo model for a good US Robotics Sportster modem. Another problem is when customers have external 28.8 or faster modems that are not plugged into a 16550 buffered com port. Internal modems do not have this limitation. What happens when the customer *has* a good modem and you're certain that the setup is correct in their machine? The last resort is to have them contact the local phone company and have their wiring checked! Now, there is a trick to this however. The phone companies like to ignore the fact that many millions of people use their phone lines for data communications. It costs them less money this way as wires that are fine for voice may be terrible for data communications. Bad grounding or tiny shorts can take a good data stream and turn it into garbage. When instructing your customers to go this route and request a phone company representative to visit them they must not mention data communications. Have them rack their brains for problems that might occur when only voice is being moved over the wires. Maybe the customer hears intermittent static, perhaps there is only trouble when it is raining or cold outside...?? They must communicate these voice problems to the trouble center otherwise their request will be ignored. I would never encourage anyone to lie to the phone company in order to have their voice/data lines checked out professionally but most customers can remember a problem or two on the phone when they've been using it for a regular voice call. Also, tell the customers to be persistent. Many technicians will come to a house only to patch into the phone line and say, 'It sounds good,' and then leave. Instruct the customer to have the lines thoroughly checked out. Many of our own patrons have had many problems fixed in this way, even to the extent of having the wiring from a phone pole to their house replaced entirely. Older neighborhoods have many more such problems than the newer ones with underground wiring. Remember, your job as an ISP is to provide services but you are also an educator! Only you have the entire gamut of information in telecommunications and you must be able to pass it on to your customers. Do not worry, if you don't know it all now you will after a year in this industry.

User Information

Make a policy early on to not divulge any user information to anyone. Not to family, not to friends and not to anyone who does not have a valid search warrant. I made this mistake twice before I learned that my best intentions are not necessarily helpful to my users who wish to remain anonymous. Protect yourself and stick to this policy, and be certain that your users know this is standard operating procedure as well. They will appreciate it.

Expirations

In your user policies you should delineate how you handle expired accounts. It's only proper to give those users who are sending checks a little bit of leeway in their payments. You can follow up with a phone call if they are late, which is a nice service touch and often much appreciated. Mistakes are made and no one wants to lose their access by accident. I suggest that you give your billed users an extra five mail days to get their payments in. If they do not pay by this time you should suspend the account. Five days later you should delete the accounts. If the user attempts to come back to the system you should charge the setup fee again. In this way you will be discouraging your users from relying on leniency each month. Whatever your policy, if you do not explicitly state the procedure your users will not be able to abide by the rules.

Trial Runs

A trial run is a nice way to assure that your users are going to be able to utilize your service. If you charge their credit card or cash their check before you know that their particular computer setup can use the system you are taking a risk. We found that we were often refunding user's money due to their inability to connect to the system. When signing up they were simply assuming that all would go well. Who would have known that you needed something better than a 286 computer to get PPP access? What? A 2400 baud modem ca not do world wide web browsing? You see where we're going with this. As a way of allowing users to try before they buy you can setup a trial run PPP account. Ideally the access on this account would be limited to three or four minutes per call. You can even disable this account during prime time if you like. This should be plenty of time to test a connection. It's not really long enough to do anything useful and will eventually drive someone mad who attempts to use it in that way. I know because we had many half insane new customers call us after attempting to use the account for free for more than an hour at a time. The Internet is like potato chips, you can't have just a couple (of minutes). Be sure to publicize the user ID and the password prominently so that users can get their software setup correctly before signing up.

Remote Reset Hardware

Even the most well maintained systems sometimes have difficulties. When you are at home in bed at 3am and the system locks up tight nothing can ruin your night, your sleep, and your next day like having to drive to the office and reset the hardware. There are boxes on the market that allow you to do this remotely by dialing over a phone line and entering a code with your keypad. If you have even rare difficulties like this that require a 'hard reset' you might want to consider one of these boxes. Keep in mind that your system must be setup to automatically resume operation after a power failure or a reset such as this. Call USA Communications Corp. at (800) 724-5434. They offer a product called 'Teleboot' which fits the bill perfectly.

Community - User Loyalty Through Thick and Thin

Your customers desire more than a modem on the other end of their phone line. We're not talking about technical support here either. To maintain your customer base you must build loyalty to your service. Every provider has outages, system failures and poor performance at one time or another. If your customers have not bonded to your company and your service they are more likely to pick up and walk during the rough times. They don't know that the provider down the street will have just as many if not more problems than you're having (hopefully). To build a bond between your customers and your company you must treat them as individuals and build community. Community can be the glue between your users and your company and it is a bond that is held on a personal basis. Community is not built with an impersonal approach. How do you build community? When you send newsletters out be sure to mention other happenings in the area that might be of interest to them. Make a habit of sending out email to all of the customers on a regular schedule, even if you don't have any system news. In these mass mailings you need to speak to one customer, not the entire customer base as a whole. Make it personal by telling of funny happenings at the company or events in the employees lives. Express opinions on the new technologies that are flying about the net, whether good or bad. Tell the users your vision and how you intend to accomplish it. Another fantastic community builder is get-togethers or user meets. Find a suitable location and provide some food or beverages and invite all of the users to attend. As your users get to know each other they often take over the technical support aspects that your help desk once offered, helping each other informally. On our system a couple that met at one of our user meets subsequently were married a number of months later. We congratulated them in our mailing and let all of the other users know. Be certain to provide electronic message bases as a public forum where users can chat and get to know each other. Be sure to participate in these forums as you have time. Another good idea is to have drawings and contests at your user meets. Get local computer shops to donate some prizes. Contact your equipment and access provider and ask for some freebies and promotional goodies.

Community is stronger than technology and adds character to a wonderful but rather sterile technology. It is a bond that will carry you and the user base through the good times and the bad.

Tech Support Failure - Hit any user to continue.

Content Draws Crowds
Content is what people on the Internet are looking for. Content is why you have dial up customers, they can reach other sources of information by connecting to the net through you. Build content that appeals to a particular niche audience and you have a marketable service above and beyond access. If you can corner a market area that really appeals to even a small number of people you can draw them from a world-wide audience. Perhaps Indian Cooking is your specialty. If only .2% of all Internet users out there are in love with

Indian cooking you can build a members-only service based on this desire for content. You may provide recipes, an online cook who will give tips each week for the site, a nationwide list of Indian restaurants and food suppliers, etc. At some point, if you've chosen your niche well and do a good job, you will have a critical mass of users and you can then begin to extract revenue from this area. Perhaps you can sell ads on the site or you can charge a membership fee for access. For new ISPs one of the fastest ways to draw a crowd is to get a current content provider to put their information up on the web. Perhaps this is a local paper or weekly magazine. Use their content to springboard your own company into the public's eye. Partner with them on marketing their content and share in the revenues.

Roaming
Roaming is a concept whereby your dial up customers can connect to other ISPs in locales that you do not directly service. They remain your customers but perhaps they need access while they're away on vacation or traveling for business. Roaming is not a new concept in theory but in practice it's been very difficult to get it implemented. There are many concerns and generally ISPs do not like 'tourists' using their dial up lines and service when they are not being directly paid for it. It's strictly a bartered service whereby a group of ISPs agree to service each others client should they be traveling for a short amount of time. All participating ISPs can thus offer temporary service to their clients when they are out of town. You may wish to file this tidbit and explore the possibilities as time allows. It is certain that many dial up customers need nation-wide access due to extensive business trips. To compete effectively with the largest ISPs you will need to offer some version of long distance access and roaming might be the answer. The i-Pass Alliance has such a 'roaming' system in place currently. You can contact them at http://www.ipass.com

Domain Name Reservation Pitch
If you've worked in the ISP business for any amount of time you've heard this pitch to a business. "We've just checked and your domain name is not currently taken. We can reserve this for your use for a one time fee of $??? plus the Internic's standard charges." For some

reason this method of generating future customer's seems to be frowned upon in the business. I'm not sure why because it really is a valid concern. Businesses want their domain name to reflect their business name or trademark, not some abbreviated version of them. If a business uses a generic word for its name (Ie. Decks, Inc.) then there is no amount of legal wrangling that will wrest decks.com from another holder. You will not be able to trademark the name and therefore you would be out of luck. If your name is being used on the web and you are lucky enough to have a trademark then you will have little problem securing this from another holder. However, what if your company is called Gatewood Enterprises and in another state there resides Gatewood Distributors, both trademarked names. If you'd like to get gatewood.com and they already have it, again, you're out of luck. Offering to reserve a domain for a customer gets their attention and potentially gets their future business for yourself. When they are ready to go online who will they turn to? Their friendly ISP who has reserved their domain name for them. A reasonable setup fee can also be applied to this service for handling the paperwork and to cover a bit of your overhead. New proposals for Top Level Domains (TLDs, ie. .com, .edu. .net, etc.) are on the table currently and we should see an explosion of new domain suffixes shortly. This should go a long way towards alleviating some of the current crowding in the market.

Patience and a Sense of Humor
Any technical field can drive a man or woman to drink. In the Internet business this can be doubly so. The smallest details left unattended can bring an entire network to its knees. When you're on your last frazzled nerve just smile, smile, smile:

Murphy's Laws on Technology
As soon as you invest in technology, the technology automatically becomes cheaper or obsolete and usually both.

Everything always costs more money and take more time than you have.

If a builder built buildings the way programmers wrote programs then the first woodpecker that came along would destroy civilization.

Chuck's Internet Addenda
What the HTML can't the CGI won't

On network outages:
When confronted, the ISP will assure you it is the carrier's fault.
When confronted, the carrier will assure you it is the ISP's fault.
When both are cornered the unanimous opinion will be that it is your fault.

33.6 modems aren't.

If technical support is pressured on issues that they have no knowledge of you will be passed on to people that know less and less about more and more until you reach a person that doesn't know anything at all. This person works for every ISP in existence and makes quite a living of it.

The net has evolved rudimentary intelligence and it knows when you've been bad or good....it just doesn't care. You're assumed to be doing bad.

As soon as you open an ISP for business you will find yourself in a life or death struggle with the local bagel shop who has also begun to offer Internet service.

The very next revision to the standard will make all of your work obsolete.

Hacker's always have the right of way.

If you build the interface to be idiot proof then the first moderately intelligent user will destroy the system, and vice versa.

'Whatever' is not a boolean search operator.

On the flakiness of the market:
In the unlikely event that you ever master database connectivity and secure transactions then popular demand would shift to fuzzy logic based on chicken entrails.

Featherkile's Rule
Whatever you did, that's what you planned!

Appendix: Case Studies

The Internet service business is by no means limited solely to access providers. The opportunities for companies catering to niche markets is as numerous as stars in the night sky. Perhaps a pure Internet access providing business is not in the cards for your own endeavor. Even so, there are other avenues to self-sufficiency and financial independence. Consider the following business ideas, all in practice today.

The common Internet services:

- General Internet access & service business
- Web design and layout
- General web content and advertising service
- Network integration and leased line provider
- Online retail sites

Slightly less common but no less viable business models:

- Specialized search engines (& advertising)
- Intranet consulting and design

- Intranet & database programming
- Internet software (news readers, email, utilities)
- Internet equipment reseller
- Online auction houses
- Online advertising networks and agencies
- ISP wholesalers (selling ISP services to smaller ISPs)
- Premium end-user services
    (Advanced Usenet, anonymous email, etc.)
- Online transaction agent (assisting buyers in meeting sellers, exporters in meeting importers, etc.)

As you can see, there are many innovative ways to make a career from the Internet. What follows are actual questions and answers from current Internet service companies. The variety of services and specialties that they cater to may assist you in understanding the many approaches available to this industry. Their words are uncut and are shown here as presented to us.

Name of Organization:	Webstart Communications
Type of Business:	Web Content, Advertising, and Advertising Affiliations
Year business founded:	1995
Number of Employees:	4
City & State of Home Office:	Berkeley, CA
Web Address:	http://www.webstart.com/
Email for public inquiries:	jed@webstart.com
Phone Number:	(510) 548-4590

Company Vision Statement:

At Webstart we are not alone in seeing tremendous value added by the World Wide Web to human communication. We are contributing where we can. We currently provide some moderately popular Web content on which we sell advertising. We are also expanding in the Web presence area for the Healthcare industry.

Company History:

Webstart was started by James E. (Jed) Donnelley and Sam Coleman. We had each started a Web indexing site (Jed, the Computer and Communication pages (C&C), now at: http://www.cmpcmm.com/cc/ and Sam, the California pages: http://www.calif.com/ca/

The C&C page set was started for practical reasons - to facilitate research in the Computer and Communications are. The California pages were started essentially as a public service. They were started with support from Lawrence Livermore National Laboratory late in 1993 (C&C) and early 1994 (California) and supported that way until spring of 1995. By that time the registrations were consuming so much time that it could not be justified as an LLNL supported activity.

We were in the same situation as many who supported index sites at that time. We decided to try to commercialize this content and see where it went. We got permission from LLNL to do so and moved the content to a commercial site (with redirections from LLNL for some time).

Main business endeavors and Internet services offered:
We currently have the two primary sets of Web content listed above. We are just now starting to list healthcare providers (only one demo site currently (12/96) listed).

We are currently delivering about 120k impressions per month (4k per day, ~12k "hits"). We give away trial advertising runs between 1k impressions for focused ads and 2k impressions for general banner ads. For people that find these trial valuable we sell advertising at competitive rates. We currently have generally between 6 and 12 sponsors per month, about half of which are paying for larger blocks of impessions. We utilize a variety of advertising tools including straight banners, DNS domain focused banners (e.g. what we call our "National Focus" advertising), map gif advertising (mostly on state and local area maps in California), and key word search advertising.

What sets your organizations apart from other Internet companies?
Generally the care we are able to devote to our sponsors. Our costs are very low (basically just our time as we trade advertising for our own Web presence) and we are able to devote some amount of attention even to sponsors that are purchasing relatively few impressions (e.g. 20-60k impressions).

What tools and technical resources do you utilize?
We run as a virtual host on Apache on Free BSD. We have developed our own accounting, banner rotation, and other administration software.

Future trends for your organization:
Our four employees currently all live in geographically separated locations, so we each use distinct ISPs (though we are close enough that we can meet fact to face at least every couple of weeks or so). We all currently have other full time employment, but two to three of

us are now considering quitting our "day" jobs and working full time on Webstart.

We are considering branching out in a couple of areas. We are negotiating with some other sites to affiliate content (us marketing the advertising and others supporting the content). We are also currently branching out in the Web presence business, with a focus on the healthcare industry.

What do you see as the major pitfall most Internet companies find themselves in:
I don't feel qualified to say what other entrepreneurs are doing wrong. I really feel that we don't even have enough experience to say what we have done wrong (though it would appear that we underestimated the costs of supporting registrations for our databases).

One thing is clear from our experience. Pricing and service quality vary so widely over the different services that the industry generally has a deservedly bad name. We constantly find ourselves combating this negative impression that people retain (when they have any experience at all). We have found cases where the same service (virtual host, so much disk space, so much traffic, similar services) was offered between $0 and $3,000 per month. Most of the serious offers we received were between $40 and $500 per month. That is a factor of 10 or more in pricing for the same proposed service. It has been our experience that you do not "get what you pay for" on the Internet today. The market is simply not developed enough and there isn't enough factual information for buyers to make informed decisions.

Any thoughts you'd like to offer:
We (I at least) feel that certificated (secure) access control will contribute significant additional value to the Internet (Intranets, etc.). This technology is just on the verge of being able to provide convenient and relatively safe access control, digital signatures, and privacy. User names and passwords are not a workable solution for these needs. We feel that our Web presence business direction will be facilitated by this technology.

One of the biggest stumbling blocks to further Internet use is the generally terrible state of personal computer software. Basically systems crash regularly (if used heavily and for a variety of purposes) and they are VERY difficult for a non-computer person to configure and use. This fact combined with the general difficulties finding information on the Internet is keeping many people from becoming satisified users. There is nothing technical preventing both of these problems from being solved. We feel that the Internet is today at a stage somewhat like the early days of the automobile. It basically takes a technically knowledgeable hobbyist to participate. We look forward to the easing of these barriers to use (e.g. the electric starter for the Internet) in the next few years and to a newly expanded level of Internet use in the home and office. We plan to be there adding value where we can.

Use of the Internet/Web in the healthcare area is significantly retarded by the above problems. We look forward to applying early solutions to the above problems to help patients, providers, and insurers communicate effectively (e.g. patients find appropriate providers supported by insurers).

Name of Organization:	Bonsai Software, Inc.
Type of Business:	Software consulting & service on the Internet.
Year business founded:	1992
Number of Employees:	8

City & State of Home Office:	Livermore, CA
Web Address:	www.bonsai.com
Email for public inquiries:	bonsai_info@bonsai.com
Phone Number:	(510) 606-5420

Company Vision Statement:

Bonsai Software leverages appropriate state-of-the-art technology to provide solutions to our customers. We invest in understanding emerging technology in preparation for its potential deployment. Often Bonsai provides middle-ware solutions which greatly enhance the capabilities of the technology.

Company History:

Bonsai's founders are Ken Sedgwick and Brent Gorda. Both come from scientific computing, specifically parallel processing. Each has a technical background in the area of Unix and networking. Ken and Brent met at the LLNL (Lawrence Livermore National Lab) where they were involved in special projects involving advanced parallel processing technology.

Some noteworthy projects:

GO/EO Connect - Bonsai designed and built the communications software for the GO Penpoint system.

Sun Performance analysis tool - Bonsai was responsible for the design and implementation of this tool for Sun Micro-systems.

SmartBookmarks - Bonsai held the contract to build this system for First Floor.

Genentech, Inc - Bonsai has been fundamental in much of the Genentech web site (both internal and External).

Webforum(tm) - One of Bonsai's early offerings. This was a Web-based news-reader (based on NNTP).

Webalog(tm) - another Bonsai tool in wide use among our associates and clients.

Many of our sites have received Internet awards in the past few years. The work we have done for the Genentech Access Excellence site has often been highlighted in the press.

Main business endeavors and Internet services offered:
Internet Auctions
Bonsai provides software technology and hosting/support services for the highest quality Internet Auctions. (An example can be found at www.numismatists.com). These full-featured auction sites are very popular and the auction segment of the Internet is growing rapidly.

With a recent site (www.easyauction.com), we offer the ability for anyone with a Web site to auction off their goods with a self-service auctioning system.

Site Sitter(tm) Remote Internet Probing Service
Bonsai offers a service which enables anyone with a net connection to have their machines watched by our computers. Our system probes from multiple locations, passes results through regular expressions supplied by the client, and notifies the person in charge of the site when an incident occurs.

We use this to tell ourselves when problems occur such as:
> Network outages
> Machine down
> Machine load averages high
> Disks filling
> Database failure
> Server errors (http)
> Third party DNS failure
> Secure page availability (SSL)

As with the EasyAuction(tm) Internet Auction Service, the SiteSitter(tm) service is self-service (after a setup and training session). Clients can then administer their probes as they see fit.

Software Engineering -
Bonsai's technical talent is second to none. We are specialists in all areas of Unix and networking issues, and utilize these capabilities to provide the best solution for our clients.

Internet Catalogs -
With our Webalog(tm) engine, we provide catalogs at the top end of the scale. Our ability to leverage database technology ensures that these catalogs are unlimited in data capability. An example (at www.edsoft.com) contains > 30,000 products.

Full Service WWW creation / hosting -
Bonsai has graphic artists on staff and relationships with other artists for use on projects. We have multimedia specialists capable of video/sound editing/creation. In addition to our technical abilities, hardware and network infrastructure, these artistic capabilities enable us to offer the full solution to our clients.

ISP - Through our T1 connection in Berkeley, CA, we provide co-location, virtual hosting services, Frame Relay, and dedicated ISDN connections. We currently host for >30 clients as well as numerous temporary hosting for projects under development. We currently have a handful of co-location, ISDN, and Frame Relay customers

Bonsai is located in the San Francisco Bay area, with offices in Livermore, Berkeley and San Francisco. Our clients, while mainly in the Bay Area, range geographically from Denver to LA, to Boston.

We believe the Internet removes geographical barriers, and use our advanced capabilities and infrastructure to do co-design and implement solutions with groups from all over.

What sets your organizations apart from other Internet companies?
Bonsai distinguishes itself from other Internet companies in our technical abilities. We were involved in consulting/contract work

long before the WWW became popular. Combined with our background and historical use of the Internet, we are very comfortable in this environment.

Other companies rush to market with less than spectacular offerings on less capable hardware. They often attempt to make up for their lack of technology with an emphasis on marketing and hype.

Bonsai is different. We have less marketing and more technology to offer our clients. Because we are small, we carefully choose what work we take on. We put a large emphasis on finding projects that we believe will succeed. Every major project is considered a partnership. Bonsai provides the technical talent, our partner the market expertise.

What tools and technical resources do you utilize?
Bonsai is a Unix shop on the technical side. We mainly work and host under Unix (any flavor). We typically provide less-technical clients with filemaker and web interfaces for the content part of the site-administration duties.

We have a solid development environment with practices such as revision control (CVS) over all WWW sites, dual disk systems where data is critical, and use of advanced database solutions (Informix, Oracle, etc) where appropriate. We rely heavily on portable communications equipment (portable computers, cell phones, pagers, PDAs) to ensure high bandwidth communications and continued smooth operations.

On the creative side, we utilize many platforms (Mac, NT, Solaris, SGI) as appropriate to optimize the solution. Software tools here mainly include the standard suite of Adobe offerings (Photoshop, Premier, Acrobat, ...).

Our in-house tool box is often in use by partners and clients once they get a taste of it. The most successful example of this is our Webalog(tm) setup which provides a TCL programming environment within each HTML page on a site. This enables simple quick programming capabilities (including access to NNTP, Informix, etc) on any page. (TCL is a standard language from John Ousterhout, currently with Sun Microsystems).

Future trends for your organization:
Bonsai will remain at the leading edge of technology. We will continue to provide the most appropriate solution possible for our clients. This requires our continued investment in emerging technology. We believe this is a path to long term stability and success.

What do you see as the major pitfall most Internet companies find themselves in:
Many companies in this area seem to be under-staffed in their technical capabilities. Since the Web and basic HTML is very simple, many companies have been built up to address this work, much like when typists were specialized talent. As HTML authoring gets easier, these companies will have a hard time surviving.

On the other end of the scale, Java brings some serious legitimacy to the picture. In order to have a good site, you need some programming on it (Java or otherwise). This raises the stakes and further pushes out those who are under-prepared technically.

Any thoughts you'd like to offer:
The Internet is a fast-paced arena that is here to stay. No one person can keep up with the advancements in technology: the hype is too large to get your arms around anymore. It takes a strong team, one that can separate the wheat from the chaff, to move forward.

As one learns in hockey: to win you must play a strong fundamental game, trust your teammates with your life, and keep your head up as you skate. You must also enjoy what you do in order to survive. Its not the potential to get rich that should drive you. As Steve Jobs puts it: The journey is the reward.

Name of Organization:	Solunet, Inc.
Type of Business:	VAR of Inter-Networking products
Year business founded:	1990
Number of Employees:	50
City & State of Home Office:	Palm Bay, Florida
Web Address:	www.solunet.com
Email for public inquiries:	sales@solunet.com
Phone Number:	1-888-SOLUNET

Company Vision Statement:

Solunet, Inc. has made a commitment to provide solutions for all of your Inter-Networking requirements. A complete inventory of the industry's finest products, a factory trained support staff, timely delivery, and our reputation for superior service make Solunet, Inc. the right choice for you. Our technically oriented sales staff can assist with solutions for your application and give you a unique, specialized service.

Company History:

In 1989, Mike Wertheimer looked back on his 20 year history working as an engineer for several leading high technology firms and decided he was not satisfied. The Internet and telecommuting had been around for years, but the business community had not quite caught up with the available technology. Mike knew this was a huge opportunity.

In 1990, he decided that it was just a matter of time before big business would stumble upon telecommuting as a means to communicate at a faster rate. He borrowed $30,000 from his father-in-law and began operations, working beside his wife Helen in their home.

Through negotiation with leading high-tech manufacturers, Mike started Solunet as a Value Added Reseller (VAR) of telecommuting and Internet equipment. With the credibility of quality equipment behind him, Wertheimer emphasized service as the Solunet advantage.

Early contracts to provide companies such as American Express and AT&T Universal Card Services with equipment and professional expertise for their computer networking and telecommuting needs gave Solunet the credibility and the money needed to face the coming competition. By providing quality service, Solunet was able to maintain a great deal of repeat business in its first five years, which is vital to success in this constantly changing environment.

Mike always has insisted that Solunet make customer service the company's top priority. He attributes this, more than anything else, as the reason for Solunet's phenomenal early success. A variety of maintenance support, including a guarantee of replacement parts within 24 hours, has earned Solunet high praise from satisfied customers. Mike's instincts about the market and the customer's need to have the complex made simple proved accurate. Solunet has tripled revenues every year since its inception. Though the company is now a power in the internetworking VAR marketplace, personal outreach is still the key. Mike wouldn't have it any other way.

In recognition for his accomplishments with Solunet, Wertheimer was a finalist for Florida's 1996 Entrepreneur of the Year Award. Solunet is also the largest VAR for Shiva, Ascend and Livingston products. They were named a Cisco Enterprise Partner in the ISP industry, a Gold VAR for Adtran, a Platinum VAR for U.S. Robotics and a Select MasterVAR for Microcom.

Main business endeavors and Internet services offered:
Our main focus at Solunet is to be the Providers Provider. We do not compete with our ISP clients by offering dial-up or leased line accounts, we provide the access equipment and technical expertise that they require to offer their services to their customers. We specialize in the internetworking arena, focusing primarily on the access devices such as routers, communication servers, ISDN equipment and modems. But it is more than just selling boxes, we integrate the equipment we sell and offer customized technical support for our users. Dealing with over 2500 ISPs worldwide gives us the advantage of seeing the good the bad and the ugly, that expertise is as close as a phone call.

What sets your organizations apart from other Internet companies?

Customer service is the King at Solunet. It is easy to sell boxes, but when you take all the pieces and integrate them seamlessly into a network that is were we shine. Solunet is more than just a supplier. We put the Value back in VAR. We are factory trained and authorized to provide technical support and consulting, giving you the Solunet added advantage. Whether you are an end user or reseller, you'll be getting support after the sale!

What tools and technical resources do you utilize?

At Solunet we have an inside technical support staff that is factory trained and certified from each of our manufacturers. Besides the technical training offered by our manufacturers our staff includes engineers from ISPs, Unix programmers, system analysts and a Web Master as well as a certified NT professional. Our outside staff of engineers are constantly doing installations at remote POPs as well as installing the new ISP's backbone's. As they say "been there, done that."

At our lab in Florida we duplicate almost every OS that our customers use with multiple digital lines to trouble shoot any problems that might occur at the customer premise.

Future trends for your organization:

As of January 1, 1997, Solunet will have completed the acquisition of Integrated Digital Networks, a Virginia-based VAR. We hope to work together with our new employees to further our presence in the Government and Commercial markets while continuing to capitalize on our substantial ISP
customer base.

What do you see as the major pitfall most Internet companies find themselves in:

The biggest problem that I see that Internet Entrepreneurs make is that they remain static and do not grow and offer value added services (ie: Intranet, Telecommuting). Doing the "me-to" thing in business and undercutting pricing to a point where they are losing money just to gain market share. Remember that low cost and quality service are exclusive items.

Any thoughts you'd like to offer:

Being in this business for five years and seeing my business grow from 300K to 30M has made me an old timer. But the scary part of this business is that we are only seeing the tip of the iceberg! The Internet is just the on-ramp to the future!

Name of Organization: WildStar Internet Services, Inc.
Type of Business: Internet Service Provider
Year business founded: 1995
Number of Employees: <10

City & State of Home Office: Norman, Oklahoma
Web Address: www.wildstar.net
Email for public inquiries: info@wildstar.net
Phone Number: (405) 447-0581

Company Vision Statement:
Wildstar Internet Services provides a variety of Internet services including: Telnet access UNIX and IRC accounts, PPP/SLIP Dialup and professional WWW design, development, and hosting services. We aren't trying to be a big company. We prefer to keep things on a reasonable scale so we can provide a good service and get to know our customers.

Company History:
Wildstar Internet was formed when its founders decided to move a public telnet service, which was originally a self learning project while in college, off of the college equipment because it had grown too rapidly and was getting too large to justify allowing it to run on the public machines. To prevent having to close the service down, members where asked to support the service with low monthly membership fees, and a private system was setup. In order to help cover the costs involved, and to help keep membership dues to a minimum, other services (Dialup access, WWW design and hosting) where offered. All 3 areas grew into what is now WildStar Internet Services, Inc.

Main business endeavors and Internet services offered:
Services Offered:
    Dedicated ISDN
    Dialup access (405 Area code)
    Telnet UNIX shell accounts
    Telnet Custom IRC (Internet Relay Chat) accounts.

Professional WWW consulting, development, and hosting services.
Network Consulting

What sets your organizations apart from other Internet companies?

We aren't trying to be the biggest company around. We do this because we enjoy working with the Internet, and working with people.

What tools and technical resources do you utilize?

We have used all sorts of equipment and operating systems. Since equipment and technology changes so quickly, email us at support@wildstar.net if you would like technical information about our equipment at that time.

Future trends for your organization:

Mainly, we plan on continuing to offer UNIX/IRC services, and working on expanding our WWW/dialup areas. Most likely we will remain local to the Oklahoma calling area (405) on our dialups. Our WWW and Unix/IRC services are offered world wide and will probably remain that way.

What do you see as the major pitfall most Internet companies find?

Failure to estimate how much initial investment will be required the first year seems to be what we see kills most providers. Failure to expand your equipment and services in a timely manner is a definite fatal mistake.

Name of Organization:	Comstar Technologies
Type of Business:	Internet Service Provider
Year business founded:	1993
Number of Employees:	Currently 1 full-time

City & State of Home Office:	Waukesha, WI
Web Address:	http://www.wauknet.com/
Email for public inquiries:	comstar@wauknet.com
Phone Number:	(414) 524-9628

Company Vision Statement:
To provide quality internet access with no busy signals.

Company History:
Comstar Technologies was founded in 1993 by Jeffrey Kirk to provide custom software for area businesses. With the growing popularity of the Internet, businesses began asking about web site development. Considering that a web site must be hosted somewhere, that the Milwaukee area had only one major Internet service provider, and that the Waukesha area is large enough to support its own Internet service, moving into the ISP business made sense. The Waukesha Network went online in early 1996 gaining major accounts from the Waukesha Area Chamber of Commerce, Waukesha County Economic Development Corporation, and the Waukesha Area Convention and Visitors Bureau.

Main business endeavors and Internet services offered:
Dial-up internet access (local to Waukesha and Milwaukee counties)
- E-mail
- web browsing
- Usenet newsgroups

Website design and maintenance
- HTML programming
- image scanning and touchup
- CGI and Java Script
- introductory web site packages

Website hosting
- all business users are given a free starter homepage
- all business users are listed in the Wauknet Business Directory

What sets your organizations apart from other Internet companies?
We have been able to maintain no busy signals for our customers. Being in Waukesha, our service is a local call to a wider area than our local competitors.

What tools and technical resources do you utilize?
Utilizing Netscape servers on Windows NT. Our Internet connection is a T1.

Future trends for your organization:
Main focus now is to find additional customers. We're beginning a broad advertising campaign in January 1997.

What do you see as the major pitfall most Internet companies find themselves in:
I think many internet companies add new customers without regard to their capacity, mostly in having too many customers per incoming modem. It is tempting to keep selling service, without expanding capabilities, to increase profits. But I think that is a poor practice if you want happy customers.

Also, poor customer service is an issue with many computer related companies, from software to hardware to internet service. As an industry we've got to start improving in this area.

Any thoughts you'd like to offer:
To keep customers happy, while not overselling your service, you must be willing to ride out the startup and early expansion expenses. Plan well, because the communication expenses are great.

It's a good idea to accept credit cards. It offers convenience for customers and guarantees that we get paid in a timely manner.

Every business should be represented with an Internet web site…and we'd be happy to host their site.

Name of Organization:	@ Online Design
Type of Business:	Web Developers
Year Business Founded:	January, 96
Number of Employees:	4

City & State of Home Office:	Louisville, KY
Web Address:	http://www.olinedsign.com
Email for public inquiries:	ContactUs@olinedsign.com
Phone Number:	(502) 852-0900

Company Vision Statement:

@ Online Design believes that every Internet or intranet site that we develop should cater to the interests and needs of targeted visitors. It is important that web content incorporates interactivity so that visitors get personalized attention and find information on the site valuable enough to visit repeatedly. We will never use technology for technology's sake, rather design sites that visitors will be enticed to return to over and over again.

Company History:

@ Online Design was founded by Susan Weiss and Barbara Lang in January 1996. BellSouth, International Tours and Cruises, the City of Danville and Boyle County KY, Imperial Military Surplus, and Southern Indiana Convention and Visitors Bureau are among a growing list of clientele. @ Online Design also offers a commercially available web-based training product called the Copyright and Netiquette Primer™.

Main business endeavors and Internet services offered:

@ Online Design offers Internet and Intranet content development. We offer a full array of web development services including pre-planning and strategic analysis, design, marketing, maintenance and training. @ Online Design also develops customized intranet training modules and has a commercially available web-based training product called the Copyright and Netiquette Primer™. The Primer educates employees about copyright issues as they pertain to intranet web page development.

What sets your organization apart from other Internet companies?
We emphasize the importance of marketing a site after it has been developed. Many other developers in the industry simply post a completed site and leave the marketing issues up to their clients. @ Online Design assesses how the web site will be used as a tool for the company to communicate with customers.

What tools and technical resources do you utilize?
@ Online Design's offices are located in a Telecommunications Research Center giving our employees access to the latest in Internet technologies. Web sites that we have developed include shopping carts, chat rooms, and other customized CGI scripts to add interactivity where it is needed.

Future trends for your organization:
We believe that web sites will become much more interactive therefore, we plan to keep up with rapidly changing technologies that will aid in developing highly interactive sites. We also believe that a new commercial intranet web-based training market will appear in the near future.

What do you see as the major pitfall most Internet companies find themselves in:
The biggest mistake that we see occur is the use of technology for technology's sake. Oftentimes, web developers get caught up in trying to use the latest new technology simply to impress even though it is not needed. Another common mistake is that web developers often include graphics and other media objects that take too long for the average visitor to download.

Any thoughts you'd like to offer:
Web page development has gone through dramatic changes in the past 12 months. Most web sites a year ago were simply marketing billboards with a few bells and whistles. Today web site design requires the developers to think about how an ongoing relationship can be maintained through a web site. Instead of waiting for a customer to return to a web site for more information, techniques can

be used to contact your visitors when sites have been updated, new promotions or events occur, etc.

Name of Organization: Deja News, Inc.
Year business founded: 1995
Number of Employees: 30
Type of Business: The most comprehensive search engine for Usenet newsgroups on the World Wide Web

City & State of Home Office: Austin, TX
Web Address: http://www.dejanews.com
Email for public inquiries: sales@dejanews.com
Phone Number: (512) 451-0433

Company Vision Statement:
The Deja News mission is to be the premier source for Usenet newsgroups on the World Wide Web by providing the best tools for searching, browsing and posting to newsgroups, and to provide high quality, well-targeted advertising opportunities for clients requiring sophisticated market segmentation.

Company History:
Deja News was founded in Austin in May 1995 by Steven Madere as a way to provide easy access to Usenet newsgroups, which serve as an on-line meeting and discussion forum for millions of computer users.

The site has received numerous awards, including being rated in the Top 5 Percent of All Sites by Pointcom, a Four-Star Site by Yahoo! Computing, a Three-Star Site by the McKinley Group/U.S. Magellan Review and honored with NetGuide magazine's first Five-Star rating. In its November 1996 article on Internet search sites, PC Magazine said of Deja News, "Its power and bevy of options make it the best site we reviewed.[...]Deja News was very fast, very accurate, and very complete." Deja News can also be found on other major web search engines as their Usenet search resource.

Main business endeavors and Internet services offered:
Deja News provides a combination of services not found in any other Usenet utility, including:
• the largest archives for Usenet newsgroup postings;

- fast search and retrieval capability;
- special Usenet queries, including author profile, date, subject, newsgroup and keyword;
- unique filtering capabilities;
- Usenet posting feature that allows users to post directly to newsgroups from the website;
- newsgroup browsing, enabling users to browse newsgroups by hierarchy; and
- Deja Read News, which allows users to read current Usenet news from favorite groups and create custom bookmarks.

Deja News provides very targeted advertising by enabling companies to sponsor the main home page, search page, search results page, articles from specified newsgroups, or keywords. With more than 20,000 topics discussed-and more than 43 million page views each month-advertisers are certain to reach a target audience interested in their product or service.

What sets your organizations apart from other Internet companies?

Deja News is unique in that it continues to be the premier resource for searching Usenet newsgroup postings. With 24 months worth of postings archived, and more than 125 gigabytes of information, it is the largest on-line text database in the world. Until Deja News, this vast amount of information was virtually inaccessible on the World Wide Web, and largely unmanageable. Deja News gives millions of users an easy, fast way to access Usenet discussion groups - "the other half of the Internet." Deja News is also able to provide advertisers with very, very targeted advertising by enabling them to sponsor specific keywords or newsgroups to reach a select audience.

What tools and technical resources do you utilize?

Through advanced search algorithms, Deja News allows users to perform complex searches through more than 125 gigabytes of data in a matter of seconds.

Future trends for your organization:

Deja News is dedicated to retaining its position as the most popular Usenet search engine, and will continue expanding its archives and search options. Other future plans include personalized e-mail alerts and a revised user interface.

In addition, applying Deja News' experience in high-volume database management to advertising banner placement and tracking has produced GlobalTrack (www.globaltrack.com), the most comprehensive Internet ad campaign management and tracking service. GlobalTrack gives anyone who places ad banner campaigns on the Internet, including interactive agencies, unprecedented control over their entire web advertising schedule.

About the Author and Farewells

Charles 'Chuck' Burke received his degree in Economics from Bellarmine College in 1994. While never practicing in a job position of pure economics the degree has served as a fantastic foundation for varied endeavors of all sorts. Involved in personal computers since age 9, he is one of the many individuals in a new generation entirely raised in a digital world. A few of the many computer fields he has worked include graphical information systems in tracking imports and exports, director of computer training and support services for General Electric Appliances, and network administration for a number of organizations. Telecommunications is still his first love in the high tech arena. Mr. Burke lives in Louisville, Kentucky, where he was born and still insists on complaining about the weather.

In February of 1996 the Shiva Systems ISP & BBS business was sold to Mikrotec Internet Services, Kentucky's largest ISP. Chuck took up residence in the Mikrotec family where he currently serves as management support and performs various work in expanding the network.

Farewell for now...

I hope you have enjoyed this second edition of the book and more to the point, I hope it helps you on your path to success in this new medium. It has been highly rewarding for me personally. It has also made me look at both ISP technology and the industry as a whole in a highly critical way. This has clarified many issues that I had feelings about on a gut level but was unable to put into words up to this point. The pace of change we are living in will not slow but will, in fact, increase as the greater portion of the population begins to find our new Oz. Unlike the story though, this land is not built on smoke and mirrors but rather solid technology, support and community.

I can assure you this will not be the last version of this book. We are only getting started and this volume will expand over time. I hope you stick with us! Be sure to visit us on the web, we are located at http://www.index.mis.net/kanti. You will find most of the links in this book organized there for your own use. You will also find other resources for the new ISP.

Be careful when choosing your partners and may the wind always be at your back.

God bless,
Chuck Burke

BIBLIOGRAPHY

Albitz, Paul, and Cricket Liu. *DNS and BIND*.
 Sebastopol, CA: O'Reilly and Associates, 1992.

Boardwatch Magazine. Littleton, CO.

Getting Connected.
 Sebastopol, CA: O'Reilly and Associates, 1994.

Kennedy, David J. *Planning for Online Services*,
 Alexandria, VA: Association of Online Professionals, 1996.

Lemay, Laura. *Teach Yourself Web Publishing with HTML in 14
 Days*. Sams Publishing, 1996.

Levinson, Jay Conrad and Charles Rubin. *Guerrilla Marketing
 Online*. N.Y., New York: Houghton Mifflin, 1996.

GLOSSARY

56K A leased line that carries 56,000 bits per second. Approximately twice the speed of a 28.8 connection.

ADSL Asymmetric Digital Subscriber Line. A high bandwidth protocol and hardware combination for achieving broadband connectivity over standard telephone lines (similar to ISDN). ADSL is a variant of the xDSL technology set. Although specs vary wildly, a user should be able to pump data upstream at 640kbps+ and receive data (downstream) at speeds as great as 6mbps (more than a few T1's worth of bandwidth). As of 1996 the technology is still under development with no recognized universal standards.

ARCHIE This is a software tool used for finding files stored on anonymous FTP sites. This software requires the user to know the exact file name, or a sub-string of it.

ANONYMOUS FTP An FTP login where the remote user is allowed to access services using the generic login name of 'anonymous'.

ARPANET "Advanced Research Projects Administration Network." A division of the Department of Defense setup in the late sixties as an experimental wide area network. Originally devised to survive a nuclear war.

BACKBONE A high-speed line or series of connections that forms a major pathway within a network. The term is relative as a backbone in a small network will likely be much smaller than many non-backbone lines in a large network.

BANDWIDTH The maximum amount of information that can be transmitted over a given medium. Ie. A 28.8 modem has a maximum bandwidth of 28,000 bits per second.

BBS Bulletin Board System. A computer based system that allows for the sending and receiving of messages and files.

BROWSER   Generically used to represent world wide web browsers. Browsers present the information that servers dish up to clients. (See Client, Server)

BUS   The copper tracings on the surface of the motherboard that transmit data between computer components.

CARRIER   (1) A long distance carrier   (2) A provider of voice or data circuits

CGI   Common Gateway Interface. An application programming interface that allows the communication of data between HTML documents and executable programs. Ie. A CGI script might take your input from an HTML form and place the information into a database or return the results of a database search to you in HTML format.

CLASS C ADDRESS   A Class C is a block of 256 IP addresses. This is what you will wish to begin with when you start your ISP. (See IP Address)

CLIENT   A software program that is used to contact and obtain data from a server on another computer. Ie. Netscape Navigator is a world wide web client. (See Server) *Also* One who pays the bills.

COFFEE Lubricating fluid for problem solving and higher thinking skills.

CSLIP   Compressed SLIP. SLIP connections with compression for a more efficient data transfer. (See SLIP)

CSU/DSU   Customer Service Unit / Digital Service Unit. A hardware device for interfacing high speed digital lines to a computer network. A T1 line plugs into a CSU/DSU which in turn plugs into a router.

CYBERSPACE   This term was coined by William Gibson in his novel Neuromancer. The term is currently used to describe the Internet and online services.

DISK CACHE   An area of memory used to store information being read and written to a disk drive. Access to the information is sped up due to memory being inherently faster than the mechanical storage of a disk drive.

DOMAIN NAME This is the name which identifies each Internet site. Domain Names have two or more parts, separated by dots. The part on the left is the most specific, and the part on the right is the most general. A machine may have more than one Domain Name but a Domain Name points to only one machine. Domain names are the human equivalent of IP addresses, which makes it much easier for us to locate resources on the Internet. For every domain name there is an IP address equivalent.

DNS Domain Name Service. DNS is a control system that provides the link between the 'human friendly' domain names and the less friendly IP addresses. Domain names and IP addresses are maintained in tables stored at Internet sites. As an ISP you will be maintaining a DNS server to provide DNS service to your local network.

DS0 See 56k

DS1 See T1

E-MAIL Electronic Mail. Messages, usually text, sent electronically from one person to another via computer.

ETHERNET A very common method of networking computers in a LAN. Ethernet will handle about 10,000,000 bits per second and can be used with almost any kind of computer. (See LAN, NIC)

FAQ Frequently Asked Questions. FAQs are documents that list and answer the most common questions on a particular subject. FAQs are maintained on almost every long lived newsgroup on the Usenet but are not limited to this area. (See Newsgroup, Usenet)

FTP File Transfer Protocol. This is the most common method of moving files between two Internet sites. FTP is a special way to login to another Internet site for the purposes of retrieving and /or sending files.

FINGER A utility to see if another user is currently connected to the Internet. *Also* A gesture often given to relay anger and/or frustration to a tech support caller.

FLAME An insult or attack on another user based on messages generally in public conferences such as newsgroups. (See Newsgroups)

FRACTIONAL T1 A portion of the channels of a T1 circuit used to deliver only a percentage of the maximum bandwidth possible. A full T1 is usually made up of 24 channels of 56k or 64k depending on how it is configured.

GATEWAY A hardware / software system that translates data between two internally incompatible formats. Also used to describe the way that one system allows access to another system. Ie. Some BBS software can be gateways to the Internet.

GOPHER (1) An Internet system for supplying menus of information across the Internet. This is being replaced by the Web. (2) A small, furry creature which lives in your computer at night and is responsible for most of your system troubles during the day.

HOME PAGE The topmost page in a collection of HTML documents.

HOST A computer that services other machines on a network. Ie. As an Internet user you connect to your Internet host. *Also* 'Good' Host, or one who has an open bar at their party.

HTML Hypertext Markup Language The main format for documents on the web. HTML is the language and syntax of web pages. (See World Wide Web)

HTTP Hypertext Transport Protocol. The protocol that moves data across the web. Mainly used to move HTML web pages but can also be used to transport binary or executable type program code.

HYPERTEXT A text document that allows you to navigate through it by choosing a 'link', usually by clicking on the link with your mouse.

IETF The Internet Engineering Task Force. A group that facilitates the creation and acceptance of new Internet standards, generally in the form of RFCs. (See RFC)

INTERNET The collective networks and individual computers that use the TCP/IP protocols to link themselves together. The Internet was born out of the ARPANET project from the late sixties. Not to be confused with 'internet' (lower case I) which refers generically to multiple networks connected together.

INTERNIC The agency that handles the registration of domain names. (See Domain Names)

IP Internet Protocol, the low level or basic protocol of the Internet

IP NUMBER / ADDRESS An Internet Protocol number or address is a series of four numbers separated by dots. Ie. XXX.XXX.XXX.XXX, 204.189.80.1, etc. An IP address is needed for any machine that is connected to the Internet in real time.

IRC Internet Relay Chat. A multi-user chat system where IRC clients connect to IRC servers and allow the users to type to each other in real time. Specialty functions built into many new IRC client software allows you to send files, audio and even video to others on an IRC server. Often compared to 'Crack' as they both can have similar effects depending upon the user.

ISDN Integrated Services Digital Network. A digital connection achieved using an ISDN line and ISDN equipment. This format for data delivery and retrieval allows for connections up to 128kbps. ISDN consists of three channels of communication for each ISDN connection. Two 'B' or bearer channels and one 'D' or delta/digital channel for signalling. Utilizing one B channel gives you 64kbps of bandwidth and inverse multiplexing allows you to combine both B channels for a maximum of 128kbps connection. ISDN comes in two sizes, BRI, Basic Rate Interface, and PRI or Primary Rate Interface. The BRI is the most common ISDN connection and the one described above. ISDN BRI connections are often shown as 2B+D which refers to the channels of the connection. ISDN PRI refers to a much larger ISDN connection which consists of 23 BRI channels and is similar to T1 wires in price and performance.

LAN Local Area Network A grouping of computers tied together through some sort of connectivity topology, usually locale specific to a particular building or facility.

LEASED LINE A data or voice line that is rented from a carrier for 24/7 usage.

LEC Local Exchange Carrier. Your local phone company. *See* RBOC

LOCAL LOOP That portion of a leased line and the cost for a leased line that refers to the distance between the POP and an end point. Ie. "I have a local loop on the phone who is browsing the web at 2400 baud!"

LOGIN (1) The account name used to access a computer system. (2) The act of accessing a computer system.

MEGALINK *See* T1

MODEM The word is derived from Modulate/Demodulate, the actions taken by the hardware that transforms digital information into analog signals to be sent over a standard telephone line. A 'modem' is hardware that performs this function. Dial up users generally use modems or ISDN equipment to dial into a computer system.

MOSAIC The first web browser. (See browser)

NIC (1) Network Interface Card, Ie. an ethernet card. (2) Network Information Center, Ie. The InterNIC handles domain name registrations.

NETWORK (1) The act of tying computers together so that resources can be used communally. (2) A group of connected computers that can share resources.

NEWSGROUP A conference or discussion area on USENET, used for reading and posting messages. There are currently over 15,000 public newsgroups carried over Usenet servers. (See Usenet)

NNTP Network News Transport Protocol. Used to transport newsgroup content from one Usenet server to another. (See Usenet, Newsgroup)

NODE A single computer on a network.

NSFNET The National Science Foundation Network, one of the major networks on the Internet.

OS Operating System. The most basic software foundation of a computer that other software relies upon to function. DOS and UNIX are two examples of operating systems.

PACKET SWITCHING The process of taking data and reducing it to smaller pieces and then transporting those pieces throughout a network. Packet switching allows many people to use the network simultaneously as packets simply line up to be transported through the same connections. The Internet is a packet switching network.

PING A utility used to check if another computer is hooked to the Internet currently. Ping also returns the round trip time for the data packet and is used to diagnose lags and other slowdowns in this way. Derived from submarine jargon when ships would send a sonar ping to check the distance to an object. Ie. ping www.cajunrecipes.com will check to see if this computer is currently reachable from your connection.

POP Point of Presence. A geographic location of a resource. Used to define the location of a switch or central office for a carrier or other provider of services.

PORT (1) An address that Internet servers use when servicing particular requests. Web servers generally 'listen' to port 80. Although non-standard ports can be defined they must be specified by the client attempting to access them through their software. (2) An input/output connection for a computer or router where data is passed from the internal hardware to external hardware or data lines. Technically speaking a router is a computer.

POST / POSTING Placing a message on a conference. You can *post* a message to a Usenet newsgroup.

POTS Plain Old Telephone Service. In the telephone industry POTS refers to plain dial tone telephone connections, the kind in most homes and offices.

PPP The Point to Point Protocol. Used to connect computers to a TCP/IP network. This protocol is improved over the older method for accomplishing this same task, SLIP. (See SLIP, CSLIP)

RBOC (Often pronounced 'R-Bach') Regional Bell Operating Company. Your phone company! Also referred to as 'Baby Bells' by some.

RFC Request For Comments. The process of creating new Internet standards is in the form of requests. This procedure creates open standards that are published for general consumption as RFC documents. The IETF does much of the diplomacy in getting RFCs applied as new standards. (See IETF)

ROUTER A proprietary device or a software package which makes a computer function so as to move data between connected networks. A router looks at the destination address of packets and moves them toward their ultimate destination.

SERVER A hardware or software/hardware combination that takes requests for data and serves the data to the requesting client. A server could also be multi-purpose and serve data for many different types of requests. Ie. You could run a Web server and an FTP server on the same machine. Ie. One who serve's the drinks. *Also see* Client

SERVICE PROVIDER Generically used to refer to a provider of Internet services, the same as Internet Service Provider (ISP for short). *Also see* Overworked Individuals

SHELL (1) An account that allows you to use the resources of another computer to access the Internet (2) Generically: A service or program that rides over top of the standard operating system in order to provide special services or functionality to a user.

SLIP Serial Line Internet Protocol. A method of providing IP (See IP) over serial connections. Generally used for intermittent connection by dial up customers. SLIP predates PPP as a method of dialing into an Internet server.

SMTP   Simple Mail Transfer Protocol. A protocol that allows for the movement of Email across the Internet.

SUB NET A portion of a network that uses a number of IP addresses from the parent network.

T1 A leased line that carries data at 1.544 megabits per second (1,544,000 bits per second). A T1 line is the most common method of connecting ISPs to other Internet providers. Also referred to as a DS1 or Megalink circuit. T1 lines can also be used to provide 'dial tone' or voice POTS. (See POTS)

T3 A leased line connection capable of moving data at 45,000,000 bits per second. A T3 is made up of 24 T1 lines. This is a BIG pipe.

T50 We made it up. As far as I know there isn't such an animal as a T50 but I'd like to have one anyway!

TCP/IP   Transmission Control Protocol / Internet Protocol.   The Transmission Control Protocol supplies an application specific interface layer to IP (See IP). TCP/IP generally refers to a suite of protocols that allow computers to network together, and more specifically, it is the protocol used to tie the Internet together.

TELNET A program (and command) that allows you to login to another computer on the Internet. (See Login)

TERMINAL An interface that allows you to remotely access a computer system.   Terminals can be either hardware or software in nature. Terminal software generally refers to packages that allow you to connect using your modem to another computer.

TERMINAL SERVER A special piece of hardware that connects many modems to a network through an ethernet connection. A terminal server handles the dial up users at an ISPs site. A multiport serial card accomplishes the same task by connecting modems to a computer that is equipped to handle dial up users. *Also* A server which is ready to keel over.

TUNNELING PROTOCOL An encrypted communications protocol used for the transfer of sensitive data over the public network. *See also* Virtual Private Network

UNIX The most common operating system for servers on the Internet. UNIX was designed to be a multi-user operating system with an extremely open architecture. *See Also* Cult

URL Uniform Resource Locator. A way of addressing resources on the Internet through the web.

USENET A system for collecting, expiring, and distributing messages. Generically refers to the entire public collection of newsgroups carried over the Internet. Not all Usenet servers must be on the Internet however, as they still serve the same purposes for private groups.

VIRTUAL PRIVATE NETWORK (VPN) A connection established over the public network (Internet) between two or more points which utilize encryption technology. Most often used to connect remote offices together in order to share sensitive data. *See also: Tunneling Protocol*

W3 See World Wide Web

WAN A Wide Area Network. A network that covers an area larger than a single building or facility. (See LAN)

WEBSITE (1) A collection of HTML documents tied together. (2) The server that hosts a collection of HTML documents.

WINSOCK A library of functions that allow Windows operating systems to connect to TCP/IP networks. You need a Winsock to connect to the Internet. The most popular shareware Winsock is Trumpet Winsock.

WORLD WIDE WEB (Aka: W3, WWW, the Web, etc.) (1) The entire collection of HTML documents and accompanying resources that are on the Internet and accessed using a browser. (2) More vaguely used to represent the entire collection of all resources on the Internet. (See Browser)

X56 A new modem technology that takes advantage of a digital connection to an ISPs POP. Requires that the ISPs analog connections be accomplished via ISDN PRI or channelized T1. Also requires an X56 enabled modem on both sides of the connection.

INDEX